# AGRARIAN ECONOMY, STATE AND SOCIETY IN CONTEMPORARY TANZANIA

# The Making of Modern Africa

**Series Editors:** Abebe Zegeye and John Higginson

# Agrarian Economy, State and Society in Contemporary Tanzania

*Edited by*
PETER G. FORSTER
*Sociology and Anthropology, School of Comparative
and Applied Social Sciences, University of Hull*

SAM MAGHIMBI
*Department of Sociology,
University of Dar es Salaam*

# Ashgate

Aldershot • Brookfield USA • Singapore • Sydney

Published by
Ashgate Publishing Ltd
Gower House
Croft Road
Aldershot
Hants GU11 3HR
England

Ashgate Publishing Company
Old Post Road
Brookfield
Vermont 05036
USA

Ashgate website: http://www.ashgate.com

**British Library Cataloguing in Publication Data**
Agrarian economy, state and society in contemporary
    Tanzania. - (The making of modern Africa)
    1. Agriculture and state - Tanzania 2. Land reform - Tanzania
    - Case studies 3. Agricultural productivity - Tanzania
    4. Tanzania - Economic conditions - 1964 -
    I. Forster, Peter G. (Peter Glover), 1944 - II. Maghimbi, Sam
    338.1'8'678

**Library of Congress Catalog Card Number:** 99-72972

ISBN 1 85972 627 5

Printed in Great Britain

# Contents

# PART II  INDIGENOUS TECHNICAL KNOWLEDGE

# PART III  CASE STUDIES

# List of Tables, Figures and Maps

# Chapter 13

# Chapter 14

# Chapter 15

# Chapter 16

# List of Contributors

**Peter G. Forster** is Senior Lecturer, Sociology and Anthropology, in the School of Comparative and Applied Social Science, University of Hull

**Sam Maghimbi** is Professor in the Department of Sociology, University of Dar es Salaam

**Pat Caplan** is Director of the Institute of Commonwealth Studies, University of London

**C.S.L. Chachage** is Professor in the Department of Sociology, University of Dar es Salaam

**G.C. Kajembe** is Lecturer in the Institute of Continuing Education, Sokoine University of Agriculture, Morogoro

**Andrew S.Z. Kiondo** is Professor in the Department of Politics, University of Dar es Salaam

**T. Lassalle** is Agricultural Officer, Department of Agricultural Education and Extension, Sokoine University of Agriculture, Morogoro

**Sizya Lugeye** is Agricultural Adviser at the Embassy of Ireland, Dar es Salaam

**Francis F. Lyimo** is Lecturer in the Department of Sociology, University of Dar es Salaam

**A.Z. Mattee** is Associate Professor in the Department of Agricultural Education and Extension, Sokoine University of Agriculture, Morogoro

**Simeon Mesaki** is Lecturer in the Department of Sociology, University of Dar es Salaam

**M.E. Mlambiti** is Professor in the Department of Agricultural Economics and Agribusiness, Sokoine University of Agriculture, Morogoro

**Malongo R.S. Mlozi** is Senior Lecturer in the Department of Agricultural Education and Extension, Sokoine University of Agriculture, Morogoro

**Stefano Ponte** is a PhD candidate in the School of Development Studies, University of East Anglia. He is also a Visiting Lecturer at the Center for International Development Research, Duke University, Durham NC

**D.F. Rutatora** is Associate Professor in the Department of Agricultural Economics and Agribusiness, Sokoine University of Agriculture, Morogoro

**John Sivalon** is Senior Lecturer in the Department of Sociology, University of Dar es Salaam

# Acknowledgements

The editors are most grateful once again to the British Council for facilitating this publication through the Link relationship between the University of Dar es Salaam in Tanzania and the University of Hull in England. This is one of several publications that have been made possible through the Academic Link, of which two other volumes were prepared by the present editors. Although the Link has now officially come to an end, it is hoped that the network created through it will continue to prove its worth for many years to come; and some new volumes are in fact already in active preparation.

It is once again pleasing to note that the influence of the Link has extended to Sokoine University of Agriculture, at which six contributors are based. The authors are also grateful for the contributions from Stefano Ponte (Duke University and University of East Anglia), and Professor Pat Caplan (Institute of Commonwealth Studies, University of London); to Ibun Kombo, who supplied information on important points of detail; and to Stella Ryan, who prepared the final version of the text.

Mention here does not imply approval of or agreement with the contents, for which the authors and editors take full responsibility.

# List of Abbreviations

| | |
|---|---|
| ACTS | Africa Centre for Technology Studies |
| AGSASU | Agricultural Sample Survey |
| ASP | Afro-Shirazi Party |
| BoT | Bank of Tanzania |
| BRALUP | Bureau of Resource Assessment and Land Use Planning |
| CAB | Central Agricultural Bureau |
| CCM | Chama cha Mapinduzi |
| CDC | Colonial/Commonwealth Development Corporation |
| CDR | Centre for Development Research |
| CG | Consultative Group (for Tanzania) |
| CIMMYT | Centro Internacional para el Mejoramiento del Maiz y del Trigo (International Centre for Maize and Wheat Improvement) |
| CODESRIA | Council for the Development of Economic and Social Research in Africa |
| CUF | Civic United Front |
| DALDO | District Agricultural and Livestock Development Officer |
| DSI | Development Studies Institute |
| EAC | East African Community |
| EALB | East Africa Literature Bureau |
| EAPH | East Africa Publishing House |
| ERB | Economic Resource Bureau |
| ERP | Economic Recovery Programme |
| ESAF | Enhanced Strutural Adjustment Facility |
| ESAP | Economic and Social Action Programme |
| EWU | Early Warning Unit |
| FAO | Food and Agricultural Organization (United Nations) |
| GDP | Gross Domestic Product |
| GNP | Gross National Product |
| ha. | hectares |
| HASHI | Hifadhi Ardhi Shinyanga (Shinyanga Soil Conservation) |
| HBS | Household Budget Survey |
| HIMA | Hifadhi Mazingira (Mazingira Conservation) |
| HMSO | Her Majesty's Stationery Office |
| HYV | High Yielding Variety |
| IBRD | International Bank for Reconstruction and Development |
| ICE | Institute of Continuing Education (SUA) |

| | |
|---|---|
| ICRA | International Centre for Development-oriented Research in Agriculture (Wageningen) |
| ICRAF | International Council for Research in Agroforestry (Kenya) |
| IDRC | International Development Research Centre (Ottawa) |
| IDS | Institute of Development Studies |
| IFAD | International Fund for Agricultural Development |
| IFI | International Financial Institution |
| IIED | International Institute for Environment and Development |
| IIED | International Institute of Economic Development |
| IK | Indigenous Knowledge |
| ILEIA | Information Centre for Low External Input and Sustainable Agriculture (Netherlands) |
| ILO | International Labour Office |
| IMF | International Monetary Fund |
| IPC | Investment Promotion Centre |
| IRA | Institute of Resource Assessment |
| ITK | Indigenous Technical Knowledge |
| JKT | Jeshi la Kujenga Taifa (National Service Corporation Sole) |
| kg. | kilograms |
| km. | kilometres |
| LSFS | Large-scale Farm Survey |
| MALCD | Ministry of Agriculture, Livestock and Cooperative Development |
| MCH | Maternity and Child Health |
| MDB | Marketing Development Bureau |
| MLHUD | Ministry of Lands, Housing and Urban Development |
| MoA | Ministry of Agriculture |
| MVIWATA | Mtandao wa Vikundi vya Wakulima Tanzania (Farmers' Group Network in Tanzania) |
| NAFCO | National Agriculture and Food Company |
| NAP | National Agricultural Policy |
| NCCR | National Convention for Construction and Reform |
| NESP | National Economic Survival Programme |
| NMC | National Milling Corporation |
| NORAD | Norwegian Agency for International Development |
| NSCA | National Sample Census of Agriculture |
| ODA | Overseas Development Administration (UK) |
| ODI | Overseas Development Institute (UK) |
| OECD | Organization for Economic Cooperation and Development |
| PANET | Pastoral Network of Tanzania |
| PRA | Participatory Rural Appraisal |
| RALDO | Regional Agriculture and Livestock Development Officer |
| SAP | Structural Adjustment Programme |
| SCOM | Strengthening Communication Project |
| SES | Socio-economic Status |
| SGR | Strategic Grain Reserve |
| SHISCAP | Shinyanga Soil Conservation and Afforestation Programme |

| | |
|---|---|
| SIAS | Scandinavian Institute for African Studies |
| STAMICO | State Mining Corporation |
| SUA | Sokoine University of Agriculture |
| TACTA | Tanganyika Cooperative Trading Agency |
| TADREG | Tanzania Development Research Group |
| TAG | Tanzania Advisory Group |
| TANAA | Tanzania Agricultural Adjustment Programme |
| TANESCO | Tanzania Electrical Supply Company |
| TANU | Tanganyika African National Union |
| TAZARA | Tanzania-Zambia Railway Authority |
| TCG | Tanzania Consultative Group |
| TCGA | Tanzania Coffee Growers' Association |
| TET | Tanzania Economic Trends |
| TPH | Tanzania Publishing House |
| TRC | Tanzania Railways Corporation |
| Tsh. | Tanzania Shillings |
| Tz | Tanzania |
| UDP | United Democratic Party |
| UMADEP | Uluguru Mountains Agricultural Development Project |
| UMD | United Multiparty Democracy |
| UN | United Nations |
| UNCED | United Nations Conference on Environment and Development |
| UNDP | United Nations Development Plan |
| URT | United Republic of Tanzania |
| VSA | Village Settlement Agency |
| WB | World Bank |
| ZNP | Zanzibar Nationalist Party |
| ZPPP | Zanzibar and Pemba People's Party |

# Introduction

PETER G. FORSTER AND SAM MAGHIMBI

The importance of peasant farming in Tanzania cannot be overemphasized. The country is heavily dependent on the peasant economy for jobs, food, raw materials for industries, and foreign exchange. The major crops which earn the country foreign exchange are all (except sisal) grown mostly by peasants. These crops include cotton, cashew nuts, coffee, tea, tobacco, and pyrethrum. In the case of food crops, it is only wheat which is grown mostly in plantations, though some peasants also grow it. The other major food crops (maize, paddy and pulses) are overwhelmingly grown by peasants.

Since the publication of the two volumes of *The Tanzanian Peasantry* (in 1992 and 1995) agricultural production has not shown much improvement. In the 1980s agricultural production tended to show a downward trend, or at best stagnate. This is clearer when one compares current output with the 1980s and the 1970s, using production data for two crops: cashew nuts (a peasant crop) and sisal (a plantation crop).

In the volumes of *The Tanzanian Peasantry*, several causes of the decline in the peasant economy and the whole rural economy were analysed. These included the abolition of cooperatives and local governments, the creation of communal (*ujamaa*) villages in the countryside and the introduction of Parastatal Crop Authorities.

Attempts made by the government to revive the peasant economy are part of what have been termed 'adjustment measures'. Local government and cooperatives were reinstated in 1985 and Parastatal Crop Authorities were abolished. From 1984 the government of Tanzania attempted adjustment measures and currently the country is in the second decade of adjustment.

Adjustment was examined in the second volume of *The Tanzanian Peasantry* but there is a need now to make detailed studies of its impact on the Tanzanian economy. It seems that although there was early optimistic evaluation of adjustment policies, their impact could have been overestimated. Up-to-date information and detailed analysis are therefore required.

During the ten years ending in 1983 the growth in GDP for Tanzania averaged just under 2 per cent (Gibbon, 1995, p. 15). This was below the rate of population growth: the average annual population growth rate was 3.2 per cent in 1967-78 and 2.8 per cent in 1978-88 (URT, 1991, p. 21).

## Table 1  Production of two major export crops

| Year | Sisal | Cashew Nuts |
|------|-------|-------------|
| 1960-1 | 198 | 40 |
| 1965-6 | 225 | 74 |
| 1970-1 | 181 | 113 |
| 1975-6 | 114 | 84 |
| 1980-1 | 74 | 57 |
| 1985-6 | 29 | 19 |
| 1989-90 | 40 | 25 |
| 1994-5 | 28 | 70 |

(figures given to nearest 1000 tons)

*Source*: MoA, 1995;  Maghimbi, 1990, p. 273.

## Table 2  Peak year and lowest year (sisal and cashew nuts)

| Sisal | | Cashew Nuts | |
|-------|-----|-------------|-----|
| 1965-6 | 225 | 1973-4 | 141 |
| 1984-5 | 28 | 1986-7 | 17 |

*Source*: MoA, 1995;  Maghimbi, 1990, p. 273.

Between 1984 and 1986 the annual GDP growth rate rose to 3.3 per cent;  for 1987-90 it was 3.7 per cent;  for 1991-3 it rose to 3.8 per cent (Gibbon, 1995, p. 15).  These later figures are all above the rate of population growth, and could be considered impressive if one bears in mind that Tanzania's terms of trade declined by 30 per cent during 1987-91.  Nevertheless, there are doubts about the real level of economic expansion which has occurred.  The unregistered economy accounted for at least 30 per cent of the total economic activity in the preadjustment period.  Thus even if only a fraction of this had been subsequently officialized as a consequence of the deregulation measures that occurred during adjustment, the GDP should have registered a significant growth.  For example, it was estimated that the partial incorporation of previously unregistered gold production into the GDP after 1989 alone accounted for 1 per cent growth in the annual GDP (Gibbon, 1995, p. 15).

Structural adjustment has not resulted in rapid advancement of the peasant economy.  There are also indications that the social sectors like education and health have been *adversely* affected. There is thus a need for new studies on structural adjustment. Initially there was a rush by policy-makers, academics, and the World Bank and IMF, to conclude that the economy and standard of living of Tanzanians was improving as a result of adjustment measures. One expert on Tanzania has been more cautious in his assessment, concluding that:

> Even taking account of the terms of trade data mentioned above (i.e. the thirty per cent decline for 1987-90) figures on export and import levels since 1986 have been disappointing. While imports have climbed steadily to around $1500 million per annum in the context of trade liberalisation, exports have remained at between only $300 and $400 million per annum, as they were when adjustment started. Inflation has remained rather high, at consistently over 20 per cent. Of more concern still are the basic social indicators. Infant mortality (deaths per 1000 live births) fell from 122 in 1980 to 117 in 1985, but this fall then slowed to 115 by 1991. Life expectancy at birth, which has been 47.2 years in 1980, rose to 48.0 years in 1985 before falling to 47.3 in 1991. Primary school enrolments, which stood at 93 per cent of the relevant age group in 1980, declined to 72 per cent in 1985 and 63 per cent in 1991 (Gibbon, 1995, p. 15).

Structural adjustment measures were expected to result in raising of producer prices and wages but as the chapter by Maghimbi on the failure of institutional, technical and structure shifts in peasant agriculture shows, increases in producer prices have been matched by increases in the cost of inputs such as fertilizer.

The failure of peasant agriculture in Tanzania to take off has contributed to the slow growth of industries and the urban economy in general. Land parcelization remains the major constraint on the advancement of peasant agriculture. Adjustment policies failed to address the question of land reform. Parcelization was an area indicated as problematic in the first volume of *The Tanzanian Peasantry* (Forster and Maghimbi, 1992, p. xix), while in the second volume (Forster and Maghimbi, 1992, p. xxi), it was argued that for rural development to occur in Tanzania there was a need to address land reform, institutional reform, community development, and technological progress. None of these four areas has been properly addressed during the era of structural adjustment in the 1990s. Some institutional reforms were attempted but these were limited and did not result in increased productivity in the peasant economy. The appearance of the present volume comes at the right time to examine why the peasant economy is not advancing in a country with a big agricultural potential. A disturbing lack of policy remains evident, despite the overwhelming preponderance of peasants in the Tanzanian population and the key importance of their contribution to the economy. The assumptions upon which *ujamaa* socialism were based have been subject to serious criticism, and there is recognition of the ineffectiveness of top-down measures in general; but there is uncertainty concerning what to put in their place.

## Structural Adjustment and Land Reform

The issue of structural adjustment inevitably dominates the discussion at macroscopic level, and also has repercussions in the local situation. It can be considered in conjunction with land reform, since there is an emphasis upon 'liberalization' and private enterprise, with corresponding pressure towards individualization of land tenure. However, the effectiveness of structural adjustment in achieving its objects can turn out to be highly dubious. Most of the papers in Part I reflect this concern.

Ponte notes that there was indeed a crisis, but that the remedies proposed were based upon a new orthodoxy which supported free market reforms. He suggests that it was more a matter of a paradigm shift than the adoption of a new strategy of proven effectiveness; and that reports of beneficial consequences were often based upon spurious or non-existent data. Failures, likewise, were explained in terms of lack of thoroughgoing implementation of free-market reforms.

However, it must be remembered that all economic theorizing and policy-making occurs in a political context, and some contributors to the present volume have seen it as appropriate to highlight the political dimension. This in turn is to be placed in the historic context of colonialism, in view of the legacy of policies which benefited settlers to the detriment of the peasantry. But, as Mlambiti shows, the importance of political factors in development continues to remain crucial, and he suggests that this has been apparent in relation to both *ujamaa* and structural adjustment. After independence a continued high profile for the state was apparent, and Maghimbi (Ch. 5) notes how other ends were set aside against the policy of a quick victory for African socialism. However, as Chachage suggests, structural adjustment might be seen as part of a global movement away from the 'big state'.

When the peasantry are being considered, the question of land tenure is obviously a crucial aspect of government policies. Kiondo notes again how colonial land policies were related to the needs of settlers, and Maghimbi (Ch. 6) examines the special case of Zanzibar, where Arab colonialism predated British penetration. Arab domination then came to be supported by the British, and land alienation was allowed to continue to a far greater extent than it occurred on the Mainland. The eventual consequence was revolution. In the case of the Mainland, Chachage shows how the settler-oriented land policies that were practised by the colonial powers continued side by side with measures to conserve traditional measures of peasant agriculture. He notes, however, that after 1945 there was a move towards a 'modernization' approach, which in its turn downgraded what peasants were in fact able to achieve.

One important issue that arises concerns the question of legal title to land, which relates to the individualization of land tenure. Maghimbi (Ch. 5) notes the problem of lack of title deeds and the difficulties arising from lack of clarity in respect of claims. He also notes that larger holdings would be needed for a 'green revolution' to occur and suggests that a major problem inherited from the *ujamaa* era is that the latter tended to preserve holdings of a size unsuitable for innovatory practices.

Some contributors point to numerous difficulties that have arisen as a result of individualization of land tenure. Mlambiti shows that policies arising from structural adjustment have led to the speculative holding of land to the detriment of the peasants, among whom poverty has increased with structural adjustment. He also notes that, as such land often stands empty, there is no benefit to national development goals in general. Kiondo also comments on this tendency, thereby refuting the idea that individualization of land holding necessarily leads to better utilization. He also notes that even illegal annexation of peasant land sometimes occurs with impunity. Kiondo continues by showing that private investors with larger holdings might be able to secure credit; but that this is to the detriment of the poor - especially the women and the younger men, whose land rights are likely to be the first to be disposed of. He sees an explosive situation as likely to develop as a result, and urges recognition of the futility of development plans which do not take peasants' needs into account. Chachage confirms that in the new situation, larger investors have pursued land alienation further, in some cases for mining; while in other cases land is acquired by rich urban people. Both he and Mlambiti see the need for land reform to be undertaken in accordance with a wider process of democratization.

Maghimbi (Ch. 5) does however argue that measures to promote equality can destroy agriculture, showing that the success of green revolution policies in India was dependent upon consolidation of land holdings and the stimulation of the richer peasants. He sees the latter as having been present among the cooperative activists in Tanzania in the past, but as subsequently destroyed by government policies. Maghimbi continues by showing that the technology for a green revolution has been available for a long time, but that without land reform it cannot be applied effectively. On the other hand, in his discussion of Zanzibar (Ch. 6), Maghimbi notes that land reform on its own is insufficient. He points out that in Zanzibar there was some redistribution of land, but that stagnation continued. He attributes this to the lack of government action in channelling credit to peasants and in the initiation of technological change - with profits channelled into other activities such as the building of residential accommodation.

## Indigenous Technical Knowledge

It is encouraging that the theme of peasant knowledge, raised in both volumes of *The Tanzanian Peasantry*, can be continued here. This is particularly relevant in the context of the lead taken by the United Nations with regard to greater environmental awareness, including the conservation of biodiversity (as Lugeye is concerned to stress). Rutatora also notes that systems of agriculture which are based upon indigenous technical knowledge are more sustainable since they use locally available materials and do not require foreign exchange. All contributors to this section recognize the need to record what peasants already know, and Lugeye argues that students of agriculture should be taught this in their curricula. Rutatora examines in considerable detail a specific system of indigenous agriculture.

Contributors to this section generally recognize that peasant knowledge is far from static. Kajembe and Rutatora show how indigenous technical knowledge can be seen as evolving through time, and they observe that there is even evidence that peasants perform experiments - though little of this has been put on record. Lugeye shows that outside knowledge is incorporated into indigenous technical knowledge where it is seen to be compatible, and Rutatora shows that it develops and adapts in accordance with land availability. Mattee and Lassalle develop themes suggested in *The Tanzanian Peasantry* (Forster and Maghimbi, 1995, Ch. 10). They show the constant process of adaptation and improvement among Uluguru farmers. They stress the importance of ensuring that extension operates within that context, with the involvement of farmers throughout.

It is again suggested that top-down approaches simply do not work, and that there is a need to examine the process of communication between peasants and researchers. Mattee and Lassalle see this as a central problem, and show the importance of a collaborative technique which will help to overcome conservative behaviour (which is displayed by researchers as well as by peasants). They see researchers as facilitating rather than leading, and they recognize the key factor in the situation as being the strengthening of communication. It is also acknowledged, particularly in relation to the case studied by Rutatora, that indigenous methods cannot now be left to function unaided. Rutatora shows that key problem-areas include population increase, reduced collective decision-making, migration to areas where the system is less effective, and the growing of more lucrative crops for which the system is also less appropriate.

**Case Studies**

The specific studies in Part III examine a number of relevant issues from different perspectives. Lyimo's two contributions deal with research in villages on the issue of peasant access to resources. In Ch. 11, Lyimo also notes the failure of top-down methods and over-bureaucratic procedures. He confirms that development needs to be peasant-centred and that communication with peasants should be a two-way process. He sees the failure of peasants to adopt improved technology, seeds, and inputs such as pesticides and fertilizers as symptomatic of inappropriate attempts at government intervention. In Ch. 12, the research in the villages is presented in more depth, and an examination is made of variation in access to the resources which are needed to improve production. Lyimo notes that there are variations both between and within villages with respect to such access.

Mlozi's contribution raises the interesting question of agriculture and the environment, but in relation to the urban setting. He shows that this activity is carried on by those of a wide range of socio-economic status. Practitioners include the elites, for whom it can be a major source of income despite their relatively high salaries. Political clout is shown to be relevant here, since influential people can ensure that by-laws aiming to regulate urban agriculture are not properly enforced.

Two contributors also show that cultural factors are not always supportive of development goals. Mesaki suggests this with respect to the Coast Region, where cultural celebrations take up a particularly long time, and witchcraft beliefs and practices can also inhibit progress. He does however see other factors as relevant, especially since the area is near to Dar es Salaam. As a consequence there is a tendency to seek paid work in town rather than engage in labour-intensive cultivation in the village.

The system of out-migration also places a greater burden on the women. This is noted by Mesaki, who quotes Caplan's work on this subject. Caplan's contribution to this volume (dealing with Mafia Island) looks further and maintains that the preference for male children is such that girls receive less adequate medical attention and nutrition, so that fewer survive to adult life. It is clear that in such a situation, development cannot be totally accommodating to cultural values and supportive of the empowerment of women at the same time.

Finally, political change is scrutinized directly in Sivalon's discussion of peasants' attitudes to the multi-party elections which were forthcoming in 1995. The results are of great interest, since multipartyism is clearly seen in the rural areas as not an improvement: even though CCM is felt to benefit the rich, the business community and foreigners rather than themselves. Women, the poor and the uneducated are shown as particularly sceptical of multipartyism. CCM is viewed critically but reform within the single party is seen as a more realistic alternative. A general feeling is apparent that all politicians, whatever their political colour, will simply come and tell peasants what to do.

## Common Themes

There is little optimism for the future. The overall message seems to be that there were many mistakes in the past but that the new system has done nothing to improve the situation. There is much recognition of the ineffectiveness of top-down measures and bureaucratic excesses, and of the need to listen to the peasants: but this is to be seen in the overall context of entrenched elite privilege which also enables the process of law to be used for personal advantage or even to be circumvented. Unregulated capitalism has not made the lot of the peasant any easier, and has deprived many of their means of livelihood. There clearly is a need to improve peasant agriculture, and culture involves some constraints as well as sometimes being responsive to innovation. An atmosphere of trust between peasants and those who make decisions of more far-ranging scope is clearly called for but in the present context there are many obstacles to achieving this.

## References

Forster, P.G. and Maghimbi, S. (1982), *The Tanzanian Peasantry: Economy in Crisis*, Avebury, Aldershot.

Forster, P.G. and Maghimbi, S. (1995), *The Tanzanian Peasantry: Further Studies*, Avebury, Aldershot.

Gibbon, P. (1995), 'Mechanization of Production and Privatization of Development in Post-Ujamaa Tanzania', in Gibbon (ed), *Liberalized Development in Tanzania*, Nordiska Afrikainstitutet, Uppsala, pp. 9-36.

Maghimbi, S. (1990), 'Rural Development Policy and Planning in Tanzania', PhD thesis, University of London (London School of Economics).

URT (1991), *1988 Population Census: Preliminary Report*, Bureau of Statistics, Ministry of Finance, Economic Affairs and Planning, Dar es Salaam.

URT (MoA) (1996), *Agricultural Policy 1995*, Dar es Salaam.

# Part I

# STRUCTURAL ADJUSTMENT AND LAND REFORM

# 1  Trading Images: Discourse and Statistical Evidence on Agricultural Adjustment in Tanzania (1986-95)

STEFANO PONTE

## Introduction

Agricultural reforms have been a constant feature of policy change in Africa since the mid-1980s.  In order to understand the historical dynamics of these reforms, the expectations built around them, and the interpretation of their outcomes, we need to analyse how market liberalization has been conceptualized and embodied in the framework of the official discourse of governments and International Financial Institutions (IFIs).  The way the 'need' for reforms is created, and the way reforms are justified ex-ante and assessed ex-post also provides a useful background to better comprehend how governments and IFIs manage to present new requests for more reforms, more time and patience, and more hardship to the public.

The idea that 'adjustment' is a particular stage in the path toward 'development' is a powerful engine for pushing for policy change.  However, the experience of African countries with adjustment has been, for the most part, a shifting target.  As soon as governments implement some reforms, there are always others to be accomplished, and the game goes on.  When it comes to assessing results, weak evidence is used to purport dubious success.  This is particularly evident in the World Bank discourse on structural adjustment and economic growth in Africa (see Ponte, 1994).  When the results are not as good as expected, governments and IFIs argue that certain reforms were not implemented properly, that the contingent or structural situation was not conducive for more positive results, or that other reforms are needed.

The first aim of this chapter is to look at how the Government of Tanzania, the World Bank and the International Monetary Fund (IMF) constituted their discourse on agricultural adjustment and how they depicted agricultural performance in official and public statements in 1986-95.  A second aim is to analyse the consequences of the creation of these official images in terms of claims for further policy change affecting rural livelihoods.  The changes in the structure of economic incentives brought by economic reforms are one key point

3

in discussion, but not only 'visible' or 'material' change is determinant. Discourse and symbolic representation shape outcomes as well as - and through - 'technical' or 'practical' intervention.

In his study of the Thaba-Tseka Project in Lesotho, Ferguson has clearly described how the production of 'development discourse' has had profound 'real' social and economic effects in the areas concerned with the project (Ferguson, 1994). Other works have been concerned with the role of 'development' discourse in shaping structural change, but have tended to analyse discourse in terms of expression of 'true' intentions versus rhetoric, where rhetoric provided international organizations with ways to achieve hidden goals (among others, see Bernstein, 1981; Heyer, Roberts and Williams (eds.), 1981; and Williams, 1986). Ferguson differs from these works in that he does not want to dismiss rhetoric only as 'untrue' and 'ideological', but to analyse it for what it does. Ferguson argues that the outcomes of planned social interventions never end up being what was intended and he dismisses the interpretation of the production of development discourse by international organizations in terms of 'conspiracy' theory (Ferguson, 1994, p.18).

In this chapter, I will described how the creation of ideas about agricultural change and performance has had an important role in the production of certain sorts of structural change during adjustment reforms in Tanzania. To paraphrase Ferguson, the aim of this study is not to analyse what agricultural adjustment does not do or might do, but to analyse what it has done and does in Tanzania. However, we will see that 'what it has done' is precisely to have introduced a particular economic credo in the rhetoric - and practice - of agricultural policy-making. What was planned by the IMF and the World Bank in the early 1980s has been carried out with accuracy in Tanzania, even if some reforms were delayed and more interventions are asked by the IFIs in order to reach a complete adjustment. 'Conspiracy' theory or not, the radical passage from *ujamaa* type of thinking to the acceptance of the conceptual apparatus of market liberalization looks more like the outcome of a planned process of ideological engineering rather than its unintended result. The way these reforms have been brought about, and the quality of the statistical evidence used to justify policy change, raise a number of issues about how ideas on the economy and economic performance have been constructed and re-constructed in Tanzania and by whom.

In the next section I will analyse how the 'need' for adjustment was progressively created in the early and mid-1980s in Tanzania. In the following section, I will trace the content and the expectations that were made around the first Economic Recovery Programme (ERP) of 1986-89. I then outline the sparkling evaluations of this programme that were made by the Government and the IFIs. I trace the disillusionment that emerged in the 1990s with slowing agricultural performance, and the difficulties that emerged in the negotiations between the Government and the IFIs. I analyse in detail one of the aspects that marked the whole period of adjustment: the repeated requests by the IFIs for more interventions and further reforms. I scrutinize the evidence which is still

4

used to purport the results of agricultural adjustment in Tanzania in the last ten years in terms of a 'success'. In the last section, I summarize the main findings and trace some conclusions.

## The 'Need' for Adjustment

In order to adjust, a country needs to have something 'out of place' which causes some kind of 'problem'. With the publication of the Berg Report (Berg, 1987), the World Bank earmarked macroeconomic policies as being 'out of place' in Sub-Saharan Africa and indicated low GDP growth as 'the problem' (IBRD, 1981). In the case of the agricultural sector in Tanzania, inappropriate agricultural policies were said to have caused low growth of agricultural GDP in the late 1970s and early 1980s; therefore, profound reforms were needed (see URT, 1985: pp. 7-10; IBRD, 1983). But how did the creation, or the realization, of these 'facts' take place?

Let us start with the external environment which Tanzania had to face during the 'crisis' period and the inappropriateness of the Government's policy-making. Several *external* factors have been indicated as having brought the Tanzanian economy into a 'crisis': (1) weak demand for agricultural products in international markets; (2) worsening terms of trade; (3) rising interest rates; (4) the proliferation of protectionism in the form of non-tariff measures by industrializing countries; (5) the oil shocks; (6) the breakdown of the East African Community (EAC) in 1977; (7) the war with Uganda; and (8) recurrent droughts (1976, 1980, 1983 and 1984). What took the lead in the dominant thinking, however, was a list of *domestic policy* factors which were said to have contributed to 'Tanzania's own bankruptcy'. Lipumba listed them as: (1) public overspending and over-interventionism of the state in the economy; (2) a corrupted and unskilled bureaucracy; (3) ill-conceived domestic economic policies; (4) the inefficiency of most parastatal enterprises (in particular the agricultural marketing boards); (5) the strategy of development of an import-dependent industrial sector; and (6) an institutional framework that discouraged individuals from an efficient utilization of resources in order to increase production (Lipumba, 1988).

Agriculture in particular was said to have suffered from strict regulation of trade and low crop producer prices. Inefficient parastatals were accused of lack of coordination, poor transportation capacity and maintenance, untimely crop collection, inadequate storing, and delayed payments. Pan-territorial pricing was said to have encouraged regions with poor transportation infrastructure to grow crops with high transport cost, which could not be stored or transported adequately, i.e. maize. Inefficiencies in the marketing system caused low availability of inputs such as fertilizers and improved seeds. By the late 1970s, most private retail shops were closed, and the Regional Trading Corporations were charged with distributing food and consumer goods. The consumers willing

5

to purchase these commodities faced rationing in the official market and unreliable supplies in the parallel markets; hence, it was said that their incentives to increase production were curtailed by the lack of access to alternative goods to buy, especially in the late 1970s and early 1980s (see Bevan and Collier, 1991; Ellis, 1988; Lele and Meyers, 1987; Lofchie, 1989; Ponte, 1994; and IBRD, 1983, 1990b, 1994).

The 'crisis' eventually brought Tanzania to the table of negotiation with the IMF in 1980, when a three-year stand-by agreement was signed. By November of the same year the programme had already fallen apart because of Tanzania's inability to meet certain performance requirements. Negotiations in 1981 did not produce a new agreement. In order to mobilize foreign exchange, the Government had to design a reform programme by itself - the National Economic Survival Programme (NESP). The NESP was followed in 1982 by another 'domestic' Structural Adjustment Programme (SAP), which aimed at dealing with the country's serious structural problems (URT, 1989a, p.2). In the agricultural sector, the SAP aimed at higher producer prices, improved input availability, and improved market structure. With the 1984-85 budget, the government more than doubled agricultural expenditure, removed the subsidy on the consumer price of maize, raised agricultural producer prices, and announced a substantial devaluation (see Gibbon, Havnevik and Hermele 1993). Shortages of petroleum and running water and the difficulty of getting credit without the IMF 'seal of approval' eventually led the Tanzanian government to endorse the Economic Recovery Programme (ERP) with the IMF in 1986. The election of the more reform-minded President Ali Hassan Mwinyi in 1985 also helped to reach the final agreement.

From the side of the 'problem' of low GDP growth, the World Bank maintains that 'from the mid-1970s to the early 1980s, there was a period of economic decline and slow growth' (IBRD, 1992, p.2). The data we find in the Tanzania Agricultural Sector Report of 1994 shows an annual growth rate of agricultural GDP of 2.11 per cent in 1966-75, 0.7 per cent in 1976-80, 2.07 per cent in 1981-83, and 6 per cent in 1984-85. The same report claims that 'in the early to the mid-1980s a series of changes in economic incentives were attempted, but failed for lack of comprehensive approach'. The implication we can trace is that 'real' adjustment, according to the World Bank, began with the ERP of 1986. If this is the case, we can understand the 'crisis' period to be between 1976 and 1985. During this period, according to World Bank data, the average annual rate of growth of agricultural GDP was a mere 2.18 per cent, which sets our 'crisis' indicator. We will return to the significance of this figure later on.

What is necessary to note here is that, by the mid-1980s, after prolonged confrontation, both the Government and the IFIs publicly announced that there was a 'need' to overcome the state of 'crisis' caused by past inappropriate agricultural policies, and the way out was spelled out within the liberalization framework of ERP. Beyond the official rhetoric, however, the Tanzanian 'crisis'

6

for the IFIs was a good chance to spread the new orthodoxy of free market reforms in the country. From the Government side, overcoming the 'crisis' meant especially being able to re-establish the flow of foreign assistance which had tumbled since the late 1970s. In the next section, I will summarize the contents of the reforms to be implemented and the expectations built around them.

## ERP and the Liberalization of Food Marketing (1986-1989)

Agriculture figured at the core of the Economic Recovery Programme (ERP). ERP officially lasted from 1986-87 to 1988-89 and was later replaced by ERPII Economic and Social Action Programme (ERPII ESAP). Accounting for 46 per cent of the GDP, 75 per cent of total export earnings, and employing 90 per cent of the workforce (1985 data), any 'appropriate' reform in agriculture was expected to have a long-lasting and positive impact on the whole economy of Tanzania (URT, 1985: p.8). ERP provided a clear indication of the parameter of reference to assess agricultural reforms in Tanzania: 'The Government will make every effort possible to sustain so that the full benefit of the initiatives already taken can be translated in *higher agricultural growth'* (URT, 1985: p.24, emphasis added). ERP also stated that 'the Government fully recognizes that it is through the agricultural sector that Tanzania's ultimate goal of *equity* and *integrated development* can best be served'. The ultimate meaning of equity in this context is rather unclear, as structural adjustment is about redirecting the economy towards more efficiency and improved allocation of resources, not about providing proto-socialistic equal opportunities to the people. Probably, the Government felt inclined to leave some reference to *ujamaa* rhetoric, in order to appease the hard-liners within the ruling party Chama cha Mapinduzi. These references, as we will see, will gradually disappear in the Government's conceptual apparatus.

The framework of reference for the reforms to be implemented in the agricultural sector was provided by the World Bank recommendations included in the 1985 *Tanzania Agricultural Sector Report* (IBRD, 1983), most of which were included in the Government's own *Agricultural Policy of Tanzania* (URT, 1983). The core requirements listed in the World Bank document comprise: (1) priority allocation of resources and foreign exchange to the agricultural sector; (2) reduction of the role of parastatals; (3) raising producer prices and retail food prices; (4) adjusting the exchange rate to reduce parastatal losses; and (5) legalization of the private sector in agricultural input and output marketing and transport (IBRD, 1983: pp. 187-188). A list of 39 detailed recommendations followed, concerning measures to be taken in agricultural pricing, food security, crop processing and marketing, export promotion, and distribution of inputs.

With obvious simplifications, this is the framework within which the Government presented its reform programme in June 1986 at the Consultative Group for Tanzania (CG) in Paris. At the same CG meeting, the IMF stated that

7

'the main emphasis of the programme is to provide to economic agents the appropriate pricing signals and to give them the necessary opportunities to act on the basis of those signals. This should provide incentives toward economic efficiency and improved allocation of scarce resources' (IMF, 1986, pp. 6-7; emphasis added). Since the Government had already started some reforms before 1986, the IMF statement conceded that a number of adjustment measures had already been taken by the government, such as a depreciation of the Tanzanian Shilling of 25 per cent, and an increase of producer prices in real terms of 10-15 per cent. However, the statement claims, 'partial attempts at correcting a fundamentally deteriorating economic and financial situation do not succeed ... in the absence of appropriate price signals' (IMF, 1986, p. 3).

From these statements we notice how the IMF insisted on a comprehensive and complete approach to economic reforms, with clear emphasis on the primary role of reforms eliminating distortions in the pricing and incentive systems. The World Bank confirmed its change of thinking which had begun with the publication of the 'Berg Report' by saying that the focus of its assistance in Tanzania would 'shift from specific investment projects to programmes which will support recovery in the main sectors - agriculture, transport and industry' (IBRD, 1986, p.2). Note that the programmes *will* - not should or might - support recovery; the implication being that future recovery is certain and that the World Bank programs will be instrumental in causing/supporting it.

In terms of timing for recovery, the Government acknowledged that 'the economic problems facing [Tanzania] today are structural in nature and will require a medium- to long-term time-frame for supply bottlenecks to be removed' (URT, 1986, p.5). This position reflects the caution expressed by the IBRD in 1983, when it remarked that the past neglect of the institutional capabilities of the Ministries of Agriculture, Transport and Education, and the national extension and research systems 'greatly reduce the response which can be expected from the agricultural sector to any short run recovery measures. Because institutional reform is so complex, recovery will be slow and difficult' (IBRD, 1983, p.xiii).

In conclusion, recovery was undoubtedly expected to stem from economic reforms, but in 1986, caution ruled over enthusiasm in terms of the time-frame of supply response. However, we will find in the next section that, as soon as rates of growth showed improvements in the first three years of ERP, cautious statements over the timing of recovery were abandoned, and enhanced growth was announced to be already under way, spurred by the economic reforms included in ERP.


**Declaring the 'Miracle': Official Evaluations of ERP**

The reforms included in ERP (1986-1989) entailed profound changes in the agricultural market environment, especially in the food sector. The Government abolished restrictions on internal marketing and movement of foodgrains; private

8

traders expanded their role in maize trading;  the role of the National Milling Corporation (NMC) was reduced to buyer of last resort and manager of food security stocks;  and panterritorial pricing was abolished.  On the side of export crops, producer prices were increased in real terms, and restrictions in the export of non-traditional export crops were relaxed (URT, 1989a: pp.16-17).

In this section, I will follow the evolution of the assessments that the Government, IMF and the World Bank made on the implementation record of ERP, and their evaluation of its response in terms of agricultural performance.  In its annual review of the 1986 economic situation, the Government forgets the carefully worded statements on the timing of supply response made just the year before, and the 'miracle view' is quickly embraced.  The review says that 'the condition of the national economy in 1986 has changed substantially ... The good rate of growth in agriculture, especially in the food sector, came from the effort of the citizens together with good weather conditions ... *The implementation of the ERP begun to yield its results*' (URT, 1987, p.1;  emphasis added).  But the government was not alone to cry at the 'miracle'.  At the 1987 CG meeting, the IMF states that 'agricultural production increased considerably, spurred by improved weather conditions, higher producer prices, the enhanced flexibility of the marketing system for domestic food crops, and generally improved availability of agricultural inputs' (IMF, 1987, p. 3).  No mention is made here for a time lag in output response.  Good luck - the weather - and good will - reform implementation - were already rewarding Tanzania with higher agricultural GDP growth.

The same story of success is reiterated by the Government in  its annual review of the economic situation for the years 1987, 1988 and 1989 (see URT, 1988, 1989b and 1990).  The Vice-Chairman of the Planning Commission, Hon. Malima, in his speech at the 1990 Economic Policy Workshop in Dar es Salaam, summarizes the Government's stance on the outcomes of ERP: 'the revival of agricultural production was, *in large measure*, the result of various policy initiatives taken under the Economic Recovery Programme, especially, the payment of remunerative agricultural producer prices, timely distribution of fertilizers and other inputs' (TET, 1990, p. 6; emphasis added).  Summarizing the achievements during the first three years of reforms, the World Bank states that 'agricultural production is estimated to have increased by over 5 per cent per year, *mainly* due to trade liberalization in food-crop marketing, the much wider range of available consumer goods in the rural areas, and reasonably good weather conditions' (IBRD, 1989, p.1; emphasis added).  The economic miracle, therefore, is on its way, thanks to agricultural reforms, and rural-based development which was envisioned, but never realized, under *ujamaa*, can be realized by following the dictates of the new economic credo.

On the other hand, the World Bank does remind the Government of Tanzania that 'more has to be done': 'Marketing costs through the marketing boards remain high ... and thus more reform is required ... Most export marketing boards continue to run heavy losses ... [and] prices which farmers receive are far lower than appropriate' (IBRD, 1989, pp. 8-9). Reforms have succeeded, but to sustain agricultural growth 'more reform is required'. This is the same line of thinking produced by the IMF in 1986, when commenting on the limits of partial reforms brought about by the Government's SAP in 1983-85. We will find arguments of this type over and over in the 1990s as well. Before coming back more in detail on this point, in the next section I will expose the change in the general mood over economic reforms which happened in the early 1990s.

## The Disillusionment of the 1990s

The need for another Economic Recovery Programme, in view of the 'exceptional' successes of the first ERP was obvious for the IMF and the World Bank. The new programme, called Economic Recovery Programme II Economic and Social Action Programme (ERPII ESAP) lasted from 1989-90 to 1991-92. For what concerns agriculture, ERPII listed as a major objective to increase domestic agricultural production of 5.5 per cent per annum (URT, 1989a, p. 15). The agricultural policy reforms included in ERPII were: (1) the redefinition of the role of the cooperative unions and the National Milling Corporation in food marketing; (2) reform of the purchasing system for the Strategic Grain Reserve (SGR); (3) reduction of the role of the export marketing boards to managers of the auctions or tender arrangements; (4) giving more autonomy to the cooperatives in terms of crop procuring; (5) recognizing the role of the private sector in export crop marketing, and (6) rehabilitation of processing and storage facilities (URT, 1989a, pp. 16-17). These and other reforms were spelled out in detail in the Tanzania Agricultural Adjustment Program (TANAA), agreed between the World Bank and the Government in 1990 (see IBRD, 1990a).

During the ERPII period, a major restructuring of NMC took place, export marketing boards were reduced to mere auctioneers and responsible for quality control; a cooperative reform was undertaken, and private traders were authorized to purchase cashew nuts. In terms of results in the agricultural sector, unfortunately the first year of ERPII coincided with the end of a three-year period of exceptionally good weather. As a consequence, the agricultural season 1989-90 marked the end of the over-optimistic assessment of economic reforms within the official discourse of the Government and the IFIs. The Government's annual economic review states that 'the performance of agricultural production in 1990 [1990-91 agricultural season] was not good, because of floods and drought ... pest and diseases' (URT, 1991, p. 114). In the Government assessment for 1991-92, the performance of the agricultural sector continues to be regarded unsatisfactorily because of drought, scarcity of agricultural inputs, agricultural tools, and high prices for fertilizers (see URT, 1992b, p. 108). It is curious that the Government was complaining about high prices for fertilizers, when these were mainly caused by the devaluation of the Tanzanian shilling included in the reform package, and later by the elimination of the subsidy on fertilizer purchases.

The last year of ERPII (1991-92) overlapped with the establishment of the IMF support under the Enhanced Structural Adjustment Facility (ESAF), which was supposed to last from 1991-92 to 1993-94. Under this agenda, the IMF and the World Bank asked the Government to consolidate the changes in export marketing introduced in 1990-91. During this time, most of the agricultural sector reforms included in the TANAA agenda have been implemented. The procurement, processing and export of coffee, cotton and tobacco have been liberalized. In 1993-94 over 50 traders were involved in procurement of cashew nuts in competition with cooperatives, 12 of whom undertook the exportation of the crop. Private traders began to procure cotton and to establish ginneries. More than 40 private traders were involved in coffee marketing in 1994-95. The procurement and distribution of agricultural inputs have been liberalized, and the subsidy on fertilizer purchases eliminated. Yet the same problems highlighted for the agricultural seasons 1990-91 and 1991-92 are found in the Government's assessments for the 1992-93 and 1993-94 seasons, where drought and delay in input distribution, together with their high prices, are said to have negatively affected production (URT, 1993, pp. 100-101; URT, 1994, p. 97). Good news came only in the 1994-95 season, when *Hali ya Uchumi* considers the production of food and export crops satisfactory, because of good weather conditions and good level of prices for export crops (URT, 1995, p. 89-91).

In these last few years, apart from the changes in weather conditions and agricultural performance, another important transition has occurred. Donors and IFIs, between 1992 and 1993, have swiftly and substantially revised their stance on the Government's implementation record of economic reforms. At the CG meeting of June 1992, the World Bank still asserted: 'the Tanzanian economy is *no longer in crisis* and ... the Government is concentrating increasingly on fundamental changes in the mode of managing the economy' (IBRD, 1992, p. 1; emphasis added). However, in 1993, the donors started complaining about the shortcomings in implementing tax reforms, too large a public deficit, excessive monetary expansion, and the failure of agricultural cooperatives to reduce their outstanding debt with the banks. The mid-term review of ESAF could not be completed and, by the end of the year, the programme had to be suspended. Even if the Government and the IMF agreed on a Shadow Programme, covering the period January-June 1994, fiscal and monetary targets were exceeded in 1993-94. The CG meeting scheduled for October 1994 had to be postponed, and all aid was frozen as a result of a tax evasion scandal.

Interestingly, at the CG meeting of February 1995 'the donors commended the government on the efforts and results achieved so far but, in view of experience, wanted more time to see that the progress [in dealing with tax exemptions and expenditure control] continues' (TCG, 1995, p. 1). The statement is ironic if we read it in connection with the IMF statement at the same meeting: 'With the support of the international community ... the authorities [of

11

Tanzania] are transforming perhaps one of the most regulated economies in Africa into *one of the most liberalized.* More could be done, but a lot has been achieved' (IMF, 1995: p.1; emphasis added). As we can recall, even at the end of ERPI we were left with a call for more reforms, but in an environment of trust between the Government and the IFIs, and with a background of good expectations for the future. In the mid-1990s, the IMF acknowledges that Tanzania is one of the most liberalized countries in Africa, yet reforms have to be implemented without financial support from the IFIs and the donors. Because of the first multi-party elections to be held in October 1995, the release of aid funds was eventually postponed to the post-election period. At the time of writing, the aid freeze was still operating because, according to the IMF Deputy Director, 'the new government [needs] to have a test of time' *(Daily News,* 11 January, 1996). It is not my intention here to elaborate further on the intermingling of conditionalities regarding economic and political reform. In the next section, however, I will analyse the meaning and the instrumental use that the IMF and the World Bank have made of the calls for more reforms.

**Asking for More**

The ubiquitous calls for more intervention and technical expertise are certainly not new in project, planning and policy reform discourse in developing countries. The agricultural adjustment experience in Tanzania does not escape this tendency. Good agricultural harvests in the second half of the 1980s allowed the Government and the IFIs to proclaim positive outcomes for their new policy direction in agriculture. In official rhetoric, the immediate response of the agricultural sector was linked to new marketing arrangements for food crops, and the restored availability of consumer goods. In some cases, the favourable weather conditions encountered in 1986-89 were also mentioned. However, to sustain agricultural growth, deeper implementation of liberalization measures was deemed necessary, and the good results were there as a testimony of the appropriateness of the path taken. In the 1990s, slowing performance was used as a reason to push for new reforms. The situation changed, but the agenda remained the same: asking for more.

Under the liberalization agenda of the 1980s, the IMF and the World Bank pushed for the divestiture of parastatals and the elimination of market controls in order to achieve a situation where the free market forces would allocate resources without distortions. It was predicted that market forces had to regulate allocation of resources in agriculture, and that this process would have led to more efficiency, and higher production. Nevertheless, when the market forces came to regulate the agricultural sector, we were told that it was not enough, and that big tasks were still ahead. The World Bank, already in 1990, had warned that further reforms were needed to address infrastructural constraints, if the agricultural growth of the late 1980s had to be maintained. The World Bank claimed that 'while addressing the marketing incentive system is a *necessary condition* to restore growth, it alone is not *sufficient*. Other policies in areas such as food security, livestock and land tenure, are important determinants of growth. Poorly performing agricultural services (extension, credit and research) and a deteriorating physical infrastructure also constrain growth and will need to be addressed if the recent growth of agricultural output is to be sustained' (IBRD, 199b, p. 73; original emphasis).

The explicit World Bank's argument for switching to a modernization/infrastructural rehabilitation strategy is that the modernization effort undertaken in the 1970s by the World Bank and the Government failed because 'bad' policies provided the wrong climate. Now we are told that structural adjustment reforms have re-addressed some of the 'bad' policies, that agricultural growth has been restored, and that, in order to sustain growth, further interventions are needed. One problem with this line of thought is that agricultural GDP did *not* increase under adjustment (see next section). However, even if the IFIs acknowledged that agricultural performance did not increase significantly in the reform period, they would argue that adjustment addressed only the 'necessary but not sufficient condition' to restore growth. Therefore, if infrastructural and institutional reforms were met, agriculture would grow faster. The 'more has to be done' argument is always applicable.

The logic of the World Bank's argument is not as solid as it might seem. First of all, the condition of infrastructure, technology, and services in the 1970s was not substantially different from the condition Tanzania is in now. *A priori* we do not know if agriculture would have grown faster had infrastructure and good services been present during the *ujamaa* era. What we are told is that policies were 'bad' and that agricultural growth was low. But, if agricultural growth has not improved under reforms, how can we know that it will in the future, and how do we know that it would not have grown under the previous policy arrangements, given better infrastructure and services? It is not my intention to defend *ujamaa* policies here. What I want to disclose is the inherent weakness of a much-celebrated argument. The counterfactual is not present, and the indication that the path taken with agricultural reforms was the 'right' one is based on belief/ideology rather than on hard evidence.

The World Bank's argument that marketing reforms were 'necessary but not sufficient', and that infrastructural development will now boost growth since an appropriate environment has been created, assumes that the liberalization process itself has *not* placed further hurdles to be overcome. All the marketing reforms are assumed to be 'good' for the development of the country, but we still have no evidence of that, since agricultural production did not increase as much as we are told it did. If this is the case, we still have to wait for another ten years, hoping that massive capital is invested in infrastructural rehabilitation (in an environment of declining aid) and that the weather will be good.

While I do not want to deny that policy mismanagement in the 1970s and early 1980s left major deficiencies in agricultural marketing, we cannot forget that some extreme liberalization measures have also created difficult situations that were not present in the past. One example is the set of circumstances that farmers have to face in the inputs market, which was liberalized in 1992-93. The latest data shows that fertilizer consumption in Tanzania dropped from 148,000 tonnes in 1991-92 to 92,000 tonnes in 1994-95. By the end of the 1994-95 cropping season, the stock of *unused* fertilizer was expected to reach 151,000 tonnes (*Daily News*, October 20, 1995). The subsidy on fertilizer, which was 45 per cent in 1992-93, was lowered to 25 per cent in the following year, and eliminated completely in 1994-95. Farmers in Iringa, in 1994-95, earned only 30,000 Tsh. from an acre (0.405 ha.) of maize compared to 39,100 Tsh. spent on fertilizers.

This evidence does not suggest that there is a current problem in availability of fertilizer, but that it is unaffordable for farmers under the free market's arrangements. This is confirmed by the fact that, owing to the last two seasons' accumulation of fertilizers, no new imports were made for the season 1995-96. The same article cites that a 'source from KILIMO [the Ministry of Agriculture] concludes that if sustained crop production is to be obtained the Government should give special treatment to fertilizers. This should include removal of taxes and return to the subsidy'. We should note that an MoA study on fertilizer production and distribution (URT, 1992a) had recommended *not* to reduce the subsidy of fertilizer with the pace it had been agreed by the Government and the donors at the 1989 CG. The document suggested retention of the 1990-91 level of subsidy (70 per cent) until 1993-94, when it could have been reduced to 4 per cent. However, the pressure for the complete liberalization of input marketing by the donors eventually led to its progressive reduction to 25 per cent in 1993-94 and complete elimination in 1994-95. At the same time, because of the contemporary problems for the cooperative unions to get cash cover to import and distribute inputs, and because of the commercialization of the National Bank of Commerce and Cooperative Rural Development Bank, obtaining inputs on credit or credit for inputs is increasingly difficult for farmers. Another relevant case in the Southern Highlands is the problem of lack of buyers. Private traders tend to eschew maize purchase in remote villages of the Southern Highlands, and if they do buy maize in these areas, their bargaining power is high. As a result, farmers either cannot sell their maize or get very low prices for it. These regions are the same that were earmarked by the Government and the World Bank in the late 1970s for the promotion of maize cultivation through the adoption of high yield varieties and input packages.

The point here is that the World Bank's return to a strategy of modernization and infrastructural rehabilitation comes in an environment where the state is withdrawing from service provision. In the case of fertilizers, for example, it will be extremely difficult to realize yield increases if the new marketing arrangements are not economically conducive for fertilizer use. The fact that all the policies reformed under adjustment are 'good' it is not clear from this evidence. Therefore, the IFIs' argument that the environment is now conducive for sustained agricultural growth in Tanzania, as well as the statistical basis on which it is constructed, is not well founded. In the next section I will expose in detail the weaknesses of the statistical evidence used to calculate agricultural GDP in Tanzania.

## The 'Numbers Tale'

One of the most interesting passages in the changing Governmental rhetoric of the early 1990s is a line from President Mwinyi's speech at the 8th Economic Policy Workshop in 1992: 'Economists ... have an important role to play in educating people of Tanzania on what constitutes sound economic policies and what are mere empty promises' (Bagachwa and Mbelle, 1993, p. 4). In the past, former President Nyerere and other 'philosophical' personalities were the ones who were supposed to educate Tanzanians; now, it is time for neo-classical economists to do so. Apparently, the empty promises which Mwinyi refers to were those of *ujamaa*, while 'realistic' expectations are those laid down within the liberalization agenda. It is necessary to verify how reliable the portrait of agricultural success under agricultural liberalization in Tanzania really is, in order to do some retrospective analysis on which false promises we should talk about.

When describing the outcomes of agricultural reform in Tanzania, the World Bank states that 'most of the measures noted in the agricultural adjustment program were put in place. Agricultural output has grown at 3.0 per cent per annum between 1986 and 1991. This is higher than the trend of 0.7 per cent per annum between 1976 and 1980, or the 2.1 percent per annum growth experienced between 1981 and 1983' (IBRD, 1994, p. 166). If we want to expand the analysis to 1994, and if we believe that agricultural GDP is a reliable figure, then in 1986-1994 we find an annual rate of agricultural growth of 5.1 per cent (calculated from URT, 1995). The indication we should get is that adjustment measures have been implemented, and that consequently agricultural growth has increased. But can we rely on this evidence to purport the 'success' of agricultural adjustment in Tanzania? That agricultural statistics are unreliable in Tanzania is not a new discovery. Nevertheless, official discourse on agricultural reform and performance is for the most part silent on the matter. In this section, I will analyse the problems of estimation of agricultural production so that we can re-read the official proclamations of accelerated agricultural growth with a different perspective.

The main providers of agricultural production statistics in Tanzania are the Ministry of Agriculture (MoA) and the Bureau of Statistics. Within the MoA, data series are published by the Statistics Unit, the Marketing Development Bureau, and the Early Warning Unit.

15

## 1) The Ministry of Agriculture (MOA), Statistics Unit

The MoA publishes a periodical review entitled *Basic Data, Agriculture and Livestock Sector*. The data on export crops published in this review comes from the Marketing Development Bureau (see later in this section). Food production estimates are gathered through the routine reporting system of the MoA, which consists of periodical estimates provided by village extension workers. These estimates are then aggregated by the District and Regional Agriculture and Livestock Development Officers (DALDO and RALDO).

This data is rife with problems. First, areas estimated are often based on the assumption that a particular fixed area is farmed by each able-bodied man, and the total area is simply obtained by multiplying this area by the number of men in the village. Another problem is that extension officers tend to inflate the figures to demonstrate that they are having an impact on local agricultural production. In the past, minimum compulsory acreages were set for certain crops, and villages were awarded for record agricultural production. Finally, these figures are likely to be revised upwards at the district and/or regional level for political reasons. In general, these estimates are subject to an inflationary chain from the village upwards. The routine data is compensated by the MoA crop-cutting surveys which have been administered annually since 1983-84. These surveys are implemented in only a couple of regions per year (from two to six depending on the year) and provide regional estimates on areas and yields for the major food crops.

## 2) The Bureau of Statistics, Planning Commission

Since 1986-87, the Bureau of Statistics has been undertaking periodical Agricultural Sample Surveys (AGSASU) which are considered the best information available on agricultural production. The sample framework of AGSASU is based on 50 village clusters. Within each village an average of 60 farming households are visited. Data collection involves interviews with smallholder farmers, crop cutting and objective area measurements. Crop cutting data is available for four food crops (maize, sorghum, paddy and bulrush millet), while interview data provides information on areas planted and production for up to 18 food crops. The results of the AGSASU for 1986-87, 1987-88, 1989-90 and 1990-91 have been published. In parallel to AGSASU, the Bureau of Statistics undertakes periodical Large Scale Farm Surveys (LSFS), conducted by mail inquiry with occasional follow-up on non-respondents.

In 1993-94, the Bureau of Statistics, in collaboration with the MoA, has conducted a National Sample Census of Agriculture It involved interviews and repeated questionnaires administered in 540 villages and 15 households per village. Crop cutting and objective area measurements were also conducted for a smaller sample of farms. A similar framework was used for the 1994-95

16

extended AGSASU. When the results are published, area and production figures will be available for main food and export crops.

## 3) Ministry of Agriculture, Early Warning Unit (EWU)

The Early Warning Unit is concerned with monitoring the food supply situation in the country. EWU collects weather and crop condition data, and elaborates forecasts of food production through a rather sophisticated yield estimate function. These estimates are then revised at the end of the farming season to provide actual production figures. To calculate production figures, however, yield estimates are multiplied by area estimates coming from the routine reporting system of the MoA, the problems of which we have already discussed. These figures, therefore, tend to be inflated. These problems notwithstanding, this is the series of food production estimates that the Bureau of Statistics uses to calculate agricultural GDP.

## 4) Ministry of Agriculture, Marketing Development Bureau (MDB)

The data on food production published in the MDB annual industry reviews is the EWU data series, and it is subject to the same problems. In terms of export crop estimates, MDB is the main provider of data. Before the liberalization of export crop marketing, MDB used to get information from the relevant Marketing Boards, since they were the sole marketing agents for the crops. The share of production which was/is exported illegally is omitted in data collection because of the difficulties (technical and political) in estimating it. Parallel exports, in principle, were more likely to have taken place in the 1970s and early 1980s, when the gap between producer price and border price was significant. The phenomenon was more likely to be relevant for coffee and cashew nuts, because cotton and tobacco are too bulky for easy smuggling. Substantial amounts of coffee are said to have been exported illegally in the 'crisis' period, especially in the border areas of the country. Mshomba estimated that about 12 per cent of arabica coffee produced in northern Tanzania between 1969 and 1985 was smuggled into Kenya (Mshomba, 1993). From the late-1980s the gap between border and producer prices has decreased substantially; therefore, parallel exports are likely to have decreased. No precise information, however, is available on this matter.

In the last few years, other problems regarding data collection on export crops have emerged. Since the marketing of these crops has been liberalized, it is more difficult to get reliable data because, for fiscal reasons, private traders are normally reluctant to declare the volume of their transactions. Traders and Cooperative Unions should report to the RALDO and to the relevant Marketing Board, but this does not always happen. There should also be information provided by the Customs Department of the Ministry of Finance, but because of the long delays in reporting, MDB tends to rely on data provided by the Marketing Boards. The recent problem with data reporting is particularly relevant in the cashew nut sector, where liberalization started in 1991-92, and where most of marketing is in the hands of the private sector. In the cotton sector, private traders only entered the market in 1994-95, buying 7-10 per cent of the cotton, so that the magnitude of the problem is smaller. Coffee marketing was liberalized in 1994-95 as well. Apart from the data that should reach the RALDOs, other data comes from the coffee auctions. A comparison of the two sets of data should give a good indication of total production, even if not all the coffee goes through the auctions as it is supposed to. The tobacco sector was liberalized in August 1994, but the buying season had already begun, so that the first season where private traders were actually on the market was the 1995-96 one. This means that tobacco figures up to 1994-95 are reliable. Pyrethrum is still marketed through the relevant parastatal, and tea and sisal are grown mainly in big estates. The production figures for these crops are normally accurate. No data is presently available on non-traditional export crops, like cocoa, oilseeds, cardamon, and vanilla.

From this review of available agricultural production data, we can conclude that production figures are generally more reliable for export crops than for food crops. However, food production estimates have become more reliable in the last few years and export crop estimates are increasingly more problematic. We are now in a better position to evaluate the reliability of the claims of agricultural success in Tanzania under agricultural adjustment. Perhaps the key aspect in assessing the reliability of agricultural GDP figures is that the Bureau of Statistics uses MDB/EWU figures instead of the more accurate AGSASU figures. We have seen that the MDB/EWU series tends to overestimate food production. The unreliability of the figures themselves provides an idea of the shaky ground on which certain claims are made. Another question, though, is to understand if the extent of overestimation during the 'crisis' period and during the adjustment period was different. If there was no difference, the claims made by the Government and the IFIs on the basis of comparable better performance in the adjustment period would be acceptable, albeit the estimates themselves would not be a good indicator of 'real' levels of production.

An assessment of the change in the rate of overestimation of agricultural production figures in time has been made by Van den Brink through a comparison of the *caloric equivalent* of major cereals calculated from the MoA production data in 1966-89 with three surveys: the Household Budget Surveys (HBS) of 1969 and 1976-77, and the AGSASU of 1986-87. Van den Brink found that the MoA figure for 1969 was similar to the figure calculated from the 1969 HBS. However, he found that food production in the MoA series was overestimated in 1976-77, and that a much higher level of overestimation was present in MoA figures for 1986-87 (Van den Brink, 1992, pp. 12-13). In order to test this apparent trend of progressive overestimation of food production figures which are used to calculate agricultural GDP, I have compared maize production figures in the MDB/EWU series with the 1976-77 HBS and the available AGSASU data.

**Table 1.1   Tanzania maize production by data source (all figures in '000 tonnes)**

|  | (1) MDB/ EWU | (2) AGSASU (Masika Season; Crop Cutting) | (3) AGSASU (Vuli Season; Interview) | (4) LSFS | (5) AGSASU + LSFS (2+3+4) | (6) MDB/ EWU Over- estimation (per cent)*** |
|---|---|---|---|---|---|---|
| 1976-77 | 1664` | - | - | - | 1623* | 2.5 |
| 1986-87 | 2359 | 1777 | 384 | 28 | 2003 | 17.8 |
| 1987-88 | 2339` | 1422 | 254 | 34 | 1710 | 36.8 |
| 1989-90 | 2445 | 1631 | 192 | 37 | 1860 | 31.5 |
| 1990-91 | 2332 | 1442 | 228 | 35** | 1705 | 36.8 |

* Derived from the 1976-77 HBS estimate of maize consumption plus exports minus imports.
** LSFS figures have not been published for 1990-91. In the other three years for which data is available they constitute an average 2.1 per cent of smallholder maize production (as in AGSASU). The calculation for the 1990-91 LSFS figure is based on 2.1 per cent of the AGSASU figure.
*** Rate of overestimation of MDB/EWU figures (column 1) in relation to the sum of AGSASU figures for both Vuli (lesser rain) and Masika (greater rain) seasons and the LSFS figures (column 5).

The trend of overestimation of maize production in the MDB/EWU series is clearly higher in the adjustment period than in 1976-77. It is particularly interesting to note that the rate of overestimation doubles between 1986-87 and 1987-88, at the height of the 'miracle' period of ERPI. This confirms and updates Van den Brink's observation of a progressively higher overestimation of the food production component of GDP since the 1970s. We can conclude that the food production component of GDP in the adjustment period was *more* inflated than in the 'crisis' period. This argument demystifies other claims that in the 1970s production figures were more inflated because of high political pressure to show good results for the villagization process. While these pressures are likely to have had an impact on production estimates in the past, the pressures to show that economic reforms work might have substituted for the original ones.

However, overestimation in the 1970s was more difficult to trace because the MoA series was the only existent one. The current situation is much less acceptable in principle, because since 1986-87 the more reliable (but *lower*) AGSASU figures have been available. The fact that the Bureau of Statistics has continued using the inflated MDB/EWU estimates of food production for the

19

computation of agricultural GDP is at least suspicious.  It is also interesting to note that the 1991-92 AGSASU was processed, but donor funds were not made available for its publication (1991-92 was a bad agricultural year).  This is surprising, since the strengthening of agricultural information services was part of the $10.8 million disbursed through the World Bank funded Agricultural Management Sector Project in 1993.  This money went into the preparation of the National Agricultural Sample Census, but not for the publication of past AGSASU.  Another peculiarity is that the census was supposed to provide regional estimates and expand the sample framework for crop cutting estimates, but this was not possible in 1993-94 because of lack of materials (1993-94 was a bad agricultural year).  However, it eventually became feasible for the 1994-95 expanded AGSASU (good harvest year).  While a 'conspiracy theory' is probably out of place, it is necessary to underline these coincidences and consider them in future research.

The reliability of data on export crops which is used into agricultural GDP calculation  is a subject for a separate discussion.  Because the profitability of smuggling abroad has decreased in the adjustment period, MDB/EWU figures for the 'crisis' period are probably underestimated, while in the adjustment period (at least up to 1992-93) they better reflect 'real' production levels.  We have seen that the extent of recent estimate distorting due to lack of reporting from private traders is still not substantial for most export crops.  We have seen that food crop production figures are more inflated for the adjustment period than for the 'crisis' period, and export crop figures are less underestimated in the adjustment period than in the 'crisis' period.  Since on the one hand we talk about overestimation and on the other of underestimation, we do not know if the aggregate result is of one type or of the other.  What we can say, however, is that agricultural GDP in 1986-94 is more inflated/less deflated than in 1976-85.  The result is that the comparison between agricultural GDP growth of 5.1 per cent in 1986-94 versus 2.18 per cent in 1976-85 is biased in favor of the adjustment period.

So what 'really' happened?  One term for comparison could be the FAO volume index of agricultural production.  According to the FAO index, Tanzania experienced an average level of growth of crop production of 1.4 per cent in 1971-77, 1.7 per cent in 1978-85, and only 0.7 per cent in 1986-93 (calculated from FAO, *FAO Production Yearbook*, various issues).  These figures, however, come from government sources, and have been revised by FAO several times.  In general, they seem to underestimate crop production.  Another indication can be found in the World Bank's own *revised* estimate of GDP breakdown within agriculture, as in the Agricultural Sector Report of 1994.  According to this source, GDP for *crops* grew at a pace of 2.5 per cent per year in 1976-80, 2.2 per cent in 1981-85, and 2.3 per cent in 1986-91 (IBRD, 1994, p. 5).  Since crop performance constitutes between 65 and 75 per cent of agricultural GDP, and crop production increase was indicated as one of the aims of agricultural reforms, the revised World Bank figures seem to give a more plausible account of comparative agricultural performance in the two periods under discussion.  If this is the case, during the 'crisis' period, crop production grew by a rate of 2.35 per cent per year, as opposed to 2.3 per cent during the 'successful' phase of agricultural adjustment! Apparently, crop performance as a whole has been quite stable in Tanzania in the last 20 years, and in the 1990s it has been lower than the rate of growth of population (currently at 2.8 per cent). From this point of view, it is clear that the 'success' claimed for agricultural adjustment in Tanzania is more an invention than a reality.

## Conclusion: Trading Images

In this article, I have attempted to delineate the transformation of official thinking on agricultural adjustment and performance in the last ten years in Tanzania, and its consequences in terms of facilitating particular types of structural change in the country. It was not my intention to provide technical advice on how to proceed next on the road to agricultural development. My aim was to disclose contrasts and frustrations, particular outcomes and significant situations related to official discourse on adjustment. The nexus of the analysis, therefore, was not to find 'what should be done', but to see 'what happened', how this was portrayed to the public, and what kind of consequences this portrait had for the assumptions made on future reforms.

Tanzania came a long way from the single-channel marketing system for agricultural inputs and outputs of the pre-reform period. Gone are the days of villagization, *ujamaa*, parastatals, consumer goods shortages, and restrictions of trade. This is evident both by looking at the present organization of agricultural trade and at the change in the official rhetoric on agricultural reforms. A new paradigm has emerged within the Government's official discourse, a paradigm that rejects old *ujamaa* policies and embraces the teachings of liberalization and privatization. As we have seen in the previous sections, the particular representations that the IMF, the World Bank and the Government made of 'necessary' policy changes and of agricultural performance in Tanzania played a central role in bringing about a specific type of structural change. As Long and Van der Ploeg argued for development in general, 'intervention should not be seen solely or perhaps even primarily as consisting of material and organizational inputs, but rather involving a kind of "trade in images" ... The construction of these images is, among other things, sustained by a process of "labelling" which functions to promote or impose certain interpretative schemata concerned with the diagnosis and solution of "development problems"' (Long and Van der Ploeg, 1989: p.231). We have seen this happening in the early 1980s in Tanzania in terms of 'labelling' the 'crisis' problem, and during the adjustment period in terms of construction and re-construction of images on 'necessary' interventions.

A telling example of this 'trade in images' is provided by two passages from President Mwinyi's speech at the Eighth National Economic Policy Workshop in 1992. In what seems an attempt to clear any doubts about the new path of

21

development for Tanzania, Mwinyi argues that 'despite the problems facing the World Trading System and the unequal exchange between the products and services of the Third World in relation to those of the developed countries, there is no escaping from participating in the world economy'. In another passage of the same speech Mwinyi declares that 'it is necessary for us [Tanzanians] to re-examine the role of the state in economic development ... State control which suffocates individual and cooperative initiative in the economy is not conducive to sustainable economic growth and social progress. Development is brought about by the people themselves' (Bagachwa and Mbelle, 1993, pp. 2-3). The ERP policy document of 1986 still mentioned 'Tanzania's ultimate goal of equity and integrated development', but now we learn that full participation in integrated world markets and state withdrawal from the economy are inescapable.

The whole liberalization paradigm in agriculture had been presented in the early 1980s by the World Bank and the IMF to the Tanzanian Government as a way to overcome low agricultural (and economic) growth. Detailed recommendations were shovelled by the IFIs and progressively included in the Government's rhetoric and actual policy change. The Government and the IFIs had high expectations concerning the outcomes of the reforms in the agricultural sector. Accelerated growth of crop production was envisioned in all policy documents. Reforms were implemented, and the official tale claimed that, as a consequence, agricultural growth resumed.

However, we have seen that the depiction of an overall agricultural 'success' in Tanzania in the adjustment period is inaccurate, and that the goals presented in the mid-1980s by the Government and the IFIs have not been achieved in terms of agricultural growth. Crop performance as a whole in the 'crisis' period is strikingly similar to the performance in the adjustment period. The Government and the IFIs knew that the basis on which agricultural figures were produced was extremely shaky, and yet we were given sparkling accounts of the success of reforms in boosting agricultural growth in Tanzania.

In the mid- and late-1980s the Government and the IFIs claimed that good agricultural performance had been stimulated by agricultural reforms and - in some instances - by good weather. In order to sustain growth, they called for more reforms to be implemented. In the early 1990s, however, it was slowing agricultural growth which was earmarked to call for further interventions aimed at addressing infrastructural constraints. More reforms were needed in a period of good performance, more reforms are needed in a period of duress. The situation changed, but the story is always the same. Any way the supply response goes, new policy reforms are needed, because the conversion to free marketing has to be complete.

The way evidence has been used in practice to push the Government to absorb more requests for further reforms has more to do with economic ideology - or faith - than technocratic and apolitical reasoning. Even if reforms are laid down in IMF and World Bank documents with the apparent flavour of 'technical' advice, when it comes to evaluation, not a doubt is cast on the appropriateness of

22

certain interventions. The lack of self-criticism about some of the measures taken in the last few years accompanied by the silence surrounding the irrelevance of agricultural performance figures are particularly disturbing. After all, we have been told that 'good' policies are ... 'good' policies.

## Note

I would like to thank officials of the Bureau of Statistics, the Ministry of Agriculture, and the UNDP, FAO and World Bank missions in Tanzania for their cooperation in providing information and documentation for this work and Lisa Richey for her comments on previous drafts.

## References

Bagachwa, M.S.D. and Mbelle, A.V.Y. (eds) (1993), 'Prelude: Opening Speech by H.E. President Ali Hassan Mwinyi to the 8th National Economic Policy Workshop' in *Economic Policy under a Multiparty System in Tanzania*, Dar es Salaam Press, Dar es Salaam, pp. 1-5.

Berg, A. (1987), *Malnutrition: what can be done?: Lessons from World Bank Experience*, Johns Hopkins University Press, Baltimore MD.

Bernstein, H. (1981), 'Notes on the State and the Peasantry: The Tanzanian Case', *Review of African Political Economy*, 10, pp. 44-62.

Bevan, D. and Collier, P. (1993), *Agriculture and the Policy Environment*, OECD, Paris.

*Daily News*, Dar es Salaam.

Ellis, F. (1988), 'Tanzania', in Harvey, C. (ed.) *Agricultural Pricing Policies in Africa: Four Country Case Study*, Macmillan, London, pp. 66-104.

Ferguson, J. (1994), *The Anti-Politics Machine: Development', Depoliticization, and Bureaucratic Power in Lesotho*, University of Minnesota Press, Minneapolis MN.

Gibbon, P., Havnevik, K.J. and Hermele, K. (1993), *A Blighted Harvest: The World Bank and African Agriculture in the 1980s*, Africa World Press, Trenton NJ.

Heyer, J., P. Roberts and G. Williams (eds) (1981), *Rural Development in Tropical Africa*, St. Martin's Press, New York NY.

International Bank for Reconstruction and Development (IBRD) (1981), *Accelerated Development in Sub-Saharan Africa. An Agenda for Action*, World Bank, Washington.

IBRD (1983), *Tanzania Agricultural Sector Report*, Report No. 4052-TA, World Bank, Washington.

IBRD (1986), 'Statement of World Bank Assistance', Tanzania Consultative Group, Paris, June 10 and 11.

IBRD (1989), 'Past Performance and Future Prospects. Presentation by the World Bank', Tanzania Consultative Group, Paris, December 18-20.

IBRD (1990a), 'Memorandum and Recommendation of the President of the International Development Association to the Executive Directors on a Proposed Development

Credit of SDR 150.4 Million to the United Republic of Tanzania for an Agricultural Adjustment Program', Report No. P-5200-TA, World Bank, Washington.

IBRD (1990b), *Tanzania Economic Report: Towards Sustainable Development in the 1990s*, vol. I: Main Report, Report No. P-5352-TA, World Bank, Washington.

IBRD (1992), 'A Vision for Sustained Growth in Tanzania', Tanzania Consultative Group, Paris, June 29-30.

IBRD (1994), *Tanzania: Agriculture. A World Bank Country Study*, World Bank, Washington.

International Monetary Fund (IMF) (1986), 'Statement by the IMF Representative', Tanzania Consultative Group, Paris, June 10 and 11.

International Monetary Fund (IMF) (1987), 'Statement by the IMF Staff Representative', Tanzania Consultative Group, Paris, July 6-7.

International Monetary Fund (IMF) (1995), 'Statement by the IMF Staff Representative' Tanzania Consultative Group, Paris, February 27-28.

Lele, U. and Meyers, R. (1987), *Growth and Structural Adjustment Change in East Africa: Domestic Policies, Agricultural Performance and World Bank Assistance, 1963-86*, Parts I and II, Research Reports No. 1 and No. 14, World Bank, Washington.

Lipumba, N. (1988), 'Policy Reforms for Economic Development in Tanzania', in S. K. Commins (ed), *Africa's Development Challenges and the World Bank*, Lynne Rienner, Boulder and London.

Lofchie, M.F. (1989), *The Policy Factor. Agricultural Performance in Kenya and Tanzania*, Lynne Rienner, Boulder and London.

Long, N. and van der Ploeg, J.D. (1989), 'Demythologizing Planned Intervention: An Actor Perspective', *Sociologia Ruralis*, 23 (3/4), pp. 226-249.

Mshomba, R.E. (1993), 'The Magnitude of Coffee Arabica Smuggled from Northern Tanzania into Kenya', *Eastern Africa Economic Review*, 9 (1), pp.165-175.

Ponte, S. (1994), *Structural Adjustment Programs and Agricultural Performance: Beyond the Policy Factor. Lessons from Kenya and Tanzania*, unpublished MA thesis, University of Chicago.

Tanzania Consultative Group (TCG) (1995), 'Chairman's Closing Statement', Tanzania Consultative Group, Paris, February 27-28.

Tanzanian Economic Trends (TET) (1990), 'Towards Economic and Social Action Programme', keynote address by Hon. K. A. Malima, Vice-Chairman of Planning Commission to the Workshop on Economic Development and Adjustment Policies After the First ERP, Dar es Salaam, January 1-4, 1990, *Tanzanian Economic Trends*, 2 (3-4), pp. 6-12.

United Republic of Tanzania (URT) (1983), 'The Agricultural Policy of Tanzania', Government Printer, Dar es Salaam.

URT (1985), 'Tanzania Government Programme for Economic Recovery', Dar es Salaam, November.

URT (1986), 'Current Economic Situation in Tanzania and the Policies and Programmes for Recovery', statement by the Minister for Finance, Economic Affairs and Planning, Tanzania Consultative Group, Paris, June 10 and 11.

URT (1987), *Hali ya Uchumi wa Taifa katika Mwaka 1986,* Government Printer, Dar es Salaam.

URT (1988), *Hali ya Uchumi wa Taifa katika Mwaka 1987,* Government Printer, Dar es Salaam.

URT (1989a), 'The United Republic of Tanzania Economic Recovery Programme II (Economic and Social Action Programme) 1989/90 - 1991/92', Dar es Salaam, November.

URT (1989b), *Hali ya Uchumi wa Taifa katika Mwaka 1988,* Government Printer, Dar es Salaam.

URT (1990), *Hali ya Uchumi wa Taifa katika Mwaka 1989,* Government Printer, Dar es Salaam.

URT (1991), *Hali ya Uchumi wa Taifa katika Mwaka 1990,* Government Printer, Dar es Salaam.

URT (1992a), 'The Study on Input Supply, Distribution and Performance of Liberalization of Input Distribution System. Volume II: Fertilizer', Ministry of Agriculture, Dar es Salaam, December.

URT (1992b), *Hali ya Uchumi wa Taifa katika Mwaka 1991,* Government Printer, Dar es Salaam.

URT (1993), *Hali ya Uchumi wa Taifa katika Mwaka 1992,* Government Printer, Dar es Salaam.

URT (1994), *Hali ya Uchumi wa Taifa katika Mwaka 1993,* Government Printer, Dar es Salaam.

URT (1995), *Hali ya Uchumi wa Taifa katika Mwaka 1994,* Government Printer, Dar es Salaam.

Van den Brink, R. (1992), 'A Review of Agriculture Statistics of Mainland Tanzania', Report for the Southern Africa Department, Agriculture Operations Division, World Bank, Washington.

Williams, G. (1986), 'Rural Development: Partners and Adversaries', *Rural Africana,* 25 (6), pp. 11-23.

# 2 Tanzania: Implementing Structural Adjustment Programmes - Learning from the Past

## M. E. MLAMBITI

### Introduction

Tanzania is a rather poor, predominantly agricultural country, with a population of 24.5 million (1990) and an area of 945,000 square kilometres. Other basic indicators are as shown in Table 2.1. The economic structure of the nation has a dual character. The rural traditional sector is involved in the production of most export items, food, and raw materials for the local industries. The urban sector is mostly involved in manufacturing and managing the service sector, and produces goods for the domestic market and a small portion for export. Both the urban and the rural sectors of the economy are highly dependent on foreign imports for their operations, hence the need for a strong export drive.

The objective of this paper is to review the country's agricultural policies before and after independence with a view to showing that political factors have an important role to play in determining success or failure of a country's development and environmental policies and programmes.

**Table 2.1   Tanzania: basic indicators**

| Population mid 1990 (millions) | Area in sq km (thousands) | GNP per capita US $ | Annual growth rate of GNP | Average annual rate of inflation (percentage) | | Life expectancy | |
|---|---|---|---|---|---|---|---|
| | | | | 1965 -80 | 1980 -90 | WB | UNDP |
| 24.5 | 945 | 110 | (130-110) -0.2 | 9.6 | 25.8 | 48 | 54 |

*Source*: IBRD, 1992, p. 218, Table 1.

# Development Strategies Carried out under the Different Forms of Government

## The Precolonial Period

No specific strategies were formulated. Settlement of the local people was mainly according to the farming systems adopted by specific groups, which were not necessarily on a tribal basis. The farming systems identified included those of agriculturalists, pastoralists, semi-pastoralists and food gatherers and hunters.

All the groups developed political systems and structures and working patterns based on their level of technological development and knowhow. For example by 1500 A.D., there were stable and permanent societies in the banana-growing areas of Kilimanjaro, East Lake, and Southern Highlands. What was grown was for domestic consumption and/or was bartered in local markets. It is difficult to say whether or not the systems were environmentally friendly, because much depended upon what the main objective was at any given time.

## The German Colonial Period

The Germans were the first formal colonialists to claim Tanganyika as their colony, in 1884. Their main objectives were to produce agricultural commodities for the mother country and to make the colony serve as the market place for the finished products from Germany. The German settlers cultivated crops needed in their country. They opened plantations for tobacco and sugarcane in the 1880s and coffee in the 1890s, and after 1898 sisal plantations were introduced, which later on became important producers of cash crops. The effects of the German development strategy cannot be clearly determined because their reign was terminated by the First World War. But obviously the opening of large plantations changed the ecological system of the areas concerned and in fact was the beginning of conspicuous environmental degradation.

## The British Colonial Period

The British were given a League of Nations mandate to administer Tanganyika after the defeat of the Germans. Although the British pattern of agricultural development did not differ significantly from the German, after 1945 there were two new departures. Between 1945 and the mid-1950s the British put greater emphasis on the principle of soil conservation to control the environmental degradation process caused by the previous farming systems. They established several development schemes in various parts of the country, such as the Mlalo rehabilitation scheme, the Mbulu scheme, the Sukuma land scheme and the groundnut scheme of 1946. Subsequently between 1955 and 1961 (when Tanganyika gained independence), the British adopted an agricultural policy of supporting the demands of the most progressive farmers by encouraging the replacement of customary land tenure by individual freehold. This policy was more or less an outcome of

27

the report of the Royal Commission on Land and Population in East Africa (1955). When this policy was announced, it was immediately condemned by the Annual Conference of the Tanganyika African National Union (TANU). As Julius Nyerere (subsequently to become president) wrote:

> I am ... opposed to the proposed Government solution to this problem of shifting cultivation. ... If we allow land to be sold like a robe, within a short period there would only be a few Africans possessing land in Tanganyika and all others would be tenants ... We would be faced with a problem which has created antagonism among peoples and led to bloodshed in many countries of the world (Nyerere [1958], 1966, pp. 55-6).

*Overall Impact of the Colonial Economic Strategies*

The colonial economic strategies had the following consequences:

1.  They intensified the existing environmental developmental situation which placed more emphasis upon environment protection but increased differences among peasants.
2.  They established plantations which remained in the hands of foreigners, and which were the major source of employment.
3.  They made certain areas of the country to become labour reservoirs for migrant workers (and consequently these remained undeveloped).
4.  They established main lines of communication between major plantation areas and centres of economic activities (the towns), widening the difference in development between the urban and the rural areas. Rural living conditions were particularly likely to suffer, especially where there were no plantations.

*After Independence but before the Arusha Declaration*

After independence the government emphasized the development of village-based agricultural production by creating the village settlement agency (VSA) in 1963. Unfortunately, most of the schemes were too expensive to run and failed to produce the expected returns. The main causes of failure include:

1.  Shortage of foreign aid and insufficient investment by the private sector into the programme.
2.  Lack of enthusiasm and dedication by the settlers in the villages, and high expectation of free services.
3.  The activity of officials in certain towns, who used the opportunity to rid themselves of groups of urban unemployed.
4.  Social conflicts which emerged, e.g. the unbalanced male to female ratio.
5.  Differences in thinking between the experts and technocrats on the one hand, and politicians on the other.

Tanzania's agricultural development policy took a different direction after the Arusha Declaration of February, 1967. The government adopted the policy of socialism, self-reliance and rural development, which stressed that in order to develop the nation needed *land, people, good policies, and good leadership* - which could all be harnessed through public and cooperative ownership of the major means of production, effective participation of the masses in development, and an equitable distribution of income and wealth. This policy was very appealing to the rural masses but was wrongly perceived.

## The Ujamaa Virus

In a country where the majority of the population are very poor and illiterate, such a strategy should of course arouse excitement because of the image that it evoked in the people - to become rich without working. Consequently, the whole nation was set on a wrong footing right from the start. As a result there was temporary achievement in the provision of social services but a near collapse of the national economy by the early 1980s, and the creation of *protected capitalism* for the people in power. Such developments are suggested in Figure 2.1 and Table 2.2.

**Table 2.2  Tanzania: capital formation by sector, 1973-1980**

| Sector | Location as Percentage of Total Investment Growth | | | | | |
|---|---|---|---|---|---|---|
| | 1973 | 1977 | 1978 | 1979 | 1980 | 1977-80 |
| Agriculture | 6.3 | 5.8 | 4.1 | 3.8 | 4.1 | 4.1 |
| Manufacturing | 11.8 | 41.6 | 36.9 | 37.8 | 34.9 | 10.2 |
| Construction | 2.3 | 3.0 | 2.6 | 3.0 | 2.3 | 8.9 |
| Electricity | 11.0 | 4.8 | 7.1 | 7.0 | 7.7 | 33.1 |
| Transport | 47.4 | 20.6 | 27.1 | 26.3 | 25.3 | 23.0 |
| Others | 21.2 | 24.2 | 22.2 | 22.1 | 25.7 | 22.6 |
| Total | 100.0 | 100.0 | 100.0 | 100.0 | 100.0 | 101.9 |

*Source*: Cheru, 1989, p. 53 (Table 3.5).

Several causes of the failure of the *ujamaa* policy have been given. The main ones include:
1. The adoption of the wrong policy of socialism, which was inappropriate for the country.
2. Deterioration of the terms of trade, as a result of the high price of imported oil and declining prices of exportable primary products.
3. The breakdown of the East African Community in 1977, which necessitated substantial investments to provide services formerly rendered by the Community.
4. The 1978 war against Idi Amin, which cost $500 million.
5. Since 1980, the recession in the West, which resulted in high interest rates and increased the country's debt service burden.

**Figure 2.1    Volume of production (officially marketed) of major export crops 1962/3 - 1985/6 ('0000 tons)**

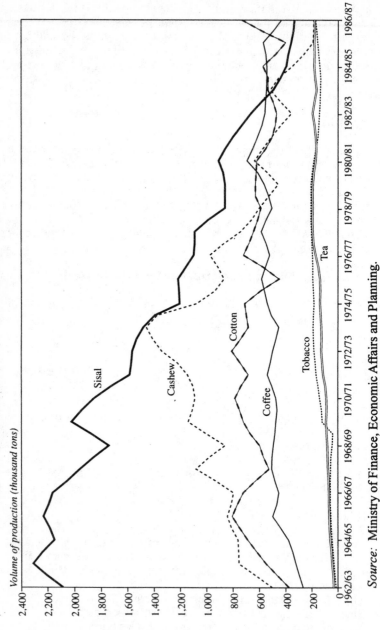

*Source:* Ministry of Finance, Economic Affairs and Planning.

30

## The Structural Adjustment Measures

From 1981, Tanzania launched two consecutive broadly-based structural adjustment programmes with similar objectives. These were the National Economic Survival Programme (NESP), launched in 1981, and the Structural Adjustment Programme (SAP) launched in 1983. These could not solve the economic crisis of the country because they lacked import support assistance. But they prepared the ground for the next economic recovery programme to be implemented under the IMF conditions. This began in 1986.

The performance of the ERP had been mixed, with good up-to-target achievements in some objectives and negative impact in other respects. Overall the economy is showing positive signs of recovery (see Table 2.3 to 2.6).
**

### Table 2.3  Tanzania: growth of production

| | | Average Annual Growth Rate (Percentage) | | | | | | | |
|---|---|---|---|---|---|---|---|---|---|
| GDP | | AGRICULTURE | | INDUSTRY | | MANUFACT-URING | | SERVICES, ETC. | |
| 1965-80 | 1980-90 | 1965-80 | 1980-90 | 1965-80 | 1980-90 | 1965-80 | 1980-90 | 1965-80 | 1980-90 |
| 3.9 | 2.8 | 1.6 | 4.1 | 4.2 | 0.0 | 5.6 | -0.4 | 10.8 | 1.3 |

*Source:* IBRD, 1992 (p. 220, Table 2).

### Table 2.4  Tanzania: agriculture and food

| Value Added in Agriculture (Millions of US$) | | Cereal Imports (thousands of metric tons) | | Food Aid in Cereals (thousands of metric tons) | | Fertilizer Consumption (hundreds of grams of Plant Nutrient per hectare) | | Average Index of Food Production per Capita (1979-81 = 100). |
|---|---|---|---|---|---|---|---|---|
| 1970 | 1990 | 1974 | 1990 | 1974-75 | 1989-90 | 1970-71 | 1989-90 | 1988 - 1990 |
| 483 | 1444 | 431 | 73 | 148 | 22 | 31 | 93 | 88 |

*Source:* IBRD, 1992 (p. 224, Table 4).

31

**Table 2.5   Tanzania: total external debt (millions of US$)**

| Long term debt public & publicly guarantee | | Private Nonguaranteed | | Use of IMF credit | | Short term debt | Total external debt |
|---|---|---|---|---|---|---|---|
| 1970 | 1990 | 1970 | 1990 | 1970 | 1990 | 1990 | 1990 |
| 180 | 5294 | 15 | 12 | 0 | 140 | 420 | 5866 |

*Source:* IBRD, 1992 (p. 258, Table 21).


**Table 2.6   Tanzania: total external debt ratios**

| Total external debt as percentage of | | | | Total debt service as percentage of exports of goods and services | | Interest payments as percentage of exports of goods and services | |
|---|---|---|---|---|---|---|---|
| Exports of goods and services | | GNP | | | | | |
| 1980 | 1990 | 1980 | 1990 | 1980 | 1990 | 1980 | 1990 |
| 317.8 | 1070.7 | 4.7 | 282.0 | 19.6 | 25.8 | 10.0 | 10.9 |

*Source:* IBRD, 1992 (p. 264, Table 24).

*SAP and the Rural Food Security Situation*

Table 2.7 shows survey results of the rural food security situation in Ulanga District between 1985 (when the IMF SAP was officially adopted by the country), and 1993 (after about eight years of its implementation). The table shows that the proportion of the rural population consuming below the critical subsistence levels for rice has increased from 50 per cent in 1985 to 68 per cent in 1993, and has fallen from 58 per cent to 52 per cent for maize, signalling that there is a shift in consumption pattern in favour of more maize. However, in general overall proportions of people consuming below the average critical subsistence level for food (i.e. both rice and maize) has increased from 54 per cent to 60 per cent.

*SAP and Rural Poverty Growth and Implied Natural Resource Degradation*

Table 2.8 shows rural poverty growth and implied natural resource degradation for severely challenged countries as observed by the World Bank report (IBRD, 1992). Tanzania, with a per capita GNP of US$110 (1990), a total population of 25 million (of which 78 per cent is rural) and projected fertility of 6.6 will have 64 million people in the year 2025, representing an increase of 167 per cent. This means that in order to maintain the current economic level, either production effort must at least increase at a similar

**Table 2.7 Ulanga District: effects of SAP on rural food security situation in District between 1985 and 1993**

| | 1985[1] | | | 1993[2] | | |
|---|---|---|---|---|---|---|
| | Rice | Maize | Total Rice & Maize | Rice | Maize | Total Rice & Maize |
| No. of households recorded | 117 | 101 | 218 | 149 | 231 | 380 |
| Average amount stored (kg) | 1091 | 707 | 1798 | 1615 | 918 | 2533 |
| Proportion of population consuming (%) | | | | | | |
| Above average | 50 | 42 | 46 | 32 | 48 | 40 |
| Below average | 50 | 58 | 54 | 68 | 52 | 60 |

*Source:* 1. Mlambiti (1992a) Table 8 (p. 59).
2. Mlambiti, Rutachokozibwa and Lugole (1993) Table 4.15 (p. 26).

rate, or some drastic measures must be undertaken to curtail population growth. A failure to do this would result in catastrophic degradation of non-renewable consumable natural resources (such as forest, water and wild animals). According to IFAD statistics reported by Belshaw (1992), the proportion of Tanzania's rural absolute poor to total population in 1988 was 47 per cent, which is relatively high compared to other developing countries. The corresponding figure for Argentina is 3 per cent, for Chile 8 per cent, and for Ghana 37 per cent.

*SAP and Environmental Problems caused by Charcoal as a Source of Domestic Energy*

One of the effects of SAP has been the increased price of imported goods, including fuel as well as cooking facilities; another has been the retrenchment of employees. Retrenched employees have less income and therefore less purchasing power, forcing them to go for cheap sources of energy for their households. In Tanzania this means consuming more forestry products, namely firewood and charcoal. Increased prices of cookers and electricity force households to go for cheap sources of energy, which means increased use of forestry products. Thus under the current situation in Tanzania, wood products are the main source of energy for the majority of urban dwellers, let alone the rural population.

The excessive pressure to remove or cut down trees, coupled with the alarming urban population growth of more than six per cent for most towns will inevitably result in environmental degradation manifested by high levels of soil erosion, crop failure, drying of rivers, silting of dams, and

33

# Table 2.8 Rural poverty growth and natural resource degradation: severely challenged countries ranked by projected population increase 1990-2025

| Country | GNP per capita 1990 ($) | Population 1990 (million) | Rural Popln. as % total 1990 | Projected Fertility 2000 | Popln. 2025 (Million) | Popln. Increase 1990-2025 as % Total 1990 |
|---|---|---|---|---|---|---|
| 1.. Rwanda | 310 | 7 | 92 | 7.6 | 23 | 229 |
| 2. Ethiopia | 120 | 51 | 87 | 7.3 | 156 | 206 |
| 3. Niger | 310 | 8 | 80 | 7.3 | 24 | 200 |
| 4. Burundi | 210 | 5 | 94 | 6.6 | 14 | 180 |
| 5. Malawi | 200 | 9 | 88 | 7.4 | 24 | 167 |
| 5. Kenya | 370 | 24 | 76 | 5.5 | 64 | 167 |
| 7. Uganda | 220 | 16 | 90 | 6.6 | 42 | 163 |
| 8. Tanzania | 110 | 25 | 78 | 6.6 | 64 | 156 |
| 8. Mali | 270 | 9 | 81 | 7.0 | 23 | 156 |
| 10. Burkina Faso | 330 | 9 | 91 | 6.3 | 22 | 144 |
| 11. Madagascar | 230 | 12 | 75 | 5.2 | 26 | 177 |
| 12. Pakistan | 380 | 115 | 68 | 4.6 | 240 | 114 |
| 13. Nepal | 170 | 19 | 90 | 4.6 | 37 | 95 |
| 14. Bangladesh | 210 | 107 | 84 | 3.3 | 176 | 64 |
| 15. India | 350 | 850 | 73 | 3.0 | 1348 | 59 |

*Source:* IBRD (1992) Table 1, 26, 27 and 31 (pp. 218-9, 268-9, 270-1, 278-9). Countries with less than five million population in 1990 have been excluded.

Note: Fertility: Total fertility rate i.e. average number of children that would be born to each woman if she were to live to the end of her child-bearing years and bear children in accordance with prevailing age-specific fertility rates.

desertification. Kimele in his study on the economics of charcoal production and environmental impact along the Dar es Salaam to Morogoro highway forecasted that about 1524 square kilometres of forest would be cleared for charcoal production in 35 years, which is equivalent to the growth period of a harvestable *Miombo* forest. A study of charcoal consumption in Morogoro (Municipal) shows that 67 per cent of the urban population use charcoal for cooking (Bwahama, 1993). At the same time TANESCO encourages people to use charcoal where lengthy cooking times are involved, in order to save electricity.

Existing literature shows that the country is losing between 300,000 and 400,000 hectares annually, while replacement has remained at 20,000 hectares. It is further reported that to date only the administrative regions of Rukwa, Lindi, Ruvuma and Tabora have in quantitative terms enough forests remaining (Mbwana, 1993). Even in those regions there are several pockets where a serious deficiency is apparent. Other causes of deforestation besides energy supply include agricultural expansion (accounting for 60 per cent of the deforestation), and wild fires that take place annually in almost all regions of the country. Hydrological balance is often affected by large-scale destruction of vegetation. Floods have become a common problem in the country because the soil retention capacity of rain water (which is normally enhanced by forests and other vegetation) is reduced by the process of desertification: causing serious damage to structures, houses and crops. Such a process has been apparent in Lushoto and Korogwe. Desertification in Tanzania is now affecting about 60 per cent of the land area, and is in evidence in Dodoma, Arusha, Shinyanga, Mwanza, Mara and parts of Iringa and Singida Regions. Table 2.9 shows indicators of the state of desertification in the twenty regions of mainland Tanzania.

*SAP and the Land Tenure System*

Since the IMF agreement of 1985, recent trends of economic liberalization have hastened the burgeoning of business interests, including foreign business and investments. This has concentrated on the tourist industry, large-scale farming, and the mining of gem stones, and has had considerable impact in high-potential districts including areas occupied by pastoralists. For example, according to Muir (1994) in Simanjiro District this policy resulted in substantial loss of grazing land to large-scale farms, the operation of businesses in the district (including the growth of tourist-related business), and the expansion of mining activities. As a consequence of population pressure from the surrounding agricultural areas there is now competition over natural resources between pastoralists and small farmers, as well as between pastoralists and large-scale farming and business interests.

The natural resources under threat in the four villages studied by Muir were loss of traditional grazing; loss of natural water sources to large-scale farms; reduced trees and browse as a consequence of opening fields and the production of charcoal; and restricted wildlife movement because of the development of large-scale farms for which wildlife could be a nuisance or a threat to crops and people.

By 1993 over 45,000 ha. had been acquired in the District for 72 large-scale farms ranging in size between 90 and 12,400 ha. (Mkamal, 1993). This figure excludes land acquisitions not lodged with the land adjudication office, and subsistence farms. In 1992 a bill abolishing the customary land tenure was enacted. But in some instances land acquisition has not followed the procedures laid down, and most land purchases are by the well-to-do people and are based on speculation; on future land markets, rather than immediate use. Thus large tracts of land between Morogoro and Kilosa are acquired properties but there are no signs of development at all. This raises difficult questions about where we are heading to. With the apparent success of the recovery programme, the government is actively campaigning for foreign investors to involve themselves in all possible areas of the economy by offering inducement conditions. It has almost put aside the role of the rural sector, since there are no programmes aimed at developing and sustaining the rural population as producers. Actually the policy which the nationalist

# Table 2.9 Indicators of the state of desertification in the twenty regions of Mainland Tanzania

| | Water short-age | Land Degra-dation | Soil Ero-sion | Water Ero-sion | Water Log-ging | Secon-dary Saline-Alkali | Defor-est-ation | Over-stock-ing | Pop-ulat-ion Press-ure | Drou-ght Haz-ards | Flood Haz-ards | Urban-ization Impact |
|---|---|---|---|---|---|---|---|---|---|---|---|---|
| Dodoma | * | * | + | + | - | - | * | * | + | + | - | + |
| Arusha | + | + | + | + | - | - | * | * | + | + | + | + |
| K'njaro | - | + | + | + | - | - | + | + | * | - | - | + |
| Tanga | + | + | + | + | - | - | * | + | + | - | + | + |
| Morogoro | + | + | + | + | + | - | + | + | + | - | * | - |
| Pwani | - | + | - | - | - | - | * | - | + | - | - | + |
| DSM | - | - | - | - | - | - | * | - | * | - | - | * |
| Lindi | + | + | + | + | - | - | + | - | - | - | - | - |
| Mtwara | + | + | + | + | - | - | + | - | - | - | - | - |
| Ruvuma | + | + | + | + | - | - | + | - | - | - | - | - |
| Iringa | - | + | + | + | - | - | + | + | - | + | - | - |
| Mbeya | - | + | + | + | * | + | * | + | * | - | * | - |
| Singida | * | * | + | + | - | - | * | * | - | * | - | - |
| Tabora | + | + | + | + | + | - | * | + | - | * | - | - |
| Rukwa | - | + | + | + | - | - | + | - | - | - | - | - |
| Kigoma | - | + | + | + | - | - | * | - | - | - | - | - |
| Shinyanga | * | + | + | + | - | - | * | * | + | * | - | - |
| Ziwa | - | - | + | + | - | - | + | - | - | - | - | - |
| Mwanza | + | + | + | - | - | - | * | * | + | + | - | - |
| Mara | * | + | + | - | - | - | * | * | - | + | - | - |

Key:  - Insignificant to wild   + Moderate   * Severe
*Source:* Mbwana (1993), Table 1.

politicians rejected during the British period is now being encouraged without any precautionary measures. The implementation of the IMF package has affected the public service sector badly, as already noted. Currently dispensaries and hospitals are without drugs, rural water taps are dry, higher education is for the wealthy people, and three meals a day are for the high-salaried class. Moreover, land is being acquired in thousands of hectares or square kilometres without developing corresponding agricultural production schemes for the rural masses in order to safeguard the future. The prospects for the common people are bleak indeed.

## Analysis of the Possible Causes of the Problem of the Tanzania Economic Development Model

As one reviews the situation, one learns that the government is far from the goal of achieving a sustainable economic development programme. Why is this so? Is it because of having a wrong policy again, or a wrong IMF package?

The analysis of the possible causes is based on Figure 2.2. This represents an economic development model which has two phases made up of six components. The state, power, and the national economic system form phase 1, while factors of production, the production process, and the propositions make up phase 2. The state is formed of the ruling party which has the mandate to appoint the leadership that forms the government (power); the leadership is responsible for making national policies which affect the utilization of national factors of production according to the given production function (process) to meet national objectives as seen by the leadership - including a safe environment and sustainable economic development by manipulating various propositions (see Figure 2.2). The process of development can be caused by positive or negative actions of the implementers. Thus we have two development paths, i.e. a positive path resulting in improved development and a negative path resulting in retarded or no development. The factors in phase 1 are indeed the principal determinants of the effectiveness of the factors in phase 2, and most developing countries are in fact caught up in phase 1. And as long as they are unable to provide a situation conducive to development in phase 1, all efforts made in phase 2 are a waste of time and resources as far as real economic development is concerned. In order to identify which particular factor in phase 1 is the main problem, the process of elimination is adopted; and the main limiting factor is the one which should be tackled first.

Thus in general it is the leadership that formulates the policies which have a direct bearing on resource utilization and consequently on the environment and development. It is the leadership that sets the objectives to be achieved. However, leadership formation depends on the national organ, i.e. the ruling party. If the ruling party has a good system of getting the right leaders as is the case with most developed nations, then there is a greater chance of success and if it does not as is the case with most developing countries then there is a greater chance of being unsuccessful.

The only way of guaranteeing a reasonably good system to get the right kind of leadership is to have true democracy, i.e. good governance and transparency at all levels of the political process. This can be achieved by giving power to the people through their representatives, with transparency being given top priority and supported by the leadership. Short of that there is little chance of having rapid economic development because the implementation of and success for any recommended programmes and strategies depend very much on the implementers at all levels.

**Conclusion**

The brief discussion presented above shows that the Tanzania government has rightly identified the country's focal point for sustainable development as lying in the rural sector, whose agricultural production is in turn heavily dependent on the traditional sector. Furthermore, the discussion also tries to show that failure of any chosen development strategy is not necessarily determined by the national policy or the development programmes adopted: but rather by the summation of many other factors that influence the economy as a whole. However, the discussion demonstrates convincingly that for any programme to be successful in accelerating the pace of sustainable economic development, the country must have a political leadership committed to the achievement of the goals of economic development, set up democratically, and must adopt an outward-oriented development policy guided by good governance and transparency. Consequently, good leadership is a key ingredient in a successful development programme.

# Figure 2.2 Organogram of Tanzania's development model

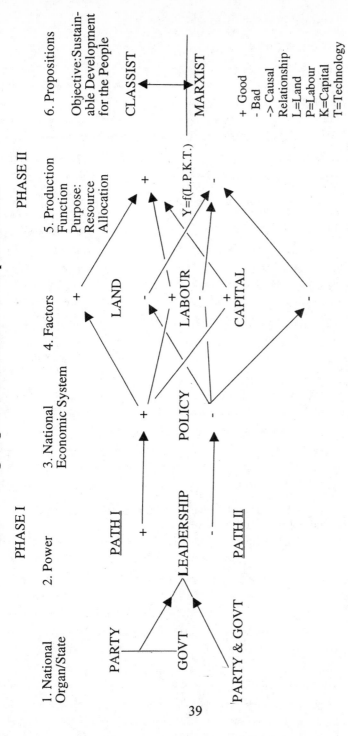

|  | PHASE I | | | PHASE II | 6. Propositions |
|--|--|--|--|--|--|

1. National Organ/State
2. Power
3. National Economic System
4. Factors
5. Production Function Purpose: Resource Allocation

Objective:Sustainable Development for the People

CLASSIST ←→ MARXIST

+ Good
- Bad
-> Causal Relationship
L=Land
P=Labour
K=Capital
T=Technology

Note: Leadership has a key role in economic development. If the leadership is committed to development, it will adopt and implement a suitable economic policy hence offer a positive impact. If it is not committed, development won't be achieved. The choice of leadership is therefore important in economic development.

39

### Figure 2.3  Marxist and classic propositions

**CLASSIC PROPOSITIONS**

| | | | |
|---|---|---|---|
| 0 | = | $f$ (L, K. Q, T) | 1 |
| T | = | T (I) | 2 |
| I | = | $\Delta Q = I$ (R) | 3 |
| R | = | R (T, L) | 4 |
| W | = | W (I) | 5 |
| L | = | L (W) | 6 |
| 0 | = | R + W | 7 |

In the long run equilibrium we have also
$\quad$ W = wL where w = minimum wage rate

**MARXIST PROPOSITIONS**　　　　　　　　　　　　**SYMBOLS**

$$0 \quad = f \text{ (L, K. Q, T)}$$
$$T \quad = T \text{ (I)}$$
$$I \quad = I \text{ (R)}$$
$$R' \quad = \frac{0 - w}{W + Q'} \quad = \frac{R....}{W + Q'}$$
$$W = W \text{ (I)}$$
$$L = L \text{ (I/Q)}$$
$$C = C \text{ (W)}$$
$$R = R \text{ (T, C)}$$

T = Technology
Q = Capital
K = Land
L = Labour
I = Investment
R = Profit
W = Wage
O = Output

The three identities are

$$0 = R + W$$
$$0 = C + I$$
$$Q' = U.Q$$

Where　U is users cost of using capital
$\qquad$ Q' is capital goods and variables used in production
$\qquad$ R' is rate of return on turnover

# References

Belshaw, D. (1994), Seminar Paper, SUA.

Bwahama, J.K. (1993), 'Availability and Marketing of Charcoal and its Impact on Environment in Morogoro Muncipality', unpublished Special Project, SUA.

Cheru, F. (1989), *The Silent Revolution in Africa*, Zed Books, London.

*East Africa Royal Commission 1953-1955* (1955), HMSO, London (Cmd. 9475).

Higgins, B. (1959), *Economic Development: Principles, Problems and Policies*, Norton, New York, NY.

International Bank for Reconstruction and Development (IBRD) (1992), *World Development Report*, Oxford University Press, London.

Kashuliza, A.K. and Mbiha, E.R. (1992), *Structural Adjustment Policy Reforms and the Performance of the Agricultural Sector in Tanzania, 1988-1990*, Wye College, Department of Agricultural Economics series.

Kimele, P.M. (1990), 'The Economics of Charcoal Production and Environmental Impact along the Dar es Salaam - Morogoro Highway', unpublished Special Project, SUA.

Mbwana, S.B. (1993), 'Brief Status on the Environmental Situation in Tanzania', Paper presented at the Seminar for Norwegian Volunteers in Tanzania, December 1993.

Mkamal, A.J. (1993), 'Land Adjudication in a Pastoral Area of Northern Tanzania', Paper presented at the PANET Workshop on Pastoral Land Use Planning held in Dar es Salaam, October 1993.

Mlambiti, M.E. (1992a), 'The Effects of Politics on Planning and Plan Implementation in Developing Countries with Special Reference to Tanzania', *Memoirs of the Philosophy of Agricultural Science, Kyoto University*, 15, pp. 2-18.

Mlambiti, M.E. (1992b), 'The Petals of Ulanga District: Potential, Constraints, Current Resources Utilization and Food Security Situation of the District', SUA, Morogoro.

Mlambiti, M.E., Rutachokozibwa, V. and Lugole, J.S. (1993), 'Socio-economic Survey of Kilombero Valley, Tanzania', Study funded by the ODA and submitted to the Kilombero Valley Teak Company, Itakara, Tanzania.

Muir, A. (1994), 'A Situation Analysis of Pastoralism in Simanjiro District, Tanzania', VETAID, Roslin (Midlothian, Scotland).

Mulokozi, B., Shellakindo, W.H. and Baguma, R. (1989), 'The Adaptation of Government to Economic Change: the case of Senegal', in Balogun, M.J. nd Mutahaba, G. (eds) (1989), *Economic Restructuring and African Public Administration Issues: Action and Future Choices*, Kumarian Press, West Hartford CT, pp. 187-202.

Nyerere, J.K. ([1958] 1966), 'National Property', in Nyerere, *Freedom and Unity*, Oxford University Press, Dar es Salaam, pp. 53-8.

Omari, C.K. (1976), *Strategy for Rural Development: Tanzania Experience*, EALB, Nairobi.

Wangwe, S.M. (1989), 'Structural Adjustment in Tanzania: Some Recent Experiences in Structural Change and Poverty', Paper presented at CDR Seminar, 23-24 February 1989.

# 3 Structural Adjustment and Land Reform Policy in Tanzania: A Political Interpretation of the 1992 National Agricultural Policy

ANDREW S.Z. KIONDO

This paper briefly reviews previous land tenure policies in Tanzania and takes the 1992 National Agricultural Policy (NAP) as a point of departure towards a World Bank framework of Structural Adjustment Programme (SAP) oriented land reform policy. The central argument of the paper is that a land reform policy that does not take into account the needs and interests of peasants in Tanzania cannot increase agricultural productivity as envisaged by the NAP. The argument also implies that market forces cannot be left to determine land reform policy direction, as they can hardly be expected to take into consideration the relevant needs and interests of peasants. This chapter will use the 1992 Land Commission Report findings (URT, 1994) and will relate some of them to a case study of two villages in the Tanga region for purposes of illustration.

At the risk of being accused of over-simplification, it seems safe to say that the land tenure system in Tanzania, as in many countries with a colonial experience, has changed roughly from the so-called *indigenous* or *communal land ownership* during the pre-colonial period to *crown land 'ownership'* with freehold entitlement to settlers, during the colonial period, to *state land 'ownership'* soon after independence and finally to the present-day pressures for some form of *individualization* of land tenure under the dictates of SAPs[1] (Izumi, 1993). Each of the above-mentioned types of land ownership had particular politico-economic goals born out of a specific configuration of political forces, and change in these necessitated policy reform. We shall expand on this below.

There is a misconception of historical reality which tries to lump all precolonial African land tenure systems together, and sees them in terms of communal land ownership alone. In reality, precolonial Tanzania (mainland), at least at the time of colonization, displayed a variety of land ownership types, from the fairly well developed feudal system of *nyarubanja* in the West Lake zone, to the communal ownership which mainly existed among pastoralists of the northern Eastern Zone.

The colonial period in Tanzania falls under two administrations: one by the Germans from the 1880s to the First World War, and the other by the British from the First World War to independence in 1961. Needless to say, both regimes had land policies motivated by settler interests. Through the Imperial Decree of November 26, 1895, the Germans declared that all land, whether occupied or not, was to be treated as unowned crown land under the German Empire. In practice, settlers owned land because they were issued with titles, while indigenous people were simply left with a recognition of permissive rights of occupancy (URT, 1994, p. 9).

The British colonial period differed slightly from the German for two reasons. One was that unlike the German period, Tanganyika under the British was to be administered as a Mandated Territory (under the League of Nations), and a Trust Territory (under the United Nations). In both cases Britain was to administer Tanganyika on the basis of that country's international status. The agreement with regard to land ownership stipulated that:

> In informing laws relating to the holding or transfer of land and natural resources the Administrative Authority shall take into consideration native laws and customs and shall respect the rights and safeguard the interests both present and future of the native population. No native land or natural resources may be transferred except between natives, save with the previous consent of the competent authority. No real rights over native land or natural resources in favour of non-natives may be created except with the same consent (URT, 1994, p. 10).

The second difference, which is by no means unrelated to the first one, concerns the British colonial policy which aimed at developing the country as a plantation/peasant economy, as opposed to a settler colony which was the ultimate aim of the German colonial policy. However, these differences notwithstanding, alienation of land in favour of settlers characterized both the German and British colonial periods. Differences in the rate and extent of land alienation were more an outcome of policy shifts within one colonial regime than differences in the regimes concerned (see Table 3.1).

**Table 3.1    Land alienation and policy shifts during the British period**

| Period | Annual average in acres (hectares) | Policy shifts |
|---|---|---|
| 1923-6 | 24,000 (9,720) | Native paramountcy |
| 1927-9 | 145,000 (58,725) | Dual policy |
| 1930-6 | 30,000 (12,150) | Depression |
| 1937-9 | 90,000 (36,450) | Recovery |
| 1940-8 | 21,000 (8,505) | War |
| 1949-57 | 260,000 (105,300) | Reconstruction and Pro-Alienation |

*Source*: URT, 1994, p. 14.

While the total area of land alienated during a period of over 35 years of British colonialism was a little more than 3.5 million (1417,500 ha.), the total land alienated during the German period of about 20 years (taking 1895 as the starting point for land alienation) amounted to a little over half a million hectares (1235,300 acres) (URT, 1994, p. 13; Koponen, 1994, p. 607).

Colonial land policy continued, to a greater extent, to influence post-independence land tenure systems in the sense that the post-colonial government inherited the legal framework upon which the colonial government based its land tenure policies. For example, during colonialism 'unowned' land was declared crown land under the colonial state, and after independence it was declared 'public land' under the post-colonial state. Also, the Governor was the sole custodian of the crown land during the colonial period, and the President was to take over the same responsibility during the post-colonial period. However, at a specific level the post-colonial government did undertake land tenure reforms which radically altered the colonial land policy. The first of these were the reforms based on Government Paper no. 2 of 1962, entitled 'Proposals of the Tanganyika Government for Land Reform'. The reforms effected through the Freehold Titles (Conversion) and Government Leases Act, 1963 (cap. 523) converted freeholds, most of which were granted during the German colonial period, into government leaseholds: thereby affecting some one million acres (405,000 ha.) of land. The impact of these reforms was more of a legal nature, rather than providing material benefit to customary land owners, as the land report hastens to add:

> It must be remembered that the conversion of the largely German freeholds to Government leaseholds was not *nationalisation* of property in the sense of taking over land of former owners. Nor did it involve any land reform in the nature of re-distribution of land to customary owners. What it did was to reduce the estate (interest) in land of the former owners from their ownership being in perpetuity to a definite period, the maximum being 99 years (from the date of conversion), including saving of derivative or secondary interests on such lands (emphasis original) (URT, 1994, p. 18).

After the conversion of freeholds in 1963, there came the Nyarubanja Enfranchisement Act of 1965 and the Customary Leaseholds (Enfranchisement) Act of 1968. The former law was enacted to enfranchise *nyarubanja* tenants in the West Lake zone where semi-feudal land relations had developed, while the latter was enacted to bring to an end all types of customary landlord/tenant relationships. An extension of the principles that lay behind the enfranchisement of tenants to rural and urban lands that were held under the statutory tenure (rights of occupancy) constituted a third and final attempt at tenurial reform by the post-colonial state. This was done through the 1965 Rural Farmlands (Acquisition and Re-grant) Act, which was meant to apply to a situation where the landowner himself was not the developer and the land was substantially developed by an occupier who was in some kind of tenancy relationship with the landowner (URT, 1994, p. 19).

The 1967 Arusha Declaration and the consequent nationalization of the 'commanding heights' of the country's economy did little of substance in relation to land reform except to prepare ground for the villagization movement which settled people without a legal land tenure framework. The process of land distribution under the village settlement movement and the legal problems it created are well documented and ably discussed in the Land Commission Report (see URT, 1994, ch. 4), and we need not concern ourselves with the details here. Suffice it to say that by 1976, the villagization movement had settled about 13 million scattered people into the so-called *ujamaa* villages. In some cases land was taken from large farmers and handed over to the villages for use by newcomers. In other cases people migrated to new, uncultivated land and there was no need for confiscation. Then in 1975 the government put in place the Villages and Ujamaa Villages (Designation, Registration, and Administration) Act to take care of land allocation in the villages. Unfortunately, the Act did not clarify individual land rights in relation to former landowners, nor did it give any guidelines to the village councils which were given the authority to allocate and control village land.

Apart from the villagization movement, nothing much took place in terms of policy initiatives on land reform until the introduction of the Structural Adjustment Programmes in the 1980s, especially the 1982 SAP. But before we examine the SAP and the socio-political forces it represented, an outline of the background that brought about a need for such a programme is appropriate. While Tanzania was carrying out the villagization movement, the country was hit by the 1974-5 oil shock which manifested itself in hiked oil prices and impacted negatively on the country's foreign reserves. This situation was made worse by the villagization movement which disrupted agricultural activities. However, the 1977 coffee boom greatly improved the foreign reserve position.

But the increased reserves resulting from the 1977 coffee boom were quickly dissipated by (i) the undertaking of unplanned industrial projects at the expense of and to the neglect of agriculture; (ii) increased unnecessary imports through the open general licence, and (iii) the 1978-9 war with Uganda. As the country was just coming out of the war, it was hit again by a series of external shocks between 1979 and 1982. Sutcliffe (1986, p. 19) has identified these shocks as (i) the oil price rises of 1979-80 which resulted in high import prices; (ii) unfavourable terms of trade resulting from rises in the prices of imported manufactured goods; (iii) decline in the price of primary products; (iv) the drying up of new loans after the debt crises of the early 1980s; (v) the rise of interest rates on international financial credits; and (vi) the rise in the international value of the dollar which further complicated the debt crisis. In 1974-5, Tanzania had faced shocks of a similar nature, but in dealing with the 1979-80 shocks the country had totally different policy choices:

> In 1974 and 1975 balance of payments needs were met through additional borrowing from foreign sources (mostly concessional) ... In the post-second-shock period, concessional borrowing was not (sic) longer an available option (Meyers, 1985, p. 25).

In the early 1980s, therefore, Tanzania faced not only a more unfavourable external environment, but also a changed attitude on the part of the international donor community.

It was within such a context that in 1981 the country devised its first reform programme - the National Economic Survival Plan (NESP). Externally the programme could not expect any support as the country faced a harsh and uncooperative environment while internally the brief flirtation with private capital during the 1977 coffee boom had been terminated.[2] Thus NESP did not indicate any role for the private sector in the country's efforts at economic survival. Nor did it contain any measures which could be seen as a sign of further retreat from the statist policies of the 1970s and a compromise to domestic private capital. Instead it deployed the mobilizational style used in the early 1970s by giving directives and moral exhortations to workers and peasants, urging them to increase production. But unlike the 1960s and part of the 1970s when the post-colonial state enjoyed a great measure of popular legitimacy, the 1980s were to be characterized by a general crisis of political legitimacy and declining state mobilizational capacity. Therefore, strategy for increasing production which relied on mobilization as the main instrument, at a time of crisis of political legitimacy, was doomed to fail from the beginning. As indicated in Table 3.2, none of the targets for 1981 were realized. Except for coffee and cashew nuts, whose targets were close to realization (78 per cent and 99 per cent respectively), the rest of the crops did very badly. In particular three crops (tea, tobacco and pyrethrum) performed below 50 per cent of the targets set by NESP.

Table 3.2   National Economic Survival Programme: target realization for 1981 (value in million Tsh.)

| Crop | Target | Realization | Percentage Realization |
|------|--------|-------------|------------------------|
| Coffee | 1327.00 | 1030.13 | 78% |
| Cotton | 626.20 | 407.79 | 65% |
| Tea | 214.67 | 103.59 | 48% |
| Cashew nuts | 461.20 | 458.66 | 99% |
| Tobacco | 247.63 | 101.69 | 41% |
| Pyrethrum | 32.20 | 11.25 | 35% |

Source: Modified from Ministry of Planning and Economic Affairs, 1981, p. 8.

After the failure of NESP, some significant economic reforms were to be made through the 1982 Structural Adjustment Programme. SAP was related to the World Bank through the Tanzania Advisory Group (TAG) which was commissioned jointly by the Bank and Tanzania. Following on from TAG's submission of its final report in April 1982, the government launched SAP in June that year, as the first serious adjustment programme for Tanzania. SAP was to be implemented in a three-year period, between 1982-3 and 1984-5. Both the government of Tanzania and the World Bank officially acknowledged that the programme, which was approved by Parliament in June 1982, was largely based on the more detailed report of the TAG (Ministry of Planning and Economic Affairs, 1982, p. 5; and IBRD, 1984, p. 71).

SAP had two aspects to it: *crisis management* and *structural adjustment*. The first aspect aimed at getting inflation under control while achieving a quick restoration of productive activities. To do this it assumed an external injection of balance of payments support. It was further assumed that the realization of the first aspect would lead to the creation of a conducive environment through which the second aspect would also be realized. The aim of the second aspect was to pursue policy measures that would reduce dependence on external support and restore growth momentum.

Crisis management envisaged restraint measures such as cutbacks on government expenditure and imports, in order to restore economic balance both internal and external. Policy instruments to be used included the budget, prices, and credit. It also meant a short-term shift away from new investments in order to mobilize and concentrate the available resources for full utilization of existing capacity.

On the other hand, structural adjustment among other things envisaged a broad set of mutually consistent and interacting policies whose general objectives were given as follows; (i) to *restructure* future economic activity, (ii) to *rationalize* production and (iii) to *improving planning and control systems* through more effective budgeting, monitoring, evaluations and enforcement of agreed priorities.

A notable weakness on the part of SAP 1982 was the lack of specific policy measures with regard to the agricultural sector, especially concerning increasing production (Skarstein, Havnevik and Mmbaga, 1988, p. 96). But this weakness was compensated through another policy document issued at around the same time as SAP: the Tanzania National Agricultural Policy (NAP). It is important to read NAP alongside SAP if one is to understand the post-1982 land policy reforms.

NAP was prepared by a committee of eleven people appointed by the Minister of Agriculture in May 1982. It was chaired by the economic adviser to the President, Professor Simon Mbilinyi. Members were picked from the Ministry of Agriculture, the Central Bank, the then Faculty of Agriculture of the University of Dar es Salaam based at Morogoro, and coopted members from the Department of Economics of the University of Dar es Salaam. During the course of the preparation of NAP, the committee 'critically reviewed the available literature on agricultural development in Tanzania, held interviews with the key Ministries, [and] closely associated with the agricultural sector'. It further 'solicited written and verbal views from members of the public, ministries, parastatals and farmers' associations, the party and government officials at regional, district and village levels' (MoA, NAP 1982, p. iii).

As a policy document NAP thoroughly covers the agricultural sector in all its aspects. It reviews, *inter alia*, various modes of production carried out in the country, the land tenure system, crop production, farm labour, agricultural marketing, the input supply and delivery system, finance, and foreign exchange allocation (MoA, 1982, pp. vii-xiv). The crucial areas that compensate for the weakness of SAP are those concerned with modes of farming and land tenure systems, agricultural prices, agricultural finance and the whole issue of the private sector. On modes of farming and land tenure systems, NAP clearly recognizes the presence and role of large-scale private farming. Although technically land still remained the property of the state, the new policy directed that its allocation for agricultural development should be on a longer term basis (with a minimum of 33 years) in order to provide for the security of private investors. To emphasize this, a special section on private sector investment was provided, with a clear directive, to 'maintain an atmosphere of confidence and security in order to attract investment in agriculture' (MoA, 1982, p. xi). The new land tenure system which sought to provide for the security of private investors introduced an element of private ownership of land as opposed to the former system where land was entirely state property, with rights to use sometimes being bought and sold.

It is important to emphasize that the new land policy born out of NAP is part of a package within the framework of liberalization under SAP, and that the main objective of land privatization under NAP was to facilitate commercial farming for foreign exchange and raw material generation for industries. It is also equally important to note that the type of land policy reforms directed by NAP were in the long run geared towards creating a class of big farmers in the rural areas, at the expense of masses of poor peasants. Reforms of the land tenure system can be taken as an example. Providing individual land users with title deeds has had two profound results, both of which have encouraged the development of a class of big farmers at the expense of the mass of poor peasants. The first result has been to transfer land ownership from poor peasants to wealthy farmers and bureaucrats. Developments noted in Dar es Salaam, Morogoro and Mbozi (Mbeya) support this conclusion. In Dar es Salaam all the good land on the outskirts of the city had been bought by wealthy bureaucrats and business people, thereby pushing poor peasants to less fertile marginal land further away from the city, or forcing them to leave Dar es Salaam altogether, or to remain as destitutes in the city. This movement has now gone as far as Kibaha (a fertile district in Coast Region, bordering on Dar es Salaam), where land is already extremely expensive to buy as most bureaucrats from Dar es Salaam scramble to secure farms there.

In Morogoro, most poor peasants are being replaced by wealthy absentee landlords who are most likely to reside in Dar es Salaam. The issue was taken before the CCM conference in Dodoma, but no solution was provided. In Mbozi, complaints have been reported in the local news media to the effect that land belonging to villages was being sold to rich people, some coming from other districts (see Readers' Forum, *Uhuru*, December 29, 1988). These are by no means isolated cases. After examining land alienation in Coast, Dar es Salaam, Lindi, Morogoro, Mtwara, Arusha, Kilimanjaro and Tanga regions, the Report of the Presidential Commission of Enquiry into Land Matters (URT, 1994, p. 33) concluded that there was a clear trend towards alienation of large tracts of village land to 'outsiders'. This trend shows that it is the large farmers who own most of the alienated land. The Dar es Salaam registry for example shows that 88 per cent of the more than 100,000 alienated acres (40,500 ha.) belong to 15 per cent of the

48

holders; while from the Moshi registry it is apparent that 33 per cent of the holders own 81 per cent of the total alienated land (see Tables 3.3 and 3.4). This trend, as we shall see in the case study below, represents a development that is taking place in many parts of the country. With inflation soaring high and further devaluations with no end in sight, investment in land has increasingly become popular as savings easily become valueless. At the same time, the satisfaction of basic needs which cannot now be met by the state (e.g. education and medicine) forces peasants to sell land, which is the only valuable property that they control. In other cases, village land is being sold by unscrupulous officials to speculators or plantations, as the case study below also illustrates.

**Table 3.3** **Alienated land:**
**Land registered in Dar es Salaam and Moshi Registries,**
**1987-1992 (August)**

| Region | Total area acres (hectares) | Number of properties (property holders) | Average size acres (hectares) |
|---|---|---|---|
| | *Dar es Salaam Registry* | | |
| Coast | 60,365 (24398) | 208 | 290 (177) |
| Dar es Salaam | 1,146 (463) | 7 | 164 (66) |
| Lindi | 865 (350) | 6 | 144 (58) |
| Morogoro | 55,270 (22367) | 40 | 1382 (559) |
| Mtwara | 1,188 (481) | 18 | 66 (27) |
| *Total* | 138,710 (56135) | 302 | 459 (185) |
| | *Moshi Registry* | | |
| Arusha | 47,074 (19050) | 64 | 736 (298) |
| Kilimanjaro | 530 (214) | 7 | 76 (31) |
| Tanga | 19,044 (7707) | 28 | 680 (275) |
| *Total* | 66,648 (269972)) | 99 | 673 (272) |
| *Overal total* | 205,358 (83017) | 401 | 1,132 (513) |

*Source:* URT, 1994, vol.1, p. 32.

The second result of the land tenure system reforms follows logically from the one discussed above. Once farmers secure title deeds for their land, it guarantees them financial credits. Since the reforms were introduced, title deeds had been issued mostly to individual farmers (for that matter big farmers only) as opposed to villages. This has meant that the big farmers who could easily secure title deeds for their land have had access to financial credits while poor peasants have not.[3] Both results of the reforms have meant the emergence of a class of wealthy farmers in the rural areas, at the expense of poor peasants.

Within the category of poor peasants, it is possible to identify some who are particularly vulnerable: these include youths and women. The plight of youths in the wake of land tenure reforms is very well illustrated by the complaints of one youth from Mbozi (Mbeya). Customarily, youths inherit

## Table 3.4    Spread of size of holdings

|  | 31-50 acres (13-20 ha.) | 51-200 acres (21-81 ha.) | 200-500 acres (81-203 ha.) | over 500 acres (over 203 ha.) |
|---|---|---|---|---|
| | | *Dar es Salaam Registry* | | |
| No. of holders | 49 | 71 | 5 | 24 |
| percentage | 31% | 45% | 9% | 15% |
| Land area (acres/hectares) | 1,947 (789) | 8,131(3,293) | 5,870(2,377) | 122,067(49,437) |
| percentage | 2% | 6% | 4% | 88% |
| Average (acres/hectares) | 40(16) | 115(47) | 391(158) | 5086(2060) |
| | | *Moshi Registry* | | |
| No. of holders | 7 | 31 | 28 | 33 |
| percentage | 7% | 31% | 28% | 33% |
| Land area (acres/hectares) | 336(137) | 3,421(1,386) | 8,960(3,629) | 53,994(21,868) |
| percentage | 0.5% | 5% | 13.5% | 81% |
| Average (acres/hectares) | 48(19) | 110(45) | 321(130) | 1,636(663) |

*Source*: as in Table 3.3.

land from their parents and as they grow up, they are given portions of land either from their parents' holdings or from unused village land. After observing village land being sold to rich outsiders, one youth complained in the mass media, posing an important question: 'If village land continues to be sold to outsiders at this rate, where shall we youths get land when we leave school?' (People's Forum, *Uhuru*, December 29, 1988).

In many communities of Tanzania, family land is still controlled by men. Women either use smaller portions of land within their husbands' bigger farms, or have their own farms which remain under their husbands' control. If a part of family land has to be sold, it is logical to expect that since women do not control land, it is their small portions that are likely to go first. Under such circumstances women are left to wander from one piece of land to another, as land formerly designated for them is sold. Already Marjorie Mbilinyi has observed that one effect of structural adjustment programmes has been the 'devaluation' of women's labour by attaching it to food production while men's labour is reserved for the market (export crops).[4] It would now seem that another effect is that as family land gets sold, women will further lose control of land as they are forced to move year after year.

More problems related to the impact of the land policy reforms centred around the land tenure system continued to emerge at the CCM conference in 1987. The delegate from Morogoro pointed out that in his region, since the new agricultural policy came into effect, only private farmers had been issued with land ownership certificates but there were none for villages. And a more alarming situation, he pointed out, was that certain individuals who were not resident in Morogoro came to buy land from poor peasants but then left it to lie idle. In the meantime, peasants had no land to farm although fertile land was left uncultivated. When asked why they did not develop the land, the landlords claimed that it was their property and that they were entitled to do whatever they wished with it. 'Fellow-CCM members', he deplored, 'if this situation is left unchecked, all the good land in Morogoro will soon exchange hands from the poor to the rich absentee landlords'.

The land problem was also raised by the Rukwa region delegate who linked it to a financial problem. 'The land ownership problem', he pointed out, 'has resulted in a financial problem. In Rukwa', he continued, 'only big farmers can currently get financial credit easily because they have land ownership certificates'. He concluded that 'The government must intervene to make sure that the small farmers get financial credit fairly easily too'.[5] These problems and others extensively cited in the Land Commission Report are well supported by the following case study.

## Case Study: Two Villages in Tanga Region

The Land Commission Report had looked into the question of land alienation and land shortage (URT, 1994, Ch. 5). Among those areas highly affected by this problem is Tanga Region. A close examination of two villages in the region where the problem is most acute provides us with the opportunity. Both of them serve to illustrate the myth which is central to the reasoning behind the NAP, and which is a major influence on land reform debates: namely that individualizaion of land ensures efficiency in its utilization. suggestions are also made as to how best to solve the problem.

Maramba is a village 30 miles (48 km) north-west of Tanga town. According to the 1988 census, the village had 10,000 inhabitants. In the past the village was reputed to be the granary of Tanga town. But in recent times it has hardly been capable of feeding its own inhabitants sufficiently. Threats of famine have been a constant menace to the poor peasants of Maramba who boast of two harvests of maize annually. The causal explanation for this unusual phenomenon had been bad rains. But beneath this explanation are hard facts of land distribution and utilization. The history of the village tells us that there is more than mere 'bad rains' behind this recent chronic threat of famine.

Those who have seen the 'good old days' of Maramba speak of nothing but plenty: plenty of land, food, forests, wild life, rains; plenty of anything but plantations and cash crops. But then in the 1930s plantations also entered into the vocabulary of plenty. It all started with sisal plantations which occupied the warmer fertile plains of the eastern part of the village, thereby pushing villagers to the fairly cool semi-mountainous but still very fertile part of the village. Behind this area were cold mountainous forests reserved for wild life. As long as the peasants were left with fertile semi-mountainous land which was plentiful, they were less worried by the sisal plantations which proliferated in the warm plains. Little did they know that a different crop which preferred a temperate climate and heavy rainfalls would spring up in the 1950s and push them further to the mountain forests.

Worries for the Maramba peasants began in 1952 when the CDC (Colonial, later Commonwealth Development Corporation) leased from the colonial government large tracts of village farmland and converted it into a cocoa estate. Since CDC actually developed a small portion of the land only,

51

the villagers were assured that they could use the rest on condition that they should neither grow permanent crops nor construct permanent buildings on the land. On this understanding, those whose houses fell within the leased land had to move either further towards the mountainous forest (within the limits of the forest reserve) or build along the main road to Tanga. Partly for this reason, the village grew into a small township along the main road. As for farmland, as long as the peasants were assured of use of land long enough for their requirement, they found no reason to continue to worry about leased land or land ownership.

During the mid-1970s when world market prices for cocoa became very low, CDC decided to move out of the cocoa business and handed over the estate to the government which in turn handed it over to NAFCO (National Agricultural and Food Company). NAFCO continued with the tradition started by CDC of allowing Maramba peasants to use the undeveloped land of the estate on similar conditions. But in the 1980s NAFCO also had to give up the cocoa business because of the increasing tendency to very low world market prices and general mismanagement of the farm and its resources. The estate was again returned to the government. This time there emerged a movement of the peasants to reoccupy the undeveloped lands of the estate on a permanent basis. The government immediately arrested those whom it considered to be the ringleaders of the movement and quickly handed over the estate to JKT (*Jeshi la Kujenga Taifa* or the National Service Corporation Sole). The JKT very swiftly enclosed all the land that belonged to the estate and declared it out of bounds to the public for 'security' purposes. The peasants were not only denied access to the small huts and farmlands that they had been using for generations, but they were also not allowed to walk through the forest land nearby that they had been forced to use after being denied the fertile land.

Meanwhile well-to-do bureaucrats and successful business people from Tanga town and beyond were busy buying and titling the remaining good land outside the estate boundaries. Most of these farms were either turned into ranches or hastily planted with a few coconut trees to ensure security of ownership. After selling their farms, some lucky peasants were allowed to remain as squatters or security guards to safeguard the farms. A good number of them had been reduced to destitutes doing petty business in Maramba township while land owned by both the JKT and absentee landlords lay idle and undeveloped.

Another case of land shortage we looked at is slightly different from Maramba but equally if not more dramatic. Dindira is a ward in Korogwe District, high up in the mountainous part. The ward is the site of Dindira Tea Estate and a number of villages. Unlike Maramba, Dindira has no idle underdeveloped land within or outside the estate. Virtually all the land is under either estate tea or village cultivation. Conflicts between estate boundaries and peasant farms began to emerge towards the end of the 1980s as the owners of the estate sought to expand acreage to increase production and take advantage of the agricultural reforms arising from SAP. The then Member of Parliament for Korogwe, Khalfan Kihiyo, is said to have firmly supported the peasants against any expansionist attempts by the estate owners.

But in recent years the estate owners have succeeded in their attempts to expand estate boundaries right into peasants' farms. The villagers believe that this has been possible because their new ward councillor (after the previous one died three years ago) lives away in Korogwe while their new MP (after the previous one lost in the 1990s) also lives in Dar es Salaam where he is a Deputy Minister. But more so, they attribute their land problems to a corrupt leadership at the district headquarters in Korogwe.

The land in dispute in Dindira Ward consists of farms of more than four villages in the ward and it involves hundreds of hectares. In 1994 when the peasants were about to prepare themselves for a new farming season, they found large portions of their farms cut and incorporated into the estate. The peasants believed that two European owners of the estate, identified as 'Richard' and 'Paul', had been allocated the portions of their farms by high-ranking officials from Korogwe District. Upon getting the necessary papers (titles) for the land, the Europeans distributed letters to the leaders of the village governments affected, warning peasants involved that if seen in the farms they would be taken to court because the estate now legally owned the land. The owners of the estate then sent copies of the letters to the primary court to register their seriousness.

The peasants then contributed money for fares and sent their representatives to the District Commissioner, Margareth Ndaga, to seek an explanation for their problem and a solution to it. Failing to get any help from the District Commissioner, they made further contributions to send another delegation, this time to the Regional Commissioner Azan Al-Jabri in Tanga. This too did not work. Meanwhile the estate owners were consolidating their claims beyond titling, by planting permanent trees along the new boundaries. They were even said to have cut down peasants' crops like sugar-canes, as if they were cattle feed. In one village known as Kwefingo, peasants took up their *pangas* and physically chased the poor workers, who were assigned to plant trees around the farms as a symbol of the new estate boundary. Then one elder from this village warned that if the government did not solve the conflict in time, there would soon be bloodshed. He was quoted as saying 'This is the land we depend on for food and livelihood for future generations and we can't allow it to be taken away by these Boers'.[6]

It is obvious that the land problems experienced in the two areas have been intensified in the late 1980s, although they may have long historical roots. It is also obvious that their intensification coincides with the post-1982 NAP government, a result of a land tenure policy which sets out to encourage agricultural investment through ensuring land ownership security without taking care of the needs and interests of the peasants.

In the case of Maramba village, food shortages are partly as a result of greatly reduced land use by peasants, in favour of the JKT which hardly uses the land for agricultural activities except growing soldiers' own food and undertaking bogus 'security' activities. A significant part of the rest of the land is either used for ranching or it is planted with a few permanent crops to serve as proof of ownership, or left idle for speculative purposes. In both cases the type of land use cannot be expected to take care of village food needs. In Dindira area we see a direct competition for land, between peasant production needs and those of export crop production. In both cases, contrary to the stated logic behind the NAP, individualization and titling of land seems not to promote its efficient use; nor does it ensure permanent ownership security, since peasants refuse to recognize ownership that is acquired undemocratically and against their needs and interests. What clearly emerges from the case study is that land privatization in Tanzania has taken two distinctive forms. One form is where the state alienates land and hands it over to its own institutions which are less concerned with agricultural production, while denying masses of poor peasants the use of that land. Another form of privatization is the purchase of village land by city-based people or companies, sometimes through 'free' will of the peasants themselves and sometimes through unscrupulous state officials.

**Conclusion**

In the light of all this, the question remains as to what can solve land conflicts and food shortages as are encountered in the case study areas. It has been shown clearly that peasants' needs and interests have to be taken into consideration when structuring land policy to undertake land reforms. Such needs and interests specifically involve minimum peasant rights to access land for food production use. It would seem that the 1982 NAP was rather motivated by political interests that were geared at mobilizing private investment in agriculture without putting into place a legal framework to protect the needs and interests of the masses of poor peasants.

As to what type of land policy is suitable for Tanzania's needs and which would also solve the acute land problems raised in this discussion, we concur with the suggestions of the Land Commission Report. In the short run alienated lands - especially where they have been abandoned or are not fully utilized for agriculture, and are in areas of land scarcity - should be redistributed to the occupiers who have been cultivating them or are landless (URT, 1984, p. 64). For long-term purposes, the need is for a national land policy that would look into the needs and interests of peasants as a starting point for minimum national requirements. Here the Report again put up a very strong argument which serves as a conclusion to our discussion:

> If we begin from the premise that Tanzania is a country of smallholders, our second premise follows inexorably. Tanzania must feed itself, which means first and foremost the peasantry must feed itself and secondly, feed the country ... The investor from outside the village community whether foreign or local, has little interest in investing in food production for the domestic market. His interest lies in high rates of profits in the first place, rapid returns in the second place, and accumulation of his profits in a 'safe' haven outside in the third place (URT, 1994, p. 137).

In line with the above argument, if Tanzania considers feeding itself as a minimum national requirement, then land must be made readily available to peasants.

In line with the above argument, if Tanzania considers feeding itself as a minimum national requirement, then land must be made readily available to peasants.

## Notes

1. This refers to a general trend only; in practice there are many variations. For example, Kenya switched over to individualization of land ownership during the colonial period while Tanganyika resisted the recommendations of the East Africa Royal Commission (1953-1955) which formed the basis for Kenya's move.
2. For details of this brief promotion of domestic private capital see Kiondo, 1989, pp. 180-88.
3. The argument that title deeds make land mortgageable and thereby increase farmers' access to credit has been sufficiently refuted in practice but in theory it continues to inform farmers' expectations - see the Land Commission Report (URT, 1994, p. 119).
4. This was a conclusion made by Professor Marjorie Mbilinyi during a seminar discussion for the African Studies Programme, New College, University of Toronto, in October 1988.
5. All references to the 1987 CCM conference held at Kizota, Dodoma, area directly taken from Kiondo, 1989. The author was an observer to that conference.
6. Author's own translation from Swahili version, quoted in a Swahili weekly, *Afrika Leo*, January 23, 1995.

## References

International Bank for Reconstruction and Development (IBRD) (1984), *Tanzania Country Economic Report*, no. 5019TA, Washington DC.

Izumi, K. (1993), 'Economic Liberalisation, Land Policy and Land Tenure in Tanzania', Draft research proposal, Department of Economics and Social Sciences, Agricultural University of Norway, 10 November, 1993.

Kiondo, A.S.Z. (1989), 'The Politics of Economic Reforms in Tanzania, 1977-1988', PhD. dissertation, University of Toronto.

Koponen, J. (1994), *Development for Exploitation: German Colonial Policies in Mainland Tanzania, 1894-1914*, Finnish Historical Society, Helsinki/Hamburg.

Meyers, K. (1985), 'Agricultural Performance and Policy in Tanzania', revised draft, World Bank Files (KBW/Agric/10-24-85), Washington DC.

Ministry of Agriculture (MoA) (1982), *National Agricultural Policy*, Dar es Salaam.

Ministry of Planning and Economic Affairs (1981), *Annual Development Plan 1980/81*, Government Printers (URT), Dar es Salaam.

Ministry of Planning and Economic Affairs (1982), *Structural Adjustment Programme 1982*, URT, Dar es Salaam.

55

Shivji, I.G. *A Legal Quagmire: Tanzania"s Regulation of Land Tenure (Establishment of Villages) Act, 1992*, IIED, Pastoral Land Tenure Series, London.

Skarstein, R., Havenvik, K.J. and Mmbaga, W.D.S. (1988), *Norwegian Commodity Import Support to Tanzania*, Norwegian Ministry of Development Cooperation, Trondheim.

Sutcliffe, B. (1986), 'Africa and the World Economic Crisis', in Lawrence, P. (ed.), *World Recession and the Food Crisis in Africa*, James Currey, London, pp. 18-28.

United Republic of Tanzania (URT) (1994), *Report of the President's Commission of Inquiry into Land Matters*, vol. 1, SIAS, Uppsala.

# 4 Land Issues and Tanzania's Political Economy

## C. S. L. CHACHAGE

### Introduction

Attempts to deal with transformations which have been taking place in rural Tanzania since the 1980s are fraught with numerous problems. Of these the major one is the nature of paradigm shifts which have been taking place in the reformulation of economic policies in general; and the *impasse* in 'development theories'. The latter have usually provided models of reference for rural studies. Changes taking place in Tanzania and Africa in general have occurred against the background of new international conditions. These have included collapse of bureaucratic state socialism in Eastern and Central Europe; severe economic crisis; and the implementation of Structural Adjustment Programmes (SAPs) sponsored by the World Bank and the IMF. SAPs have insisted on the liberalization of the economy, more reliance on market forces, and less state intervention - as a means to stimulate production of traditional exports and to overcome the crisis. The classic assumptions associated with Adam Smith, in accordance with which the sovereign has the task of maintaining law, order, defence, and public goods but merely provides the framework for efficient functioning of private enterprises has been resurrected (Pickett, 1989).

The same period has also witnessed attempts to restructure and reshape power relations. It has been an era of the reawakening of people and their mobilization for democratic rights against the monopolization of politics by the dominant structures of the state. This process has been accompanied by a growing critique of the role of the state and its role in human liberation (Kothari, 1984, p. 14). The developmentalist models of accumulation and accelerated development of the first decade of independence had been characterized by a high degree of state intervention as a means to achieve industrialization; but the policy of a high degree of economic control and a high level of unified political loyalty has increasingly become discredited. Instead, there has been a reconsideration of the relationship between the state and civil society, with the latter as an autonomous expression of human social will. The whole process of decentralization and rediscovery of identities is involved.

# Brief Overview of the Post-Independence Economy of Tanzania

Tanzania inherited an agriculturally-based economy which depended on the export of coffee, cotton, sisal, tea, tobacco and cashew nuts. These financed the bulk of the imports, as they accounted for more than 80 per cent of the exports. Broadly, the models for accumulation and accelerated development in Tanzania in the first decade of independence, formulated by the World Bank (cf. Little, 1966), stressed the need for state intervention in society and economy, as a means to achieve industrialization and modernization.

Such models recommended the country to embark on industrialization for import substitution for the processing of raw materials for export. Since the government had limited resources for investment, private investors were to be encouraged; and these were mainly Asian or foreign. It was necessary for the government to offer inducements, and to take action against political pressures that might be brought to bear against making of profits. Tanganyika was advised to sell raw materials, food and labour at a competitive price in the world market if capital was to be attracted.

The model was premised on the need for concentration of powers in the executive arm of the state, and on the erosion of people's capacities for social and political organization. The state was supposed to bring social services, industries, and infrastructure to the people, who in turn were expected to accept a high degree of economic control and to offer the state a unified political loyalty. Consequently, the government introduced measures such as detention without trial, which militated against the rights of people in the name of development; and there were further measures to control or abolish organizations of peasants, workers, youth, women, students, likewise trade unions, professional organizations and cooperatives. The nationalist leaders were committed to modernization/developmentalism, and the general tendency was to view the mass of the people as ignorant, superstitious, primitive, lazy, resistant to change and backward.[1]

Some rates of growth were apparent on this basis. Despite the lack of support from foreign capital, policies concerning basic consumer goods were more or less achieved by 1967 (URT, 1969, p. iii). It was noted in the 1970s that there was a growth of value added of more than 13 per cent annually in manufacturing, for the period 1965 to 1974. The growth rate in the manufacturing sector during this period was 7.5 per cent annually. Between 1965 and 1975, the percentage share of agriculture in GDP fell from 56 per cent to 42 per cent, while that of manufacturing rose from 4 per cent to 11 per cent between 1961 and 1975 (ILO, 1975, pp. 84-5).

With such developments, it had become difficult for agriculture to sustain any further import expansion by 1974, as no significant technical transformations had taken place within that sector. In that year, the volume of exports fell by 35 per cent. The situation was made worse by the forcible villagization of the peasants (which halted production in most regions), droughts, and the rise in oil prices.

To make things worse, many government-owned agricultural boards, commercial and industrial enterprises which had been an important source of funds for the governments in the 1960s, were already making huge losses by the mid-1970s. Fortunately, many of them, especially in agriculture, were supported by donors in terms of capital and personnel. By the 1970s, the government was no longer gaining from these parastatals, as it was in the 1960s. Agricultural marketing boards, for example, were appropriating an increasing proportion of the producer price themselves. They were also becoming a drain on government finances: for example, nine agricultural parastatals had combined losses of Tsh. 692 million, and overdrafts held by parastatals stood at Tsh. 5,127 million. The latter accounted for 80 per cent of loans outstanding to the National Bank of Commerce by 1981-2.[2]

By 1980, the symptoms of the crisis were widespread. They included deterioration in the balance of trade, a fall in agricultural production (food and export crops), negative per capita growth, high inflation rates, acute shortage of essential consumer goods, low industrial capacity utilization, deterioration in the budgetary position and general deterioration of the conditions of the working people. In that particular year, the value of exports was only equivalent to 43 per cent of the imports and the trade gap was over Tsh. 6 billion. Similarly, industrial capacity utilization was between 30 and 50 per cent on average and at this time the manufacturing sector accounted for only 5.8 per cent of a smaller GDP, as compared to 1977 when it accounted for 10.4 per cent. As far as foreign reserves were concerned, they peaked at $281.8 million in 1977, fell to $99.9 million in 1978, and finally to $20.3 million in 1980.

It was within this context that Tanzania started negotiations with the IMF. She was forced to devalue her currency in 1979, and the negotiations broke down immediately as Tanzania rejected the conditions. These required her to devalue significantly, freeze wages, increase interest rates, decontrol prices, relax import controls, and reduce government spending by cost-cutting on social services. Tanzania negotiated for a three year standby facility in July 1980. This agreement collapsed after four months as Tanzania exceeded the domestic budgetary ceiling.

With the failure to come to terms with the IMF in 1979-80, Tanzania formulated her own home-made programmes to deal with the crisis. These were the 1981-82 National Economic Survival Programme (NESP), the 1982 Structural Adjustment Programme (SAP), the 1982 National Agricultural Policy (NAP), and the 1986 Economic Recovery Programme (ERP). The latter was implemented with the support of the World Bank and the IMF with donor support. External assistance to the country increased from $287 million (1985) to $680 million in 1986 (as a result of the signing of the IMF accord), and to $850 million in 1989. About 47 per cent of this came from import support.

More fundamentally, as was noted by the World Bank (IBRD, 1991, p. 60), the growth in GDP has resulted from the unification of official and 'parallel' markets under liberalization, especially through the inauguration of the 'own-funded import scheme' since 1984. It is for example noteworthy that while the value of official exports was $424 million and imports were worth $1,380 million in 1989/90, imports through the 'own account' scheme were worth $38 million in 1988. At the outset of the crisis in 1980, exports covered 43 per cent of import requirements. By 1985, they covered less than one third. Under SAPs the position has actually worsened. Exports financed only 28 per cent of imports in 1992 and 25 per cent in 1991.

On the other hand, one of the things to be noted within this trend is the general stagnation in traditional as opposed to so-called 'non-traditional' exports - the latter comprising mainly manufactured and semi-processed goods, minerals, forestry and marine products, and services such as tourism. Officially, traditional exports fell from around 70 per cent of all exports by value in 1981-6 to about 46 per cent in 1990-91 and 41 per cent in 1991-2. Therefore 54 per cent and 59 per cent respectively of total exports came from non-traditional sources in the latter years. Earnings from non-traditional exports decreased from $242 million, in 1989 to $86 million in 1986, but a substantial recovery took place from 1987 when they accounted for $146 million. Average annual growth in the export value of these goods in the period 1986-90 was almost 24 per cent. In reality, estimates by the Board of External Trade show that unrecorded exports of both traditional and non-traditional products could amount to more than $500 million per year. These estimates are based on calculations from impounded products like minerals, trophies and crops.[3]

There is evidence that real (and probably environmentally irreversible) 'growth' has occurred and still occurs in activities exploiting wildlife products (ivory, crocodile skins, ostrich and other exotic birds), forest products (black woods, mangrove, mahogany, medicinal plants, etc.), marine products (prawns, lobster, sea slugs etc.), and mineral products. Some 564 tusks were seized by Dar es Salaam police in May 1993. These were worth Tsh. 72 million. According to estimates, the country produces between 10 and 16 tons of gold annually while the banks have been able to purchase only 12 tons since 1989. About 80 per cent of gemstones are exported unofficially.[4]

Since the mid-1980s there has been a partial shift in these activities from illegal to legal circuits in each of the areas under the guise of liberalization and SAPs. Alongside these activities has been the growing incidence of drug trafficking, whereby between 1986 and 1991 there were 468 Tanzanians netted abroad for this offence and 19.7 tons of bhang were impounded in 1991 alone.[5] Police were able to seize 46,193 kg. of drugs between 1991 and May 1993.[6] Many more young men were netted within the country in 1994. The so-called booming import-export trade needs to be seen in the context of these unrecorded and recorded activities.

By 1992 it had become evident that the process of 'officialization' of hitherto illicit activities had been accompanied by one of the de-officialization of legal ones. Just as 'own funds imports' continued to boom, so it became clear that the 'official' importers were evading - flagrantly and on a spectacular scale - the basic requirements of import support and the open general import licence to deposit with Tanzanian banks in local currency coverage for the forex they were obtaining. Evidence suggests that tax evasion has reached a colossal scale. The government lost Tsh. 715 million ($1.5 million) through tax evasion by manufacturers of aluminium articles and soft drinks in 1990-91 alone.[7] It has also sanctioned tax defaulting by giving exemptions against its own regulations. Towards the end of 1994, it was revealed by the government that tax evasion for that year amounted to around Tsh. 70 billion, while unwarranted tax exemptions amounted to about Tsh. 30 billion.

There is an inextricable linkage between these booming 'new' exports, corporate fraud against the state and the ongoing significance of the 'own funded import scheme'. The former two, recorded and unrecorded, fund the last, and also fund unknown levels of unregistered and unrecorded imports. Liberalization has resulted in the expansion of combined legal-illegal import-export trade and conditions whereby previously mainly legally marketed commodities can enter illegal circuits, and illegally acquired goods can enter the market legally.

## 'Agricultural Development Policies' and Land Tenure Issues

The general consensus in Tanzania is that there is no national land policy, and that the existing legal framework is outmoded, unworkable and full of contradictions in many areas.[8]   This framework is governed by the Land Ordinance, Cap. 113, 1923, which has also constituted the basic grounding of all the subsequent legislation.[9]  With this legislation, all land is supposed to be public and the president was granted powers to make land grants and leases if he/she deemed this to be for the benefit of 'public' national interests. There are two sets of law relating to land tenure:  (a) Statutory law which governs lands which have been granted by the government (such as the land held by private companies, state farms, and large and medium scale farmers). These rights are also known as 'granted rights of occupancy';  and (b) Customary law, which governs all untitled land under smallholder production.  These have also been called 'deemed rights of occupancy' since 1928 (Chidzero, 1961, p. 223).

Under German colonial rule (1885-1916) all land was decreed to be 'ownerless crown land'.  It was only settlers and plantation owners who possessed documentary evidence of actual ownership.  Africans were given rights of occupation.  The German policy of administration was geared towards plantation and settler agriculture.  Massive land alienation took place in due course, to the extent that by the eve of the First World War some 1,300,000 acres (526,500 ha.) of the best lands in northern Tanzania and the coast had been alienated to immigrants (URT, 1994, p. 9).  The number of Europeans in the country had grown from 1,390 to 4,998 between 1904 and 1913.  Of these, 882 male adults were involved in agriculture - a number almost equal to that of Kenyan settlers (Iliffe, 1979, p. 141).

German administration had already started to reconsider its policies towards Africans by 1907 as a result of the Maji Maji war of resistance (1905-6).  Henceforth, forced labour and land alienation was undertaken more cautiously and the colonial state turned to what it termed 'scientific colonialism'.  This policy was guided by the principle of 'how to make the desired profits in the surest fashion' without necessarily depriving the original population's 'place in the sun' (Gann and Duignan, 1977, p. 75). It was in this way that the administration reached the decision that it was more desirable for the country to remain a peasant colony.

The British were well aware of these aspects when they took over the country in 1917.  In a minute by the Private Secretary to the East African Protectorates Acting Governor in the same year, it was admitted that there was a lot of anti-European feeling in the country. The minute considered how best to implement a definite policy of encouraging strong and isolated tribal nationalism at the 'most effective barriers against a Pan-African upheaval' (Lonsdale, 1972, p. 20). The first governor, Horace Byatt, was to give priority to the establishment of native authorities, and this culminated in the promulgation of the Native Authority Ordinance no. 16 of 1921. When the Land Ordinance was passed in 1923, the Native Authority Ordinance was being amended. All these policies were consolidated in 1927.

The philosophy underlying the policy of Indirect Rule and the Land Law was the same. They aimed at dealing with the problems arising from the 'conflict of interests of the African population and those of European enterprise'. The government became convinced of the necessity of incorporating the 'natives' and some aspects of their outlook (those favourable to the creation of colonial capitalism) in the government for its own use (Hailey, 1950, p. 212). Western civilization demanded raw materials and food crops which were necessary to the living standards of the 'principal nations', and this is what constituted the 'empire problem'. Therefore, either the tropical inhabitants produced them or they were compelled to do so, or they gave way to some other race which could do so. According to the colonial officials, it was the honest and final settlement of the land question which determined the policies, given the general insecurity which was becoming widespread, as a result of which no African believed a word the Europeans said in so far as this question was not settled (Chachage, 1986, p. 148). In a nutshell, peasant production was more favourable for the colonials in the interwar period since it made it possible to avoid conflicts. Hardly any further land alienation for settlers was undertaken during this period, beyond the auctioning of 'enemy property'.

Since the policy of the colonial government was based on the belief that the organization of Africans followed communal tribal lines, it was necessary, in the view of the colonialists, that land policies should operate on the same basis. They believed that the land of the tribe was normally occupied in as much as people chose to do so, and that occupation was generally concentrated round the village of the chief for the purpose of safety; and that it was European occupation that had led to a tendency to spread outwards. In this way, the colonialists started concentrating population by force in the 1920s. This was done in the whole of western Tanganyika, Lindi and other parts of the country, under the guise of sleeping sickness eradication. The motives behind these concentrations were administrative expediency, labour recruitment, efficient peasant produce collection, soil conservation, and game conservation. Development reasons were being quoted in the proposals for concentration in the 1940s. Concentrations were described as local points for purposeful government action, services and fast economic development (such as medical aid, education, extension work, and markets).[10]

The interwar period witnessed the escalation of sensitivity about the control of land and labour; there were some cases of rebellion as a result. Some of the government moves mentioned above resulted from increased differentiation among rural producers - an aspect which was erroneously referred to as 'population increase and settled cultivation'. By around 1927

62

for example, the Chagga in Kilimanjaro had begun to buy and sell land, and were even demanding written titles and claiming that freehold tenure was Chagga tradition (Iliffe, 1979, p. 275). This was also happening in Bukoba, Arusha, Tabora, Mwanza, and in Nyakyusa territory.

It was in the 1940s that the colonial government began to pay increased attention to the possibility of utilization of immigrant communities, while at the same time leaving it open to the indigenous population to participate. European agriculture was increasingly seen as the only means for attainment of fast expansion and growth of the economy, given the crisis which followed the Second World War. It was argued that peasant agriculture was inefficient because of the systems of land tenure which were marked by lack of personal interest and mitigated against improvement, and further that the systems of land use (e.g. shifting cultivation and the use of fire to clear farms) caused reduced soil fertility and diminishing yields. Only European methods were seen as capable of sustained development, with machines, chemicals and improved seeds. Therefore, it was argued that even Africans had to be compelled to adopt the same methods of agriculture. Such methods were duly embodied in the Land Development and Soil Conservation Schemes.

There were no more pretensions by the 1940s concerning 'preservation of peasant agriculture and the fabric of African society' or that land could not be alienated for private use without consideration of the needs and interests of the indigenous inhabitants. The era of 'modernization' and 'modernizing imperialism' had dawned. The colonies were increasingly seen as dominated by dual economies: traditional and modern, community and society, agricultural and industrial, rural and urban, particularistic and universalistic, low achievement orientation and higher achievement orientation - and similar dichotomies. Societies were seen as needing to be transformed from the traditional subsistence stage to that of modern production.

Changes in conceptions of development resulted in change of land policies. Land alienation for the immigrant communities was undertaken on a greater scale than ever before in the history of British colonialism. Between 1945 and 1955 British settlers increased their holdings from 287,635 acres (116,492 ha.) of land on lease to 1,301,654 (527,170 ha.), Greeks increased their holdings from 90,803 acres (36,775 ha.) to 294,649 acres (119,333 ha.); Indians increased theirs from 68,110 (27,585 ha.) to 237,515 acres (9,546 ha.). The Overseas Food Corporation with its Groundnut Schemes had initially aimed at clearing 3 million acres (1,215,000 ha.). It acquired 480,000 acres (194,400 ha.) leased for 35 years (but succeeded in clearing only 50,000 acres [20,250 ha.]). Of the cultivable land surface by the 1950s 40 per cent was owned by capitalists, primarily Europeans but also Asians, Arabs and later Africans (Bates, 1957).

The famous Meru Land Case (1951-3) and the fear of land alienation were the forces behind the mobilization of Africans against colonial rule and the formation of the Tanganyika African National Union (TANU). The 1954 UN Mission pointed out that land and its use and tenure was the outstanding economic and political issue for Africans (Cliffe, 1972, p. 20). The rural protest began to have an impact at governmental level from this period. Wherever the leaders of Tanganyika African Association (the predecessor of TANU) went in Dodoma, Arusha and Mwanza, land and the ownership of

63

land was an issue about which African peasants were particularly responsive (Listowel, 1965, p. 214).

Politically, these conflicts were reflected in Nyerere's critique of those Europeans and Africans who stood for 'multi-racialism' in 1950. Their views were denounced for wanting to substitute the money bar for the colour bar, i.e. perpetuation of minority domination over the majority. Their land reform proposals which stood for recognition of individual rights and the purchase of land by all persons of all races (in the footsteps of the case which had been pushed forward for individualization of land ownership by the East Africa Royal Commission [1955]) were rejected. According to Nyerere, it was only the immigrants with money and backing from overseas who would be able to afford land. Nyerere suggested rather that in Africa, land tenure was based on primary needs and usage rather than buying, selling and speculation.[11]

The latter view of land ownership became part of TANU economic policy. When the government proposed to move towards freehold tenure, including the process of titling and registration, in 1958, TANU rejected the policy. The government had couched its arguments for freehold in terms of considerations of efficiency, whereby land would become marketable and could be transferred to the efficient users, and could also provide security to the users. Here was an attempt by the government to abandon the policy of land alienation which was proving catastrophic, by replacing it with a policy of land deprivation based on the tenurial system. It was an attempt by the colonial government to resolve a crisis that it had created.

TANU did not necessarily oppose private ownership of land, but it was opposed to alienation to individual non-Africans. It was quite willing to accept a lease of land to the African commercial corporations if beneficial to the country's economy.[12]  After independence in 1961, the government of Tanganyika converted all freeholds into government leases, which were turned into rights of occupancy in 1969. In other words, land was nationalized without necessarily any legal backing.

The independent government had inherited a thriving capitalist agriculture based on plantations and settler farms, and an expanding African capitalist agriculture. Except for the latter, this did not expand substantially after independence. African small capitalist farmers' production continued to expand with cotton at 13 per cent, coffee at 12.5 per cent, and cashew nut at 9 per cent annually. Between 1961 and 1966, GDP grew at the rate of 4.8 per cent annually in real terms and there were surpluses in the balance of payments (Coulson, 1982, p. 148). Settlers and plantation owners had begun leaving the country from 1960 onwards, taking most of their capital with them - at least £3 million ($8,430,000) (Coulson, 1982). This capital flight was due to insecurity  which some of the immigrants felt, given the revocation of freehold and some of the pronouncements made by certain nationalists, which could be perceived as hostile to capital or to certain sections of it.

Various 'rural development transformation' strategies were to be designed after independence, with important ramifications as far as land matters were concerned. Through the Department of Community Development, the government embarked on the 'local point' or 'improvement approach' which had been introduced by the colonial government in 1956 and was recommended in the Three Year Development Plan. In this programme, the government undertook to supervise and to provide extension services and credit facilities to small farmers so as to improve agriculture. The move involved concentration on small selected 'progressive farmers', in the hope that the benefits (methods, techniques, attitudes, etc.) would trickle down to other peasants. This involved the establishment of rural elites with 'progressive' attitudes. There was a proposal in the first Five Year Development Plan of 1965 to establish more than 60 pilot settlement schemes by 1970 with 'progressive farmers', and it was hoped that the number of these settlements would rise to 200 by 1980 (Coulson, 1982, p. 147).

The above approach was abandoned in 1966 as a result of failure to create a capitalist class of farmers. Instead, African capitalist farmers were expanding independently in Mbulu (Arusha), Ismani (Iringa), Maswa (Shinyanga), Urambo (Tabora), Usambara (Tanga), the northern shore of Lake Nyasa, Kilimanjaro, Bukoba, and in the cashew nut growing areas on the coast. It is these which accounted for the increase in agricultural production. There was also increase in the marketed produce as a consequence of expansion of the acreage involved in small owner peasant production all over the country: partly because of compulsion by the government. Rules and laws had been set up in almost every district and village which stipulated the minimum acreage of certain crops to be grown by 1965 (Bienen, 1967, p. 347).

Just like the colonial government, the post-colonial successors intervened in agricultural production and marketing. It was a commitment to modernize the country by the nationalists and the educated in general, who believed that they, rather than the workers or peasants, had the answers to the problems of development. In the first Five Year Development Plan, for example, the dominant view was that peasants were primitive, backward and stupid - generally inferior human beings (Coulson, 1982, p. 161). By 1962 the Minister for Agriculture was empowered to declare an area controlled whenever he was satisfied that the production, cultivation or marketing of any agricultural goods was likely to advance and improve the area. It was within this context that agricultural marketing boards were created by 1963 in almost every region. The boards were empowered to direct all producers to sell through their agencies - the cooperatives. They also had the discretion to determine the price of goods (Fimbo, 1974, p. 259).

Despite the socialist rhetoric, the underlying assumptions remained fundamentally the same. Their perspective was modernist, and the aim was to squeeze agriculture for development of other sectors. The villagization programme of 1973/4, for example, aimed at settling peasants into 'modern settlements', i.e. 'with houses placed together, in straight lines, along the roads, and with fields outside the villages, organized in block farms ... each block ... with only one type of crop, and readily accessible for control by agricultural extension officers' (Boesen, 1976, p. 13). The process involved large-scale relocation of rural dwellers (9 million by the end of the process, and thus the existence of 8,299 villages by 1979) into villages without regard to the land tenure systems. The attitude of the officials towards the ordinary people was not different from that expressed by the colonial agents before independence and in the first Five Year Development Plan. Villagers were viewed as ignorant, lazy, and useless to listen to; it was therefore thought unnecessary to consult them (Boesen, Madsen and Moody, 1977, p. 155).

The same modernist assumptions led to the creation of large-scale state farms in those years. With the 1967 Arusha Declaration, the state nationalized some of the large farms and began to open new ones. This involved alienation of large tracts of land in many regions. By 1976 there were 108 parastatal enterprises in farming. Many of them were making huge losses, but were being supported by the World Bank and other donors in terms of capital and personnel. The Netherlands and Denmark supported sugar production, Canada wheat production, and North Korea rice production, while activities supported by the World Bank included ranching. Most of these farming projects involved the displacement of people and communities; one typical case was that of the Barabaig in Hanang (Arusha), where the Canadians assisted in the establishment of wheat farms.

By the mid-1970s, agricultural production was more or less under the control of the state through its various organs. Under such circumstances, in the mid-1970s peasants began to withdraw into production systems which they were capable of controlling. The tendency was to withdraw from those crops which were bureaucratically controlled, and to become involved in those that were not, and which required less labour and material inputs and were sold at buoyant prices. This was the case with the Kilimanjaro coffee growers, who started cutting down coffee in favour of production of tomatoes and onions; and with the coastal cashew nut growers who abandoned weeding the cashew groves in favour of charcoal burning.

In some cases crops (both food and export) were merely withdrawn from the official markets and sold to the unofficial markets - and some were marketed in neighbouring countries, namely Kenya, Zambia, Malawi, Zaire (now Congo Democratic Republic), Burundi, Rwanda and Uganda. Rice from Rukwa and Kigoma is still exported to Zambia, Zaire, Rwanda and Burundi, and coffee is exported to Kenya. The decrease in officially marketed produce was a result of undemocratic state intervention in the conditions of peasant production, and could be seen as a mode of resistance. It was a withdrawal into those crops and activities which have traditionally been ignored by official support, administratively and technically. This meant also a reduction in the use of inputs and hence, the decrease in production of staples such as maize and other grains.

The severe economic crisis in the 1980s led to doubts being cast about the rural development strategy which had been applied in the past. This was at the time when the government was attempting to formulate its own home-made SAPs after failure to strike a deal with the IMF. A commission was formed in 1982 to make recommendations on a national agricultural policy, and a new policy towards land was recommended (URT, 1982). This involved abandonment of the previous insisted on communal use of land and encouraged individualization as an incentive to producers. In this new policy, medium and large-scale farmers were encouraged to expand their investments and to title their lands. Agricultural growth was now seen as depending upon the emergence of entrepreneurs in agriculture. The decline in production in the previous years was attributed to dominance of 'traditional' forms of production. This policy also introduced village titles.

The aim was to have all village lands demarcated and titled, on the pretext that such a measure would protect villagers from outside encroachment. Village governments would sub-lease land to villagers and provide security of tenure and encourage more investments in the land.

This agricultural policy marked a real ideological shift in state policies. Despite the fact that there were no changes made in the legislation, its impact was immense. There are few villages which attempted to survey their areas. But more important was the fact that the policy initiated a partial return to pre-villagization land patterns. Villagers were given a go-ahead to return to their old plots, only to find that their land had been absorbed by new settlements. At the same time original inhabitants in the nucleated villages started claiming their lands, which had been given to those who had previously moved in. Villagization and concentration of farms had increasingly resulted in land shortages and therefore social differentiation - with most school leavers becoming landless. Some villagers were being forced to walk between 5 to 10 kilometres to their farms. A whole chain of legal actions and land litigations started.

This was only one level of the impact. Since it was the liberalization policies which guided the shift in the land policy, what has been witnessed since then is the increase in number of large, medium and small-scale 'investors' (local and foreign) in land and other natural resources. There began an acquisition of land on a large scale, mainly through government allocation: for example the massive alienation of land in Arusha Region which mainly aimed at displacing the Maasai pastoralists. Such was the decision in 1994 to hand back 381,000 acres (134,629 ha.) of land in Mondali and Kiteto Districts (Arusha) to a foreign investor. The problem extends beyond farmland; a case in point is the scandal of secret granting of 4,000 square kilometres of Loliondo Game Reserve in Arusha to an Arab hunting sheikh. Since the National Investment (Promotion and Protection) Act, 1990, and the establishment of the Investment Promotion Centre (IPC) under the President, it is reported that between July 1990 and August 1993 the number of investment projects approved in the country was 80 in tourism, 58 in agriculture, and 41 in natural resources.

On the other hand, mining companies began to appear in the country in 1984 on the basis of the framework set by the 1979 Mining Act (amended further in 1982-3). Between 1989 and 1992, for example, the government granted eight reconnaissance licences, 75 prospecting licences, and 17 mining licences. By 1992 there were also 67 companies licensed in mineral drilling.[13] In addition to gold, these licences covered minerals and metals such as nickel, cobalt, precious metals, diamonds, graphite, gemstones, bauxite and beach sands. By 1992 it was estimated that there were about 500 gold and about 300 gemstone mining sites operated by small-scale miners. Officially there were 1,440 small-scale claim holders and 480 prospecting certificate holders in 1993. At a very conservative estimate of 10,000 people per site, it is possible that there were about 900,000 people involved in small-scale mining and auxiliary activities - a number which is larger than the official figures of those in the formal wage sector.

Most foreign 'large-scale' operations which have entered the picture turn out in practice to be rather small and probably incapable of large-scale investment. This is the case for most investors in all sectors. Interestingly, none of the foreign companies which were given exclusive rights in mine development since the mid-1980s have opened new mines, except in the case of gemstones. For example, Dar Tardine Tanzania Ltd (the representative of a Swiss company) was given five licences in 1984 to an area which covered 80 per cent of the most attractive gold prospects around Lake Victoria zone. By 1988, the company had managed to shut out other investors from the area but had not explored or developed new prospects. Instead it was involved in an experimental treatment of tailings in the old mines by cyanide leaching, producing officially only 40 kg. per annum. It was also involved in a project with the State Mining Corporation (STAMICO) to send teams of purchasers into 'illegal' gold mining areas to buy gold at an open market price (Jourdan, 1992, p. 8; Chachage, 1995). In fact, the so-called 'illegal' mining areas were places in which the company had sub-leased to small-scale miners. The company fell under parliamentary investigation for smuggling in the same year.

The liberalization policies were also responding to a growing interest in rural land by town dwellers such as government officials, civil servants, traders and businessmen with the expansion of informal land markets and various forms of privatization. Land grabbing by people with authority and wealth, alienation and allocation of village lands to the rich, and dubious land allocations by government officials, had become the norm in the 1980s. Some land grabbers sought future security, or were motivated by speculation, and did not necessarily aim at investment. They were speculators who obtained title to their lands, given that it had become easy to strike deals with village leaders. The Land Commission has demonstrated that incidence of deals between village leaders and outsiders who have secured large tracts of village land are numerous (URT, 1991).

Land markets in urban, peri-urban and some rural areas have been developing very fast. This has occurred despite the official policy that land was public and had no value (a policy which has absolved both colonial and post-colonial governments from compensating those dispossessed of their lands for 'public interest'). The 1982 agricultural policy recommendation on land tenure had in a way coincided with the interests of SAPs in general. SAPs had originally recommended individualization, titling and registration of lands for African countries. The assumption was that indigenous land tenure systems were obsolete, and that they discouraged economic development (e.g. they were seen as an obstacle to investments, credit and agricultural productivity improvement). The aim of the new policies was to secure land rights.[14]

In view of the inconsistencies concerning land tenure, two initiatives towards legal reforms (with different motives) arose. A Presidential Commission of Inquiry into Land Matters was appointed to investigate and propose a land policy. Around the same time, the Ministry of Lands, Housing and Urban Development (MLHUD) created a Committee for the same purpose. The Presidential Commission arose as a consequence of the number of complaints received from the public on land conflicts and litigations. The aim was to resolve the land problems. The Ministry was motivated by what were considered to be inconsistencies in the existing outdated land law, which made it difficult to plan and administer land matters.

In a nutshell, the Presidential Commission was to point out that the powers given to the Executive in all land matters by virtue of the fact that it owned all the land resulted in failure to administer land in such a way that security of tenure could be extended to customary land holders. There were too many government bodies which were involved in land administration, and too much interference from different bodies, Acts, and policies. What it advocated was a separate body - a Board of Land Commissioners - which would be answerable to the National Assembly. The Commission recommended that all land be divided into National Lands and Village Lands and that the president be divested of the radical title to land.[15]

The main concern of the Ministerial Committee was with addressing inconsistencies and lack of clarity in the existing land law.[16] It raised the problem of how the government could effect development in the desired direction without being hampered by the confusions under the existing law. The Ministry wanted land legislation which would be in line with government policies as pursued since the 1980s. It was not interested in the complete restructuring of the system, but rather in streamlining so that responsibilities could be more clearly defined and delegated. Its stated main concern was how to protect smallholders' rights to land from land grabbers, while at the same time responding to interests of 'investors' who had been approved by IPC. It was in this respect that the government passed the Regulation of Land Tenure (Established Villages) Act, 1992,[17] which extinguished the customary land rights which were affected during villagization, with the express aim of nullifying all cases in land disputes. It is clear that this Act was inspired by the spirit of the Ministerial Committee. The Act was finally thrown out in a court of law in 1994.

From the documents of the National Land Policy Workshop held in January 16-18, 1995, it is apparent that the government has rejected the question of introduction of a multiple tenure system as too complicated administratively. It has also rejected the question of divesting land from the executive arm (the president) as unjustified since it would mean that the president had to be a 'beggar'; whenever the need for land for public interests arose. Such a proposal was viewed as detrimental from the state's point of view if it had to alienate land for 'development projects' (including land use and planning) or investors. In actual fact, what the government is saying is that control of land means power, and that if customary rights were to be extinguished land for investors who had been accepted by IPC would be easily available. Since it could not accept the proposal of the Land Commission, it hired Tropical Research and Development, Inc. from the United States in 1994, to write a technical report quickly, financed by the World Bank, in preparation for the January 1995 policy meeting.[18]

## Concluding Remarks

What the economic liberalization measures have been able to achieve in the country has been to free private capital which was fettered by the state regulations in the 1970s. It has brought a restructuring of capital around the most profitable branches of the economy (especially import-export) and the creation of alternative forms of exploitation. For the working people it has meant further marginalization, aggravation of tensions and more hierarchization. It is clear from the above that the actual interests being defended by the state, given the particular forms of accumulation in the last two decades, are mercantilist with the import-export bourgeoisie at the centre of the process. The particular forms of production sustaining these forms of accumulation are parasitic, based on the plunder of natural resources. It is for this reason that the terms and conditions of how land and natural resources are used have become very important, given the increased conflict that has occurred in relation to such issues.

There is nothing more erroneous than to think that issues of land tenure merely involve the relationship of men and women to natural resources (as is believed by those who look at natural resources from the point of view of 'economic growth'). This way of conceiving land tenure systems does not necessarily address itself to the questions of redressing imbalances, inequalities, relations of domination, or exploitation. The only interest is in the setting up of 'land tenure systems' which will protect the smallholders, enhance investments, and improve productivity.[19] Those concerned with serious social problems in relation to land tenure need to consider this question from a democratic angle, with sensitivity to social and political, as well as economic factors. Bhaskar suggests that concern should be 'with the persistent relations between individuals (and groups) and with the relations between these relations (and between such relations and the nature of the products of such relations)' (Bhaskar, 1979, p. 34). Emphasis should be on viewing society from a relational point of view, whereby collective phenomena are seen primarily as expressions of enduring relationships. Bhaskar continues by noting that such a conception entails 'a transformational model of social activity', with emphasis on the question of change and history.

With such premises, land issues can only be examined from the point of view of relations among people, and people and the state, and how any differences and contradictions are treated and/or resolved. It is important to consider how the differences between workers and bosses, peasants and merchants, students and teachers, men and women, youths and elders, Muslims and Christians, Africans, Asians, Arabs and Europeans, majorities and minorities, people and state, etc. are handled. To take land issues as part and parcel of the struggle for democracy, it means one must focus on the people rather than the state. One important issue should be that of the vision of the type of society that people would like to build. Matters to be dealt with would include motive forces in society, organization of production, evidence of accumulation, sources of demands for land tenure reforms, and social and political dimensions of land tenure.

Land reforms as part of the struggles for democracy and human rights are supposed to be part of the process of transforming the state. They require one to focus on the politics of social and political emancipation of the people. Land reform makes sense only when linked to the whole question of restructuring of social relations so that individuals, groups and people in general are able to pose the question of land and natural resource control and the issues of social and political emancipation more sharply.

Beyond questions of economic growth, it is essential to take into consideration (a) the satisfaction of human needs of the majority (the marginalized, the oppressed and the exploited), focusing around the question of eradication (not alleviation) of poverty; and (b) integrated economic activities which ensure a self-centre process of capital accumulation together with a social project which focuses on the question of redressing imbalances, inequalities, oppressive and exploitative relations (i.e. which aims at restructuring relations among people). Projects which increase inequalities are fundamentally oppressive. The history of Tanzania shows that tenure insecurity has mainly been caused by government development programmes (including SAPs) with assistance from foreign consultants and donor agencies, and land grabbing by the wealthy and those in authority.

## Notes

1. The first Five Year Development Plan of 1968 talks a lot about modernization of the peasants, about whom it speaks in such derogatory terms.
2. For most of the information here see Lele and Christiansen, 1989, p. 15.
3. For details see Chachage, 1995.
4. For further details see Maliyamkono and Bagachwa, 1990; also Chachage, Ericsson and Gibbon, 1993.
5. *Daily News*, 28 July 1992.
6. *Uhuru*, 28 July 1993. In the second half of 1993, a Kenyan national was netted with drugs worth about Tsh. 3 billion in Dar es Salaam.
7. *Daily News*, 7 February 1992.
8. See URT, 1994. This Commission was led by Professor I. Shivji. The government also accepted that there was an absence of coherent land policy in its National Land Policy Draft (MLHUD, 1993).
9. This statute has undergone some amendments over the decades. Most of these took place after independence. For details, see URT, 1994; Shivji, 1995; and Tenga, 1992.
10. For details of such developments see Chachage, 1986, pp. 89-91. Also Kjekshus, 1977, presents a more comprehensive treatment of this matter.
11. Nyerere, 'Contra Capricorn', in Mss Afr. s. 1681, 'The Papers of African Bureau' (Nyerere Papers and Lectures 1956 to 1964, Rhodes House, Oxford.
12. Mss Brit Emp s.332 Creech Jones Papers, 'East Africa and Rhodesia - February 1958, Extracts from a Visiting Mission', Report to UN Mission on Tanganyika, p. 762.
13. *Daily News*, 5 August 1992.
14. The 1990 World Bank Report (IBRD, 1991), pointed out that there was an increasing problem of land disputes and delayed demarcation and registration of

land. It emphasized the need for donor support in research and policy studies on land matters, so that individualization could proceed smoothly.
15. URT, 1994. There are other proposals on the judicial system, demarcation of village boundaries, land registration, etc., but these cannot be pursued here.
16. See MLHUD, 1993.
17. For critical comments on the Act, see Shivji, 1994.
18. See MLHUD, n.d.
19. The 'new' political vocabulary in Tanzania nowadays is devoid of words such as exploitation, class, and imperialism. Instead, words like participatory/grassroots development, economic liberalization and donors/partners have become so ubiquitous.

## References

Bates, M. (1957), 'Tanganyika under British Administraion', PhD thesis, Oxford University.
Bhaskar, R. (1979), *The Possibility of Naturalism*, Harvester Press, Brighton.
Bienen, H. (1967), *Tanzania: Party Transformation and Economic Development*, Princeton University Press, Princeton, NJ.
Boesen, J. (1976), *Tanzania: From Ujamaa to Villagisation*, Institute for Development Research, Copenhagen.
Boesen, J., Madsen, B. Storgaard, and Moody, T. (eds), (1977), *Ujamaa: Socialism from Above*, SIAS, Uppsala.
Chachage, C.S.L. (1986), 'Socialist Ideology and the Reality of Tanzania', PhD thesis, Glasgow University.
Chachage, C.S.L. (1995), 'The Meek shall inherit the Earth but not the Mining Rights: The Mining Industry and Accumulation in Tanzania', in Gibbon (ed), pp. 37-108.
Chachage, C.S.L., Ericsson, M. and Gibbon, P. (1993), *Mining and Structural Adjustment: Studies in Zimbabwe and Tanzania*, SIAS, Uppsala.
Chidzero, B.T.G. (1961), *Tanganyika and International Trusteeship*, Oxford University Press, London.
Cliffe, K. (1972), 'Nationalism and the Reaction to Enforced Agricultural Change in Tanganyika during the Colonial Period', in Cliffe and Saul, vol. 1, pp. 17-24.
Cliffe, L. and Saul, J. (1972), *Socialism in Tanzania*, 2 vols, EAPH, Nairobi.
Coulson, A. (1982), *Tanzanai: A Political Economy*, Clarendon Press, Oxford.
Creech Jones Papers, Rhodes House, Oxford.
*Daily News* (Dar es Salaam), 7 February 1992, 28 May 1992.
*East African Royal Commission 1953-1955: Report* (1955), HMSO, London (Cmd 9475).
Fimbo, G.M. (1974), 'Land, Socialism and Law in Tanzania', in Ruhumbika (ed), *Towards Ujamaa*, EALB, Nairobi, pp. 230-74.
Gann, L.H. and Duignan, P. (1977), *The Rulers of German East Africa, 1884-1914*, Stanford University Press, Stanford, CA.
Gibbon, P. (ed) (1995), *Liberalised Development in Tanzania: Studies on Accumulation Processes and Local Institutions*, Nordiska Afrikainstitutet, Copenhagen.

Hailey, W.M. (Lord) (1950), *Native Administration in British African Territories*, Colonial Office, London.

IBRD (1991), *Tanzania Economic Report: Towards Sustainable Development in the 1990s*, Washington, DC.

Iliffe, J. (1979), *A Modern History of Tanganyika*, Cambridge University Press, Cambridge.

ILO (1978), *Towards Self-Reliance in Tanzania*, Addis Ababa.

Jourdan, P. (1992), *The Mineral Industry in Tanzania*, Institute of Mining Research, University of Zimbabwe, Harare.

Kjekshus, H. (1977), *Ecology Control and Economic Development in East African History*, Heinemann, London.

Kothari, R. (1984), 'Communications for Alternative Development: Towards a Paradigm', *Development Dialogue*, 1-2, pp. 13-22.

Lele, U. and Christiansen, R.E. (1989), *Markets, Marketing Boards, and Cooperatives in Africa: Issues of Adjustment*, MADIA Discussion Paper no. 11, IBRD, Washington, DC.

Listowel, J. (1965), *The Making of Tanganyika*, Chatto and Windus, London.

Little, A.D. (Inc) (1966), 'Tanganyika Industrial Development', in Smith, H. (ed), *Readings in Economic Development and Administration in Tanzania*, Institute of Public Administration, University College of Dar es Salaam, Dar es Salaam, pp. 269-284.

Lonsdale, J. (1972), 'Some Origins of Nationalism in Tanzania', in Cliffe and Saul, Vol. 1, pp. 25-8.

Maliyamkono, T.I.M. and Bagachwa, M.S.D. (1990), *The Second Economy in Tanzania*, James Currey, London.

MLHUD (1993), *National Land Policy Draft: Technical Report and Synopsis of Special Studies*, Dar es Salaam, May 1993.

MLHUD (n.d.), *Tentative Government Position on the Report on the Presidential Commission into Land Matters: Land Policy and Land Tenure Structure*, Dar es Salaam.

Nyerere Papers and Lectures, Rhodes House, Oxford.

Pickett, J. (1989), 'Reflection on the Market and State in Sub-Saharan Africa', *Africa Development Review*, 1 (1), p. 59.

Shivji, I. (1994), *A Legal Quagmire: Tanzania's Regulation of Land Tenure (Establishment of Villages) Act 1992*, IIED, London.

Shivji, I. (1995), 'Problems of Land Tenure in Tanzania: A Review and Appraisal of the Report of the Presidential Commission into Land Matters, 1992', Paper prepared for IIED, presented at the National Land Policy Workshop, Arusha, 16-19 January 1995.

Tenga, R. (1992), *Pastoral Land Rights in Tanzania: A Review*, IIED, Patoral Land Tenure Series, London.

*Uhuru* (Dar es Salaam), 28 July 1992.

URT (1969), *Five Year Development Plan,* Government Printer, Dar es Salaam.

URT (1982), *The Tanzania National Agricultural Policy,* Government Printer, Dar es Salaam.

URT (1991), *Presidential Commission of Inquiry into Land Matters*, Government Printer, Dar es Salaam.

URT (1994), *Report of the Presidential Commission into Land Matters, Vol. 1, Land Policy and Land Tenure Structure*, MLHUD/SIAS, Uppsala.

URT (1991), *Presidential Commission of Inquiry into Land Matters*, Government Printer, Dar es Salaam.

URT (1994), *Report of the Presidential Commission into Land Matters, Vol. 1, Land Policy and Land Tenure Structure*, MLHUD/SIAS, Uppsala.

# 5 The Failure of Institutional, Technical and Structural Shifts in Tanzanian Peasant Agriculture: Some Lessons from India's Green Revolution

SAM MAGHIMBI

Peasant farming in Tanzania has not made much progress since 'modern peasant farming' was introduced by the Germans in the 1880s and 1890s. Such a designation may be misleading because it is only new crops and new markets which have been introduced since the country was initially colonized. Technology has basically remained traditional, with the peasant using the hand hoe and *panga* (machete) as the principal tools in agriculture. Some arguments have even been advanced that at least in some parts of the country agriculture was performing better in terms of productivity of land and labour in the pre-colonial period compared to the colonial and post-colonial period (e.g. Kjekshus, 1996; Koponen, 1988).

The most commonly cited explanation of low production in agriculture is technology. Kuznets has shown how the basic problem of underdevelopment is that too little is produced by each individual, when compared with developed countries. Production of food in most underdeveloped countries could eventually be trebled or quadrupled if measures like good fertilization, improved seeds, improved cultivation, and control of diseases and pests were undertaken. The capital and skills requirements needed to improve agriculture are not beyond the reach of countries like Tanzania. There is a scarcity of natural resources in the underdeveloped countries but this is primarily a consequence of underdevelopment, rather than underdevelopment being a consequence of scarce natural resources (Kuznets, 1973, pp. 2-11).

Technology seems to be a favoured explanation in understanding why peasant farming in Tanzania is not making a breakthrough. However technology never functions in a social-institutional vacuum. In this chapter I will consider the absence of the necessary institutional, technical and structural shifts (e.g. land reform, marketing strategies and a green revolution) needed to transform Tanzania's peasant agriculture. Examples drawn from the green revolution in India will be related to the situation in Tanzania.

Landlessness is not as widespread in Tanzania as it is in India; indeed there are many places in Tanzania where peasants could expand their farms

75

using land which is not cultivated at present. However, there are places in Tanzania where peasants are faced with land shortage but are not aware of the presence of good land in other places. Or, more importantly, peasants may be aware of unoccupied good land somewhere but may not have the capital to reach such land and to cultivate it.

In India land reform in the first phase attempted to abolish the vast estates of the *zamindari* type in 1948-52. In the second phase of land reform (from 1952 to the end of the 1950s) numerous legislative measures were undertaken to regulate tenancy relations. The aim was to provide security of tenure, to fix rent, and in many cases to provide opportunities for the tenants to become owners by buying the land they tilled (Sharma, 1973, p. 87).

The third phase in land reform in India (late 1950s to early 1960s) saw attempts to put ceilings on the size of individual holdings. The hope was to create a pool of excess land that could be distributed to landless labourers and to small peasants. However, the laws on land ceilings had many loopholes and exemption categories and they prescribed too high ceilings on the existing holdings. Landlords were able to take steps in advance of impending legislation to divide their large holdings into small parcels. These were registered in the names of real or fictitious relatives. However by the early 1960s the structure of land relations in India had assumed a more or less stable form. The old *zamindari* type landlords and the various intermediaries had certainly been eliminated, at least in their earlier forms (Sharma, 1973, pp. 88-90).

When viewed from a populist point of view, land reform was a failure in India because it did not alleviate the conditions of the masses of rural people. The highly skewed pattern of cultivation holdings and the size of the landless workforce were not altered. But diverse systems of land tenure had been changed into more uniform, simpler ones. All owners of land were brought into direct relation to the state (Sharma, 1973, p. 88). Land reform paved the way for the new capital intensive agricultural strategy which was introduced in the late 1960s. One writer has commented that the dream of progressive farming amongst the gentry was realized in India in the late 1960s (Bernstein, 1966/7, p. 40). Land reform brought the consolidation of landholdings in India. The fragmentation of landholdings had long been a characteristic feature of Indian agriculture. The farmer's total land was often divided into numerous and widely dispersed pieces. Large-scale consolidation was achieved during the land reform, often by special legislation making such consolidation compulsory. By the end of 1969 some 29.5 million hectares of land had been consolidated and during the fourth Five Year Plan an additional 28.3 million hectares were consolidated. Sharma (1973, pp. 91, 100) has argued that without this transfer of land into compact units, mechanized farming could not possibly have emerged.

The fifteen years of implementation of land reform legislation helped in creating and consolidating a class of rich peasants who by the mid-1960s were all set to embark upon modern capitalist agriculture or to undertake what has been termed the 'green revolution'. They consisted mostly of former *zamindaris* and other landlords. This class also included the top stratum of peasant proprietors and some former tenants who enjoyed superior and permanent rights. This class had begun to feel firmly secure in its position despite the rhetoric by populist scholars and politicians on the ineffectiveness of land reform in India.

The social conditions for agricultural take-off exist in Tanganyika (mainland Tanzania). Rich peasants (sometimes called kulaks) exist but they are not secure in the rural economy and are not consolidated as a class and they have not consolidated their land ownership to undertake a green revolution. Rich peasant households represent a tiny fraction of households in the poorer parts of the country but in other areas they number nearly thirty per cent of all households in the village (Maghimbi, 1990, pp. 304-17). These are peasants who have accumulated some wealth and are able to hire labour or some machines on a more or less continuous basis. My field research in Simanjiro District in Arusha Region took me to an area near Engasummet where nearly every Maasai head of household I interviewed was a rich peasant who hired labour for farming and other activities. I interviewed 67 heads of household and all said they hired labour. These were very rich peasants because of their large herds of cattle (sometimes in excess of 1,000 head per person). Nevertheless, no green revolution (crops), or white/red revolution (milk/beef) or blue revolution (fish) was occurring in Maasailand. These rich peasants with so much wealth in cattle were experiencing a marketing crisis.

The backwardness of peasant agriculture in Tanzania can be explained in terms of two theories. One is a marketing theory and the other a production theory. Rural areas in Tanzania fall under broadly two categories. There are those areas which are poor and backward because the peasants produce so little, for a number of reasons such as lack of high-yielding seeds, localized land shortage, lack of capital, low prices, failure to utilize land and ground water, labour shortage, and the growing of crops which are not suitable for the local environment. Then there are those areas like parts of Maasailand, parts of Gogoland, and parts of Sukumaland, where the wealth is already produced but the marketing is so poorly organized that the peasants are no better off compared to peasants in the production crisis areas.

Both the British and the nationalist government in Tanganyika had a view of a stolid, homogeneous African peasantry, easy to control politically and easy to dominate socially. Thus the British government passed legislation to restrict activities of African peasants, in respect of credit, trade, and lease land ownership (Maghimbi, 1990b, p. 115). Lease land consisted of large surveyed farms and these were also situated on the best agricultural land. Peasants were discouraged from hiring labour under British rule and under the nationalist government until the 1990s. As long ago as the 1930s the British colonial government was remarking that'

> A number of wealthy natives employ labourers to cultivate for them on Crown Land ... A native should only be allowed as much land as he and his family can cultivate (McCarthy, 1982, p. 125).

There has never been land consolidation in Tanzania and land fragmentation in peasant farming is extreme (Maghimbi, 1990b, pp. 138-42). This does not help the advancement of peasant capitalist farming. There is no landlordism in Tanzania but the peasants have no security in respect of

77

land ownership because the government has never instituted a mechanism for giving peasants title deeds for their land. Land is held under customary law and peasant land does not qualify as collateral when seeking farm credit. The tendency is to parcelization of land when a household head dies. The peasants' farms are not surveyed and they hold no title deeds; they are thus at the mercy of the state. When peasants were moved from their farms *en masse* in 1969-74 by the government, they could not fight legally as they had no certificates of occupancy. This was the period when the state attempted to create nucleated villages and to force peasants to undertake commercial farming. One cannot therefore understand the failure of peasant capitalist farming without understanding the nature of both the colonial and the nationalist states.

The colonial state favoured small peasant farming because it was politically safe. At the same time it contributed to the growth of accumulation of capital in Britain with the minimum investment. For example, in 1939 the British government appointed the Tanganyika Coffee Growers' Association (TCGA) as the sole purchasing agent for all coffee in Tanganyika (Maghimbi, 1990b, p. 146). TCGA and another marketing institution, Tanganyika Cooperative Trading Agency (TACTA) made contracts with the British Ministry of Food to deliver coffee to British traders via the Ministry, at prices very much below what would prevail on the open market. Indeed, the British Ministry of Food prices were always fifty per cent or less of those prevailing on the open market (Maghimbi, 1990b, p. 147). We can thus see how peasant production in Tanganyika contributed to the growth of capitalism (and industrialization) somewhere else but not at home. This process seems to be continuing and Tanzanian scholars face the challenge of further research here. Bernstein has done some work to show how agriculture (peasant or slave or feudal) in one place can stagnate but contribute to industrial growth in another place within the same country or in another country (Bernstein, 1966/7, pp. 37-51).

The nationalist state was best described by Gibbon and Neocosmos (1985, p. 193), as one which displayed petty-bourgeois character. Petty-bourgeois policies found their maximum application in the attempt by the state to force all peasants in the late 1960s and 1970s to live in nucleated communal villages known as *ujamaa* ('socialist') villages.

Gibbon and Neocosmos show how the Tanzanian state has systematically failed to develop, implement and sustain consistent policies and means of monitoring them, and has instead sought quick victory for African Socialism; and has bombarded the population with ever-new commands, institutions and campaigns. This was a state which combined the reactionary and the progressive, the bureaucratic and the popular, the statist and the anarchist, the modernist and the nativist, the consumerist and the ascetic, the cynical and the idealist, the aggressive and the timid, the grandiose and the apathetic (Gibbon and Necosmos, 1985, p. 193). It is thus not strange that the current policies aimed at economic recovery and the promotion of liberal capitalism have overwhelmingly been formulated, directed and funded by international and global agencies of capitalism like the World Bank and IMF and not by the local state.

Land reform remains one of the most important structural shifts to be made in Tanzanian agriculture if peasant capitalism is to advance to a stage of regular growth and contribution to the country's industrialization. The peasants' farms are just too parcelized for green revolution farming methods to be applied. Equally important is the fact that because of the absence of the necessary structures to consolidate land, it is still the case that, even when new farm land is opened, it is parcelized into tiny plots when the peasant's children divide up the land. Also relevant to the situation is the absence of an advanced land market. Both the colonial and the nationalist governments discouraged the development of land markets and its concomitants like labour hiring. In any case it is hard to sell land which is not surveyed and backed by certificates of occupancy. Peasant entrepreneurs are reluctant to buy such land because relatives of the seller can later claim that it is family or lineage property and that the seller never consulted them. Such cases abound in areas where there have been sales of farms by peasants. Cases concerning unsurveyed land must be taken to primary courts and can only be heard directly by magistrates' courts after the plaintiff seeks leave of the High Court. Thus the law discourages a market in land and inhibits the growth of peasant capitalism. Major changes in land law are clearly necessary for the advancement of peasant farming.

In order for this to be achieved, there must be the necessary resources for mechanization and capitalization of the kind that took place in India during the green revolution which started in the 1960s. The newly emerging class of rich peasants in India made some capital (about 6,000 million rupees in cash and in government bonds) from the compensation obtained when *zamindari*-type landlords were abolished. Cooperation in farming was encouraged by the government since 1954 and cooperative farming societies were in the hands of rich peasants who obtained large, long-term loans for capital investments (Sharma, 1973, pp. 91-2).

Many new measures including institutional changes from the 1950s benefited the richest stratum of the Indian peasantry, enabling it to prepare for and carry out the green revolution from the 1960s to the present. Specifically these measures began after the launching of the five-year plans in 1951. The Community Development Programme which started in 1952 succeeded in pouring vast amounts of public resources in the countryside to help schemes to construct facilities such as new roads, schools, health centres and recreation centres; also irrigation projects, wells, drainage systems; storage facilities and warehouses; and soil conservation. Further capital was injected into the villages through the Agricultural Credit Societies. These had existed before but they were greatly expanded; their number increased from 195,000 in 1951 to 212,000 in 1961 and the total amount of loans and advances rose from 229 million rupees in 1951 to 2 billion rupees in 1961 (Sharma, 1973, p. 92).

During the same period (1951-61) in India there was expansion in various kinds of marketing and distributive cooperative societies. In the early 1960s the rich peasants and landlords had begun to invest their savings in wholesale trade, in food grains, and in the rapidly expanding road transport system. Rural industry fell into the hands of this class. As electricity began to reach the villages, small-scale rice mills and wheat flour mills began to operate within the villages and in nearby towns. In some areas sugar refineries were opened on the principle of cooperative ownership. The rich peasants and landlords constituted the major membership of these cooperatives and used them to expand their economic activities beyond farming (Sharma, 1973, p. 92-3). The economic success of the rural elite helped industrial growth in India and it was estimated that in 1960-61 the richest ten per cent of the rural people provided a much bigger market for industrial consumer goods than did all the urban people put together (Sharma, 1973, p. 93).

Rich peasants had started to invest in industry in Tanganyika earlier than the 1950s and 1960s. In areas like Mwanza, Songea, Bukoba, Shinyanga, Musoma, Kilimanjaro and Iringa, they had invested in corn mills, rice mills, tractors, and coffee pulping mills for the 1920s, when cooperatives helped in popularizing and marketing machines and other farm inputs. As was the case in India, the cooperatives were in the hands of the rural elite. The rich peasants in Tanzania were possibly more advanced in farming and in institutions supporting farming in the 1950s and early 1960s; they controlled the largest cooperative movement in Africa and the third largest in the world. By 1968 cooperatives in Tanzania were handling 49 per cent of the country's annual exports (worth £27.4 million [$65,725,000] in 1968). Only in Israel and Denmark were cooperatives marketing a greater proportion of a nation's overseas business (Maghimbi, 1990a, p. 85).

From 1967 when the Tanzania state started to pursue its populist policies of *ujamaa*, the rich peasants' economy and institutions which supported the rural economy were destroyed. The Department of Community Development was abolished as a government department and with it the country's community development programme. Cooperatives were abolished in the early 1970s but were reintroduced in the mid-1980s after it was clear that the rural economy was nearly collapsing. However, the new cooperatives have never been able to regain the strength of the old ones. The abolition had sent them off course and the peasants lost much property such as factories for ginning cotton and curing coffee, and other buildings; as well as trained personnel and morale. When some of their property was given back to the peasants in the 1980s by the government, it was dilapidated and damaged. We can thus see that the significant difference between India and Tanzania in the 1960s was social rather than technical and economic. In India there was a state which encouraged peasant capitalism through land reform. In Tanzania there was a state which discouraged peasant capitalism through an institutional shake-up and measures like villagization.

Other important institutions in Tanzania which could have helped the advancement of farming but which were abolished by the government in the 1970s and 1980s were local governments which were organized around district and town councils. District councils had played a very important role in building and maintaining rural roads. They had helped in enforcing agricultural by-laws which they had the power to pass, and quite often they were asked by cooperatives to pass such laws (Maghimbi, 1990b, p. 158). One of the factors which contributed to the decline of the peasant economy in the 1970s and 1980s was poor transport. Many parts of the country with major agricultural potential have not been able to advance because of the failure to get crops and animals out of the villages to local and foreign markets. The problem currently persists in many villages and this is one of the reasons why the areas of the country mentioned earlier as having no production crisis remain poor and backward. At the national level marketing institutions are weak. There has, for example, been failure to capture the large market for live cattle, goats and sheep in the Middle East. With 14,902,000 cattle, 3,728,000 sheep and 9,370,000 goats Tanzania has the largest herd of such animals in the world (URT, 1982, p. 23). What are needed for such massive wealth to be turned into capital are the kind of structural shifts which occurred in India in the 1950s and the 1960s: notably land reform, especially land consolidation and improvements in security of tenure; also better marketing and credit supply by measures such as the strengthening of cooperatives and other institutions; and technical improvements on a wide scale.

Let us now consider technological change. According to Griffin (1979, pp. 2-3), the term 'green revolution' has been used to mean two different things. Some scholars use the expression when referring to a broad transformation of the agricultural sector in undeveloped countries - to a reduction in food shortages and in undernourishment, and to elimination of agriculture as a bottleneck to overall development. Other scholars use the expression when referring to specific plant improvements, notably the development of high yielding varieties of rice and wheat. The vocabulary of propagandists is sometimes enriched in this latter context by the addition of yet another misleading phrase, namely 'miracle rice'. In the case of India there has been success with high yielding varieties of rice and wheat but some other changes have also occurred as we saw earlier. Some scholars have argued that the green revolution is a technological package produced in the laboratory to fit the needs of the rich to increase output. This type of farming needs fertilizers, machines, water and supervision; and when one of the components of the package is missing, farming cannot be undertaken. Because many rural dwellers are not credit-worthy and have no access to government sponsorship because of their inferior social positions, the green revolution has increased the polarization of the Indian peasantry. However, the aim (as with all capitalist farming) is not to reduce inequality. Reducing inequality is the kind of populism which nearly destroyed Tanzanian peasant agriculture. Under the policy of *ujamaa* villages in the 1970s and 1980s the government was trying to increase agricultural output and at the same time to reduce rural inequality. When the government moved peasants to *ujamaa* or communal villages in the late 1960s and 1970s the rich peasants' farms were divided up among the poorer peasants. Some of these rich peasants had large commercial farms which measured up to 65 hectares or more (Maghimbi, 1990b, p. 260). There were some rich peasants who tried to resist but the problem was that they were geographically scattered throughout the country; and after the abolition of cooperatives they lost the last economic institution they controlled, and they therefore had no forum in politics.

Before the green revolution, India was faced with slack growth in agriculture and there were periodic famines. The green revolution consisted basically of adoption of high yielding wheat and rice seeds from Mexico and the Philippines. Some seeds when used led to trebling of production. The

81

high yielding varieties (HYV) programme began in 1965 under the 'new strategy in agriculture' of the Union Food and Agriculture Ministry (India). Limited experiments with the dwarf Mexican varieties of wheat had already been conducted during the two previous years. A model for the new strategy existed in fifteen districts distributed throughout India. In these an Intensive Agricultural Development Programme had been started by the Ford Foundation in 1961. In 1965, 250 tons of Mexican dwarf heat variety seeds were imported, and by the end of the decade the HYV programme had been extended to large parts of India. In addition to wheat, the programme included the production of rice, maize, and several varieties of Indian millet (Sharma, 1973, pp. 77-8).

The results of the green revolution are visible in output figures. As against the record crop, prior to the green revolution, of 12.3 million tons of wheat in 1964-5, production rose to 16.5, 18.7, and 20.0 million tons in 1968, 1969 and 1970 harvests respectively. Significant improvements were also recorded in other cereals like rice and maize. Total food grain production rose from 88.4 million tons in 1964-5 (a record year) to 106 tons in 1970-1. India became self-sufficient in food in the 1970s (Sharma, 1973, p. 78).

On the technical side a number of changes occurred in agricultural operations and these have implications for Tanzania's own agricultural advancement. When HYVs are cultivated, seeds require increased amounts of chemical fertilizers and water to ensure high output. Consumption of nitrogen fertilizers in India increased from 538,000 tons in 1964-5 to 1.2 million in 1969-70. A total of 70,000 private tube wells were sunk in 1969-70 alone. In 1968 unsold tractors had accumulated at the two factories in production: however by 1970 prospective tractor buyers had to make written application and wait one or two years before delivery. By 1973 five factories were producing 187,000 tractors per year and in 1969-70 an additional 35,000 tractors were imported. Consumption of pesticides increased from 10,304 tons in 1961-2 to 28,200 tons in 1968-9. Between 1960-61 and 1967-8 the area under irrigation increased from 45 per cent to 70 per cent in some districts. This was mainly due to the rapid installation of tube wells. In some districts fertilizer use per cultivated area increased more than 123 times between 1960-61 and 1967-8. Between 1965-6 and 1968-9 the area under the new Mexican dwarf varieties expanded from 69 hectares to 171,600 hectares, or 90 per cent of total average under wheat in one district. In the same district, yields increased by over 120 per cent between 1960-61 and 1968-9 (Sharma, 1973, pp. 78-9).

The big question now is why did the breakthrough occur in India at the time it did, and why it is not occurring in Tanzania. The level of development of many villages in India and Tanzania was comparable in the 1950s and 1960s, before India initiated the green revolution.

Sharma (1973, pp. 79-80) observed that the government of India had systematically tried to affect agricultural productivity since 1952, when community development and agricultural extension programmes were instituted. Thousands of government-employed village-level workers all over India were, with little if any success, pleading with farmers to adopt measures such as new and better seeds, fertilizers, and improved tools. Even increased irrigation facilities were reported to have been unused or underutilized. Numerous American teams of experts came and went under the auspices of various bodies, yet agriculture remained stagnant.

Sharma goes on to argue that to attribute development in agriculture to a sudden technological breakthrough, as is often done, is overly simplistic. He notes that the supposedly 'new' technology underlying the green revolution was hardly new. Most of the new inputs, including the Mexican dwarf varieties of wheat, were known for quite some time to Indian agricultural experts who had also been trying to introduce them to Indian farmers. This leads to the main thesis by Sharma. He emphasized that the green revolution in India occurred not because of the *introduction* of new technology, but because of *acceptance* by farmers. Sharma further argues that this acceptance owes little if anything to the numerous social scientists, Indian and American, who for two decades were engaged in research. These were studying the so-called diffusion process, identifying variables (cultural or otherwise) which affected the process (Sharma, 1973, pp. 80-81).

For Sharma the success of the green revolution in India lies in the institutional and structural shifts (e.g. land reform [including land consolidation and security of land ownership], strengthening of marketing cooperatives, the growth and consolidation of the rich peasantry, and credit flow to the rich peasants), which Indian rural society had been undergoing in the previous two decades. These institutional and structural shifts created the prerequisites for a section of the Indian peasantry to stage the technological breakthrough.

Whitcombe provided a good summary of capitalist agriculture in India when he wrote:

In the new capital-intensive agricultural strategy, introduced into the provinces in the late 1960s, the Congress government had the means to realize the imperial dream: progressive farming amongst the gentry. Within a year or two of the programme's inception, virtually every district could field a fine crop of demonstration ex-*zamindari* - the Rai Sahibs with their 30-, 40-, 50-, 100-acre holdings, their multiplication farms of the latest Mexican wheat and Philippines paddy, their tube-wells gushing out 16,000 gallons an hour, much of it on highly profitable hire. Their tractors, their godowns stacked with fertilizer, their cold-stores ... in short, a tenth of the *zamindari* but ten times the income (Whitcombe, 1980, p. 179).

Peasant farming in Tanzania was advancing well in the 1950s and 1960s. In the entire period from 1954 to 1960 Tanzania was the only country in Africa which consistently maintained a growth trend in food production higher than that of population growth (Maghimbi, 1990a, p. 84). We saw earlier how the populist policies of *ujamaa* and the abolition of cooperatives helped to strangle the rich peasants. Moreover the state has never undertaken systematic measures to promote peasant capitalism as was the case in India in the 1950s and 1960s, as already noted. Thus we can rightly say that when the Indian state was pursuing policies to promote the green revolution, the Tanzanian state was pursuing policies which would maintain the smallest scale peasant farming on tiny plots of land. Rural development has never been institutionalized in Tanzania.

83

As indicated earlier, attempts at institutional and structural changes in Tanzania have come as a consequence of external pressure. In the early 1980s the Scandinavian governments had rejected an expansion of financial assistance to Tanzania without an IMF agreement. Thus, in the 1984-85 budget, agricultural producer prices were raised significantly, and a large devaluation was announced; as well as removal of subsidies on the staple food (maize) and to a lesser extent on agricultural inputs. The 1984-5 budget also considerably weakened the earlier emphasis on social services and education. Businessmen were from then on allowed to import goods freely if they could raise foreign exchange on their own, on a 'no questions asked' basis (Gibbon, Havnevik and Hermele, 1995, p. 53).

The government of Tanzania had replaced cooperative marketing with parastatal crop authorities when cooperatives were abolished in the early 1970s. However, the crop authorities were very inefficient and bureaucratic, and could not provide price incentives to peasants. The near-collapse of the rural economy and the World Bank/IMF pressure forced the government to attempt adjustment measures and currently the country is in the second decade of adjustment. An Economic Recovery Programme (ERP) was prepared during 1985-6 in close cooperation between the World Bank and the Tanzania government and was used as the basis for concluding the negotiations with the IMF in August 1986. The Tanzania government undertook to raise the producer prices of agricultural crops by five per cent per year in real terms, or to the level of 60 to 70 per cent of the world market price, whichever was the higher; to introduce an active exchange rate policy aimed at removing the overvaluation of the Tanzanian shilling; and to further the liberalization of external and internal trade (Gibbon, Havnevik and Hermele, 1993, p. 53).

Marketing boards and cooperatives were reintroduced in the mid-1980s. The marketing boards had previously been abolished, with the cooperatives. Marketing boards advise the government on the marketing of crops from cooperative unions, for export or local sale. Cooperative unions now once again buy and export crops from primary cooperative societies, which buy directly from peasants. However the monopoly of cooperatives has now been abolished, and crop merchants can buy crops from peasants for export.

In conclusion we can evaluate the current measures like ERP and relate them to the chances of a breakthrough occurring in peasant farming in Tanzania. The major objective of ERP was to raise agricultural producer prices in real terms and to tilt the terms of trade in favour of the agricultural sector. However Gibbon and his colleagues observe that:

As late as in January 1990 the World Bank claimed that 'Measures being undertaken in the agricultural sector are already significantly improving the standard of living of the rural population through improved prices received for production'. This statement was simply untrue. In its 1991 report the World Bank clearly spelled out that ERP had not led to the anticipated overall rise in farmers' income through an improvement of their terms of trade (Gibbon, Havnevik and Hermele, 1993, p. 54).

They go on to show how there might have been no increase in capital available to peasants in both the pre-ERP period and during the ERP period itself. The mid-1970s to 1984 saw a decline in terms of trade for both crop authorities/marketing boards and producers by about 50 per cent. The four years following the onset of the devaluation in 1984 saw the terms of trade for marketing boards improve by more than 100 per cent. Producer terms of trade increased by about 30 per cent during 1985 but they failed to improve in subsequent years. Moreover the nominal increases in producer prices failed to reflect the full extent of devaluations but increases in input prices did so (Gibbon, Havnevik and Hermele, 1993, pp. 54-5).

It seems that marketing boards and cooperative unions absorbed nearly all the benefits of the improved terms of trade in agriculture. Farmers were not reached by the benefit because of the lack of full adjustment of the agricultural producer prices to reflect exchange rate movements. Thus contrary to the objectives of the ERP there was a drop in the farmers' share of the final export value of major crops from around 80 per cent in 1986 to only 35 per cent in 1988, although in 1989 an improvement of around 50 per cent was recorded. Depreciation of the Tanzanian shilling and rising input costs far outweighed the nominal increase in producer prices. For example, while the average cotton producer price increased by 70 per cent, the average price of agrochemicals for cotton went up by 475 per cent from 1985-6 to 1988-9. Contrary to the aims of ERP there was a decrease of 14.6 per cent in the producer prices in real terms over the period (Gibbon, Havnevik and Hermele, 1993, pp. 54-5). The new cooperatives inherited many problems from the government including debts. Their performance is very poor when compared to the old ones. Their failings have also been based on gross incompetence and corruption (Gibbon, Havnevik and Hermele, 1993, p. 63). By 1992 cooperative unions had an accumulated debt of 51 billion shillings for twenty cooperative unions which showed signs of economic viability. Not much is known about the debt because information was inadequate in newspapers and radio, and government policy on cooperation is not yet clearly spelt out. It seems that the government did not actually write off the debt but undertook to act as a guarantor for the debt so that the Unions would continue to get credit for buying crops from banks.

Allowing private crop merchants to compete with cooperatives in buying crops implies less accumulation of capital by rich peasants. Moreover the short experience with these local and foreign crop merchants shows that they offer to peasants prices which are lower than those of cooperatives. They have taken advantage of delays by cooperatives, and have bought crops from peasants at lower prices.

There thus seems to be a flimsy institutional and structural basis for a green revolution to occur in Tanzania now. In the ten years ending in 1983 the growth of GDP in Tanzania averaged under two per cent per year, which is below the rate of population growth. The annual GDP growth rate rose to 3.3 per cent in 1984-6, 3.7 per cent in 1987-90, and 3.8 per cent in 1991-3. The later figures are all above population growth rate but according to Gibbon (1995b) there are serious doubts about the real level of expansion in economic activities - even if these figures are impressive in view of the decline in Tanzania's terms of trade by 30 per cent during 1987-91. Gibbon maintains that the unregistered economy accounted for at least 30 per cent of the total economic activity in the preadjustment period and that even if only a fraction of this had been subsequently officialized as a consequence of adjustment deregulation measures, the GDP should have registered a significant growth. It was, for example, estimated that after 1989 the partial incorporation of previously unregistered gold production alone accounted for one per cent growth in the annual GDP (Gibbon, 1995b, p. 15).

Figures on export and import levels in Tanzania since 1986 reflect a disappointing performance in agriculture. Imports have increased steadily to around US$ 1500 million per year in the context of trade liberalization, but exports have remained at between only US$ 300 and 400 million per year. Exports were at that level before adjustment started. Inflation has remained consistently at over 20 per cent annually. Because most of the exports consist of peasant crops like coffee, cotton and cashew nuts we can see that the peasant economy is not doing well. Very few peasants will be able to save under such conditions. In order for the big revolutionary potential of the country to be tapped in a revolutionary peasant economy led by rich peasants, much needs to be done. The state must first of all accept that the presence of a modern peasant economy is necessary for industrialization and overall national development. This acceptance must be translated into systematic policies like those which occurred in India in the 1950s and 1960s. The large irrigation potential of the country must be utilized. Tube wells and water pumps must be introduced on a large scale. Cooperatives must be strengthened by injecting more capital, and supervision from the government. Railway, road and water transport improvement must target high-potential areas such as those which have no production crisis. Most importantly, the government's industrial policy must reflect its commitment to agricultural transformation. Maximum support and protection must be given to factories which make tractors, water pumps and other farm inputs.

The green revolution technology is available and known to peasants in Tanzania. The use of tractors has a long history in the country and peasants know how to operate and repair them. The expansion of the use of tractors halted when cooperative unions were abolished. The latter had been instrumental in marketing tractors and arranging for credit for their members. There are many HYV seeds in the country. Some have been developed by the Ministry of Agriculture's numerous research stations and others have been imported, such as rice seeds from Japan. Peasants know how to use the HYV seeds but quite often lack capital to afford the full green revolution package. Fertilizer was applied only on ten per cent of the cultivated area in 1987-8 (Gibbon, Havnevik and Hermele, 1993, p. 56). It is, however, possible that less fertilizer is used now, and by fewer farmers, because of price rises which are a result of removal of government subsidies, and also because of devaluation. Government investment in agriculture seems to be declining. ERP claimed that it was focusing on the productive sector but government allocation of development resources to agriculture declined from 31 per cent in 1986-7 to 20 per cent in 1988-9, and allocation to industry remained at around 10 per cent (Gibbon, Havnevik and Hermele, 1993, p. 59).Maize is the staple food in Tanzania and HYVs of maize seeds have been used haphazardly from the 1970s or earlier. Maize has other uses besides human food. It can be used for making products such as animal feed, and beer; and it can be exported. Tanzania's green revolution could thus focus on maize. In the case of rice some relevant projects have been attempted, notably those in Lower Moshi and in Ndungu. Both are funded by the Japanese government and technology is imported from Japan. These particular projects have resulted in increased output but the problem is that on their own they are insufficient to result in a green revolution. There is also a danger that such projects will flounder when the donor agency leaves, as has been the case in other development projects. However, the Lower Moshi and Ndungu projects have demonstrated that if the right measures are systematically undertaken, a green revolution is possible in Tanzania. Moreover, Tanzania has the advantage of having much unfarmed land - unlike India.

# References

Bank of Tanzania (BoT) (1995), *Economic Bulletin for Quarter ended 31 December 1995*, vol. 24, no. 1.

Bernstein, H. (1966-7), 'Agrarian Questions Then and Now', *Journal of Peasant Studies*, 24, pp. 22-59.

Bernstein, H. and Campbell, B.K. (eds.) (1985), *Contradictions of Accumulation in Africa: Studies in Economy and State*, Sage, Beverley Hills LA.

Cole, J. (1976), *The Poor of the Earth*, Macmillan, London.

Gibbon, P. (ed.) (1995a), *Liberalized Development in Tanzania*, Nordiska Afrikainstitutet, Uppsala.

Gibbon, P. (1995b), 'Merchantisation of Production and Privatisation of Development in Post-Ujamaa Tanzania', in Gibbon (ed.) (1995a), pp. 9-36.

Gibbon, P., Havnevik, K.J. and Hermele, K. (1993), *A Blighted Harvest: The World Bank and African Agriculture in the 1980s*, James Currey, London.

Gibbon, P. and Neocosmos, M. (1985), 'Some Problems in the Political Economy of "African Socialism"', in Bernstein, H. and Campbell, B.K. (eds.), pp. 153-206.

Gough, K. and Sharma, H.P. (eds.) (1973), *Imperialism and Revolution in South Asia*, Monthly Review Press, New York.

Griffin, K. (1979), *The Political Economy of Agrarian Change: An Essay on the Green Revolution*, Macmillan, London.

Kjekshus, H. (1996), *Ecology, Control and Economic Development in East Africa*, James Currey, London.

Koponen, J. (1988), *Ecology, Control and Economic Development in East Africa*, James Currey, London.

Kuznets, S. (1973), *Population, Capital and Growth: Selected Essays*, Norton, New York.

Maghimbi, S. (1990a), 'Cooperatives in Agricultural Development', in O'Neill, N. and Mustafa, K. (eds.) (1990), *Capitalism, Socialism and Development Crisis in Tanzania*, Avebury, Aldershot, pp. 81-100.

Maghimbi, S. (1990b), 'Rural Development Policy and Planning in Tanzania', PhD thesis, University of London (London School of Economics).

McCarthy, D.M.P. (1982), *Colonial Bureaucracy and Creating Underdevelopment: Tanganyika 1914-1940*, Iowa University Press, Arnes, 10.

Sharma, H.P. (1973), *The Green Revolution in India: Prelude to a Red One?*, in Gough and Sharma, pp. 77-102.

Sklair, L. (ed.) (1994), *Capitalism and Development*, Routledge, London.

United Republic of Tanzania (URT) (1992), *Agriculture Statistics 1989*, Bureau of Statistics, Dar es Salaam.

Whitcombe, E. (1980), 'Whatever happened to the Zamindars?', in Hobsbawm, E.J., Kula, W., Mitra, A., Raj, K.N. and Sachs, I. (eds.), *Peasants in History: Essays in Honour of Daniel Thorner*, Calcutta, Oxford University Press, pp. 156-80.

# 6 Revolution and Stagnation in the Peasant Economy of Zanzibar

## SAM MAGHIMBI

This contribution is partly intended to fill a recognized need for a chapter on Zanzibar, since the two volumes of *The Tanzanian Peasantry* had concentrated on the Mainland. However, a study of the peasantry in Zanzibar is interesting for its own sake and is rich in events. The 1964 Revolution mainly occurred because of the land question, namely the grabbing of the best land from African peasants by Arab slavers and planters from the 1830s, when cloves were introduced in Zanzibar. This chapter explains the conditions which led to the 1964 Revolution. The plantation economy and marginalization of the peasantry are considered, and the land reform which came with the revolution is described. Finally an attempt is made to analyse the current stagnation of the peasant economy in Zanzibar.

## The Squatter System

The growth of the peasant economy in Zanzibar (i.e. the islands of Unguja and Pemba) has never been spectacular. The peasants had lost the land to Arab slavers and colonizers who planted cloves and coconuts from the beginning of the nineteenth century. Cloves were introduced in Zanzibar in 1839 (Sheriff, 1991, p. 112); coconuts are an indigenous crop in Zanzibar and other parts of East Africa.

In a classical case of internal colonization the Omani colonizers who had invaded Zanzibar and the coast of East Africa decided to settle in Zanzibar. The Sultan of Oman (Seyyid Said) declared Zanzibar his second capital and moved in 1849 to settle there with his followers to facilitate their exploitation of East Africa on the basis of the slave trade and slave plantations (Cooper, 1980, p. 2; Bader, 1991, p. 165; Mlahagwa and Temu, 1991, p. 146). A quick survey of both islands will reveal, even to the person who has little background in Zanzibar history, that the Arabs grabbed the most fertile land in the two islands. Thus since the days of slavery the African peasantry was marginalized and peasant farmers were found in the less fertile areas like the stony coral regions of the eastern part of both islands. Slaves were thought to work in the plantations from many parts of Africa, including Tanganyika Mainland, Zaire (now Congo Democratic Republic), Malawi, Kenya, Uganda and Zambia. Some local Africans in the two islands were also enslaved (Mlahagwa and Temu, 1991, p. 152).

89

The slave trade was abolished in 1873, and the legal status of slavery in 1897. This was undertaken by the European powers; notably Britain, who colonized Zanzibar in the 1890s. The British preserved the rule of the Sultan of Oman. Zanzibar thus suffered double colonization because the country was simultaneously an Arab and a British colony. It must however be stressed that only Africans experienced double colonization. For the Arabs the British were co-colonizers, while British colonialism in Zanzibar rested politically on Arab sub-imperialism. Omani Arab colonization of the two islands began in the 1780s and as mentioned above Seyyid Said of Oman moved to settle permanently in Zanzibar in 1840 (Clayton, 1981, pp. 1-2). Later Arab landowners claimed that they were holding their land under Islamic law; but the (best) land of the indigenous people of the two islands was alienated through intimidation and outright violence. Both the British and the Arabs have in the history of Zanzibar tried to use Islam as an ideology to justify land alienation. In the case of the Arabs the ideology was even used to justify slavery. Nevertheless, this kind of deceit did not prove effective in the long term, as was clearly illustrated in anti-Arab upheavals and the revolution of 1964.

Arab colonization of Unguja meant, for the indigenous people, forced labour and uprooting. The Arab administration forced the indigenous people and slaves from the Mainland to work (often in gangs) in farming, in building Zanzibar town, and in various forms of slavery on their clove and coconut plantations or villeinage (Clayton, 1981, p. 2). Pemba is generally more fertile than Zanzibar but it seems that the indigenous African people of Pemba were more successful in resisting land alienation by the Arab slavers. 85 per cent of the cloves in Zanzibar were grown in Pemba, and some were grown by the indigenous Pemba people themselves. Arab torture and cruelty were in evidence in Pemba, but Arab plantaions were smaller there, and the Pemba also owned some of the clove plantations (Clayton, 1981, p. 3).

When slavery was abolished the former slaves became squatters in the plantations. There was increased unwillingness to work as labour for the Arabs and the solution to the plantation labour requirement was sought in migrant labour from the mainland. This recruitment of mainland labour began in the 1890s and continued to the 1964 revolution. As Clayton explains:

> Since the indigenous were reluctant to undertake plantation labour, there could be no reduction of immigration by means of a new young generation of Zanzibar-born labourers. Mainland labour, seen as migrant and temporary, was believed to be the only solution (Clayton, 1981, p. 10).

Clayton estimates that from the turn of the century the mainland population of Zanzibar increased by 1,500 to 2,000 people per year on average (Clayton, 1981, p. 11). Currently mainland labourers still migrate to Zanzibar and Shao (1992) is of the opinion that migrant labour from the mainland comes in numbers of 500 to 2,000 per year depending on time and season. Most of the migrants to Unguja are Sukuma and Nyamwezi, while those to Pemba are Luguru and Makonde; but during the clove picking season all four ethnic groups are found in Pemba, which has more cloves than Unguja (Shao, 1992,

p. 70). In 1974 there was the largest influx of mainlanders to Zanzibar. These people were running away from villagization which was disrupting their agriculture and forcing them to abandon established farms and even homes. The majority of these migrants were Sukuma or Nyamwezi from Tabora, Mwanza, and Shinyanga. They had no serious problem in finding jobs in the islands because some of them had been labourers in the islands before (Shao, 1992, p. 70).

The total slave population in Zanzibar in the mid-1890s was 40,000 (Clayton, 1981, p. 7). As indicted above, after abolition of slavery the ex-slaves mostly became squatters. There were also some local Africans who became squatters. Some had lost their land to the Arab colonizers, while others lived in the coral areas. Squatting and landlessness thus became the most remarkable feature of Zanzibar's agriculture. All the best land was covered by cloves and coconuts (Cooper, 1980, p. 282). This meant that even those Africans who had some land had to squat in the more fertile plantation land to be able to survive. At the same time the number of squatters increased year after year as migrant labour arrived from the mainland. Stories of abuse of squatters by the plantation owners are widespread in Zanzibar and many adults clearly remember the system. The squatter had to provide labour but his bargaining position was weak because he was already residing on the plantation owner's land. The squatter was not allowed to grow permanent (tree) crops and had no security of tenure. The number of days during which the squatter had to work in the plantation were fixed; but this could be up to four days per week without any pay (Sheriff, 1991, p. 118).

Immediately after the abolition of slavery, squatters were paid nothing and the use of the planter's land for subsistence was considered their payment. However the system was not likely to work, especially when we consider that the Arabs had lost considerable political power to the British. Sheriff explains how the system had to change:

> This *burre* (free) system was in fact a system of labour rent, and it diverged so little from the preceding slave system that in the decade following emancipation only 17,000 individuals were formally freed. However, it proved extremely difficult to get this new type of labour (squatters) to work for nothing during these four days and the *burre* system had to be abandoned by 1900. Squatters, then, had to be paid a regular wage when picking cloves, and the only obligation that remained was to help pick the landowner's cloves first (Sheriff, 1991, p. 118).

As mentioned, squatters had no security of tenure and were not permitted to grow tree crops. Although they were paid when they worked they also provided unpaid labour because when they cultivated food crops between the trees they kept the plantation clean from bush and weeds (Sheriff, 1991, p. 18). Moreover if there were no regular tilling of the land between the trees the output of the tree crops like cloves and coconuts would go down because of decreased absorption of rain water by the plants and loss of soil nutrients to grass and bush.

91

**The 1964 Revolution**

The uprooting of the people of Zanzibar from their best land and the squatter system of serfdom and wage labour which resulted was potentially explosive. Peasants were also uprooted from the best land in Tanganyika and to a greater extent in Kenya and Zimbabwe. In Kenya the evidence of the Mau Mau war and in Zimbabwe the liberation war both help us to understand the political significance of large-scale land alienation. A brief explanation of the 1964 Revolution will be made here so as to provide appropriate historical contextualization. It is the revolution which led to the land reform and the land redistribution which accompanied it. These will be described in the next section.

The chief crop of Zanzibar (cloves) and the second crop (copra) were both sold in the world market. Thus the peasants in the fringe areas of Unguja and to a lesser extent Pemba, the squatters on both islands, and the mainland migrants who worked in plantations and in town, all lost income in times of depression and lost security and independence in times of prosperity (Cooper, 1980, p. 281). Marketing and most of the effort by the colonial state to improve crop production focused on cloves and coconuts. If peasants had surplus crops they were sold internally. The local market was small. This meant that there was little chance for the peasant economy to expand. The peasant economy could not expand because the planters had all the good land, and relations were always tense between squatters and landlords (Cooper, 1980, p. 280).

Some of the local people of Unguja like the Hadimu had a village and kinship structure that gave them defined rights in land (Cooper, 1980, p. 262). However, it needs to be emphasized that the natives of Zanzibar were pushed to marginal areas and that traditional guarantee of access to land was now different since there was less land, and available land was of inferior quality. In the case of the ex-slaves, even the minimum security provided by what was left of tribal land did not exist, and they were wholly dependent on the roots they established in plantations and in town. As the Hadimu became more dependent on Arab plantations for work they were faced with the necessity of developing ties with other squatters. This would be expected as the two belonged to one class which had common interest against planters. However, it must be emphasized that in Zanzibar all indigenous Africans developed a common anti-Arab and anti-Sultan attitude. This cut across class and was nurtured by the cruelty of Arabs against Black people and the privileges which Arabs maintained for themselves. Scholars like Abdul Sheriff and Abdulrehman M. Babu have tended to discount and accord a minor role to the race factor in fuelling the revolution, and in Zanzibar history generally (Sheriff, 1991, and Babu, 1991). But both scholars contradict themselves because in their works one can find examples where stratification and conflict took racial rather than class lines. For example, Sheriff shows that there were poor Arabs but he maintains that forced labour was imposed on Africans only, without explaining why this kind of coercion was not put on poor Arabs (Sheriff, 1991, p. 12). Moreover, Babu cannot show why, for example, before the revolution a section of the Zanzibar Nationalist Party (ZNP) broke away and joined the Afro-Shirazi Party (ASP).

ZNP was a party of planters which attempted to hide its ethnic (Arab) particularism by seeking to find themes that would unite all Muslims (Cooper, 1980, p. 286). This party was not anti-colonial as Babu claims (1991, p. 225). It supported the Sultan and for the majority of Zanzibaris this was an internal colonial system worse than British imperialism (which had at least abolished slavery and moderated Arab tyranny).

The ZNP had among its members the educated urban petty bourgeoisie (Babu, 1991, p. 229). These formed the Umma Party which entered into alliance with the ASP although the Umma Party as an organization was banned by the ZNP government on January 1964 (Babu, 1991, p. 238). The ASP was composed of the majority of non-Arabs, first in Zanzibar, but in 1963 the majority of Africans in Pemba had also joined (Cooper, 1980, p. 236). The point is that extreme oppression in the two islands took racial lines; and there is no need to attempt to derive a 'materialist' theory in the fashion of Sheriff and Babu to explain this away. Moreover, Sheriff and Babu display little sociological understanding of Zanzibar. Many of the so-called 'Arabs' were (are) actually Black people who had originally adopted an Arab ethnic identity, to avoid enslavement and other kinds of oppression by Arabs. These were 'ideological' Arabs (and in any case it must be recognized that race is ideologically constructed). The ideological Arabs who were more educated were more likely to see through the illusion that they were Arabs; and this explains why the Umma Party joined ASP when it was clear that conflict along racial lines was supreme and a reality. The Umma Party alliance with ASP was not tactical as Babu claims. The alliance was real; and Babu himself actually shows that political divergence in Zanzibar took racial lines (1991, p. 235).

The economy of Zanzibar depended mostly on cloves and copra. Conflict had to centre on land. In mainland Tanzania land alienation did not reach the magnitude of Zanzibar. However, in areas of comparable land alienation, such as Meru, there was tension of a kind which was marked by the Meru land case in the 1950s. In Zanzibar as ex-slaves became squatters they were more and more likely to identify themselves with others of 'squatter' status. Thus it was noted in the 1930s and 1940s that ex-slaves were increasingly calling themselves Hadimu or Pemba. In 1948 it was found that 53 per cent of the Africans of mainland ancestry were born in the islands, and the percentage was even higher in rural areas. Cooper argues that such data suggest that many 'mainlanders' in the islands were of ex-slave origin (Cooper, 1980, p. 283). From the data we can also conclude that many 'mainlanders' were squatters or were of squatter origin because slavery as abolished at the end of the 1890s and most of the ex-slaves became squatters.

Squatter/landlord relations could not hold Zanzibar society together for a long time. Squatters could still be thrown out if the landlord felt that they agitated against landlordism and Arab privileges (Cooper, 1980, p. 282). Arabs were favoured not just in land ownership but in marketing and loans. As early as 1927 the Arab Advisory Committee was created as the sole body representing clove producers and the channel through which clove bonuses were to be paid (Sheriff, 1991, p. 132).

The bad economic condition of the squatters became clearer during the Second World War. Up to then squatters were still not charged rent but they had to work for wages for the landlords. They could grow and even sell food crops but usually not fruit trees and never cloves. During the Second World War the squatters and non-squatting peasants were encouraged to grow more food as in the First World War, to meet shortages. Although this could have enabled squatters and non-squatting peasants to earn more cash, they could not do so because the best land was covered with clove and coconut trees (Cooper, 1980, p. 282). Moreover, land alienation was still going on between the 1940s and 1964 (Shao, 1992, p. 25). As mentioned Arabs were favoured by the state in land ownership and in marketing (Sheriff, 1991, pp. 132-3). During the 1940s even food rationing was organized according to race and not according to financial status (Shao, 1992, p. 24).

The first recorded anti-landlord unrest occurred in Zanzibar in 1927. Cooper traces this to the conflict between the lower classes of Zanzibar and the landlords.

> Patterns of social unrest suggest how deeply the connections between workers and peasants, Wahadimu, ex-slaves, and migrants, city and countryside, were interwoven for the lower class of Zanzibar island. The urban poor who had no access to the means of subsistence, had the least margin in their dealings with landlords, and the attempts of landlords in the African quarter of Zanzibar town to raise rents in 1927 led to the first disturbances. The threat to civic order was sufficiently strong for the Government to block arbitrary rent increases, but it also arrested and deported the alleged leaders of the disturbances.(Cooper, 1980, p. 283).

A revolutionary climate was brewing in Zanzibar. In 1944 there were dock workers' and transport workers' strikes (Shao, 1992, p. 38). The economic condition of the migrant and the squatter had deteriorated considerably by the 1940s, and a longer period of work was needed before a migrant could return home; while a casual labourer was faced with the need for a higher cash income but also faced greater competition (Cooper, 1980, p. 284). The main demand was higher wages and the strike spread rapidly from port workers to government employees and domestic servants. The strike embraced all the segments of Zanzibar town: ex-slave, migrant, and the indigenous Zanzibari population. Women boycotted Indian and Arab shops as the men stopped work. The government attempted to divide the African population by recruiting Tumbatu in their home land and bringing them as strikebreakers. However, the Tumbatu refused to work and left the work place (The Tumbatu, like the Hadimu and Pemba, are indigenous to the Zanzibar islands).

In 1938 there were anti-Arab riots which spread to rural areas. The cause of these upheavals was, as would be expected, the land question. The best land was occupied by plantations As landlords increased their grip over squatters and other peasants, less food was produced. Between 1950 and 1959 the government spent on average 37 per cent of its revenue to import food. However, by 1957 out of the government revenue of £2,340,000 ($6,575,400) the amount spent to import food was £1,746,267 ($4,907,010)

94

(Shao, 1992, p. 36; Cooper, 1980, p. 284). Squatters were evicted in direct violation of established custom and were not compensated. Those squatters who refused to leave the plantations were taken to court and fined or imprisoned. In a court system which so overtly favoured Arabs against Africans, the squatters expected the worst.

In the 1950s and early 1960s the social and political situation in Zanzibar was tense. The 1957-64 squatter evictions were serious and helped to create a revolutionary situation. Shao is of the opinion that the 1957-64 evictions were serious because some landlords who used to live in town returned to their estates. The reason for the return of absentee landlords was the sudden drop of clove prices in the world market of the late 1950s (Shao, 1992, pp. 36-7).

Squatters found themselves with no land to cultivate after the evictions. They had no shelter because they had left their houses in the plantations. They had nowhere to graze their animals because Government Decree no. 2 of 1958, the Zanzibar Rural District Administrative Order of 1960, and the Pemba District Administrative Authority of 1962 stipulated that nobody was allowed to graze, cultivate or erect structures on any land without the written permission of the owner unless the person doing so held possession of the land by virtue of lease or other contracts of a similar nature (Shao, 1992, pp. 36-7). Some landlords even went to the point of refusing squatters permission to draw water from wells on their land. The landlords formed a social group which claimed that it held land under Islamic law. In reality because the plantation land was acquired through force and cheating, it would in fact be seen under Islamic law as having been acquired by unclean (*harm*) means, and therefore be illegal. In Islam the holding of such land in itself would be considered to be an unclean act.

In the 1958 anti-Arab uprising the squatters damaged property and there were sporadic outbreaks of violence. Besides the evictions the Arab landlords were also forcing squatters to be their political followers. Cooper observed that:

> Some landlords insisted, as they had once demanded of their slaves, that their dependants follow their political lead, this time by supporting the planter-dominated Zanzibar Nationalist Party (ZNP). Some were evicted for refusing. ZNP backers also tried to install clients in waterfront jobs (Cooper, 1980, p. 284).

The planters attempted to use coercion and ties of dependence to prevent tenants and workers from involvement in independent politics. This was met by squatters' refusal to fulfil their weeding obligations. Squatters also planted crops in between clove trees, so as to damage the trees. African organizations developed settlement schemes for evicted squatters, and there was vigorous competition in finding waterfront jobs. Arab shops were boycotted and there was political challenge to the very legitimacy of Arab landlordship (Cooper, 1980, pp. 269-85).

Clearly the land question was central to Zanzibar's politics. In 1961 there were election riots in town but they quickly spread to the (rural) plantation areas where they continued for several days. Africans and Arabs attacked each other in town and in rural areas. Gangs composed of Africans of many tribes from the squatters on nearby farms went around town. In rural areas squatters and villagers went around paying off old scores against Arab landlords and shopkeepers. Tension continued and urban labour disputes erupted even after the riots. Given the history of Zanzibar there was genuine fear among the Africans that if the British left under that situation, the Arabs would take over and reinstitute slavery (Cooper, 1980, p. 285; Babu, 1991, pp. 229-31).

The African Association was formed in 1935. Originally it primarily had mainland membership, according to Cooper, but Shao argues that it represented the majority of the urban workers who were predominantly Africans (Shao, 1992, p. 40; Cooper, 1980, p. 285). The Arab Association was as much a planters' organization as an ethnic one, and it dates back to the 1920s. It gave birth to the Zanzibar Nationalist Party in 1956. The ZNP unsuccessfully tried to invoke Muslim unity and anti-British feelings and to split the Africans on ethnic lines before the 1961 elections. The African Association denounced the impoverishment of Africans, domination by Arabs, and the alliance between the Arabs and the colonial state.

The Afro-Shirazi Party was formed in 1957 out of the merger of the African Association and the Shirazi Association (Babu, 1991, p. 225). The latter was formed in 1940 and Shao argues that it represented the interests of the more indigenous Africans (1992, p. 40). The ASP was formed with the support of the Hadimu but without the participation of the Pemba. The Pemba formed their own small party, the Zanzibar and Pemba People's Party, which was led by a landowner and a former school principal (Cooper, 1980, pp. 284-5).

Shirazi identity was associated with indigenous people who owned some good land and therefore trees, and these were mostly found in Pemba. However, Cooper argues that the trend towards smallholder production never did end the unequal distribution of land and trees in Pemba which favoured Arabs, and it never shook off the domination of Arab planters in Unguja (Cooper, 1980, p. 285).

Cooper shows how the meaning of Shirazi identity had changed from the 1920s. Shirazi identity finally lost its connection with owning trees and came to embrace all Hadimu, Pemba and Tumbatu. The ex-slaves who had acquired local culture also eventually identified themselves as Shirazi, and Shirazi identity became a challenge to Arab hegemony (Cooper, 1980, p. 286). Shirazi identity thus came to mean the same thing as local African, native African, or indigenous Africa.

The Zanzibar and Pemba People's Party (ZPPP), which supported the ZNP in the 1963 election, failed to move the support of the upper crust of the peasantry to ZNP. By 1963 the majority of all African voters in Pemba had joined ASP. Some Pemba Shirazi were better-off peasants but they were faced with the realities of Arab planters' domination and tyranny. Thus the Pemba Shirazi shifted their support and identity to the African side. In the 1963 elections the ASP won by a majority in the two islands. Nevertheless flagrant gerrymandering and cheating gave the Arab-dominated ZNP/ZPPP coalition victory and it formed a government in 1963. The ASP had more votes than ZNP or ZPPP combined but it had fewer seats in Parliament (Babu, 1991, p. 239).

On 12 January 1964 the Arab-dominated government was overthrown in a popular uprising. The ASP had throughout the late 1950s and early 1960s demanded land redistribution. The ASP argument was that 80 per cent of the fertile land and the bulk of trade and industry were in the hands of a tiny minority and that all important government and other positions were in the hands of the same group (Shao, 1992, p. 42). The revolution was led by the ASP which mobilized the ZNP and ZPPP and formed a government in 1964. The Sultan and many Omani Arabs had to flee Zanzibar during the revolution and 'Wamanga' (Arabs) in rural areas were murdered (Cooper, 1980, p. 287; Babu, 1991, pp. 238-40).

### Agriculture in Zanzibar after the 1964 Revolution

Agricultural production in Zanzibar is not high despite the land reform which the revolution brought. Distribution of plantation land started on 11 November 1965 and went on until 1967. However, emergency distribution of land went on until 1974 (Shao, 1992, pp. 50-52). By 1969, 8,000 plots of land were distributed in Unguja and 6,800 plots in Pemba. These plots distributed by the Revolutionary Government of Zanzibar measure three acres (1.22 ha.) each. Up to 1974 a total of 66,573 acres (26,962 ha.) of land hand been distributed among 22,251 families. Fifty-two landlords were expropriated and these had owned 745 farms. Some of these landlords were well-known thorough scoundrels who had evicted peasants who refused to part with a fixed portion of their crops as land rent. My student, Mr Said Juma Othman, who was born in Zanzibar after the revolution, was able to mention the names of 23 landlords. Out of these, four were relatives of the Sultan, four were other Arabs, and five were Indian merchants. All of these owned plantations in Unguja. Others were five Arab landlords and four Indian merchants who owned plantations in Pemba. He mentioned only one African, an owner of plantations in Pemba. Indian merchants had acquired plantations in Unguja and Pemba when Arab landlords failed to pay back loans taken from them.

The striking feature of agriculture in Zanzibar is the stagnation and decline in agricultural output. This is clearly indicated in Table 6.1.

The labour shortage in agriculture is serious and has a long history as a problem for Zanzibar. This is related to the seasonal character of the main crop, cloves. As long ago as the 1890s the colonial state had tried to regulate labour supply. Local herdsmen were coerced, and rewarded with salary increased when they offered assistance in recruiting labour. The British set up labour centres to distribute clove pickers among landlords and in 1904 over 8,000 Pemba peasants were recruited for such work in the island. In 1907 the local herdsmen (*mashehe*) were suspended or forced to pick cloves themselves if they failed to produce a certain number of pickers. Coercion in recruiting labour was only abandoned in 1916 (Sheriff, 1991, p. 120). Another method used by the colonial government to recruit labour was to introduce a hut tax or ground rent on peasants, and to offer exemption for those who were prepared to pick cloves. This tax was abandoned in 1912 because peasants managed to evade it but the Masters and Servants Decree made the labourer liable to give up half a month's wages or to be imprisoned for up to a month for breach of contract. In 1940 the penal sanction under the decree was abolished for all classes of labour except for clove pickers (Sheriff, 1991, pp. 120-21). The *kipande* system of the Tanganyikan plantations[1] was also introduced in the 1940s, together with a more sophisticated system based on piece work. However, after the revolution it was politically no longer possible to recruit labour in accordance with slave and colonial styles.

Clove picking requires much seasonal labour. For example in the 1940s there were about 30,000 clove pickers every year in Unguja and Pemba. Some were from Pemba and the mainland but the majority were from Unguja. For example in 1943 a total of 18,662 persons travelled from Unguja to Pemba to pick cloves (Sheriff, 1992, pp. 121-2).

Some of the poor peasants (i.e. agricultural labourers) got some land after the revolution and this cut the supply of labour available for cloves. In 1977 only 1,000 tons of cloves were produced compared with 24,000 tons in 1958. Clove output nearly collapsed in the 1970s, and in 1977 only 66 tons were produced. The main cause of the decline seems to be the shortage of pickers, and Shao (1992, p. 63) shows that 40 per cent of cloves were unpicked in the 1970s. Zanzibar agriculture failed to capitalize on world clove price rises in 1969-82.

There has been some decline in the world clove prices such as 1987-8 and 1988-9. However, such declines are secondary in explaining the poor performance of agriculture in Zanzibar because even in years of good prices the performance has remained bad. The government failed to channel the necessary credit to peasants after 1964 and to initiate technological change. Just as on the mainland, farming by peasants is done on the smallest scale with hand hoes and *pangas* (machetes). Clove picking is not easy to mechanize but most of the other farming activities are also carried out manually.

It seems that the Revolutionary Government was channelling the profit from cloves towards activities such as the building of residential accommodation in the 1960s and 1970s. This did not help farming as the producer prices declined. There have since been some improvements and the producer price of cloves rose from 4.09 per cent of the world market price in 1976 to 62 per cent in 1989 (Shao, 1992, p. 65). However the problem of labour relations remains critical and the government needs to formulate appropriate policies if Zanzibar is to restore and maintain her place as the world's leading clove producer.

Labour shortage for clove picking and all farming is a complicated phenomenon especially when we consider that there is little industrialization in Zanzibar and very rapid population growth. The main industries recorded decline in the 1980s and 1990s. Sugar output was 954 tons in 1989 and only 671 tons in 1995. Cigarette production was 134,940,000 in 1980 and only 5,362,000 in 1995. Even the production of bread went down from

## Table 6.1 Marketed production of Zanzibar main export commodities (in metric tons)

| Crop | 1982 | 1983 | 1984 | 1985 | 1986 | 1987 | 1988 | 1989 | 1990 | 1991 | 1992 | 1993 | 1994 | 1995 |
|---|---|---|---|---|---|---|---|---|---|---|---|---|---|---|
| Cloves | 2931.0 | 6843.0 | 10815.0 | 1548.0 | 11303.0 | 1880.0 | 9992.0 | 4192.0 | 2004.0 | 15394.0 | 1692.0 | 1843.0 | 4927.0 | 1575.6 |
| Copra | 8014.0 | 11804.0 | 9757.0 | 3769.0 | 6379.0 | 4812.0 | 759.0 | 141.0 | 6926.0 | 3691.0 | 167.0 | 1304.0 | 3292.0 | 3292.0 |
| Chillies | 0.3 | 0.3 | 0.0 | 0.0 | 0.1 | 0.1 | 0.2 | 3.2 | 4.2 | 2.0 | 1.2 | 2.1 | 1.6 | 2.9 |
| Clove stems | 469.0 | 57.0 | 279.0 | 155.0 | 115.0 | 130.0 | 108.0 | 1053.0 | - | 482.0 | 943.0 | 35249.9 | 450.4 | 117.7 |
| Sea-weeds | - | - | - | - | - | - | - | - | - | - | 2885.4 | 2644.7 | 2811.0 | 4975.0 |

*Source*: BoT, 1995, p. 47.

99

10,127,000 loaves in 1989 to 6,519,000 loaves in 1995 (BoT, 1995, p. 50). The population of Zanzibar was 354,815 in 1967, 476,111 in 1978, and 640,578 in 1988. The annual average intercensal growth rate was 2.7 per cent for 1967-8 and 3.0 per cent for 1978-88 (URT, 1988, p. 21).

Zanzibar imports much food especially rice and wheat. Urban dwellers form a greater proportion of the population than is the case on the Mainland (30 per cent as opposed to 5 per cent). Poor state planning, especially in marketing, meant that Zanzibar's agriculture failed to capitalize on this relatively large food market. There has been little diversification from cloves and coconuts and considerable resources have been wasted on experimenting with state farms, which are very inefficiently run and are loss-making. The same money would have reaped better return if it had been invested among the more hard-working and innovative peasants.

There are many entrepreneurs in Zanzibar who could have invested in farming. Some entrepreneurs from Zanzibar are very successful businessmen on the mainland. Tanga town alone has a Pemba trading community of 10,000 people and there are more Zanzibar traders in Dar es Salaam. The government of Zanzibar has failed to channel the investment of local entrepreneurs into agriculture. The lack of interest in investment in agriculture could be a consequence of bureaucratic control of farming (especially marketing) by the state. However, we have to be careful in our analysis of Zanzibar agriculture. For example, decline is noted even in the case of products for which state control has not operated in spheres such as pricing. The output of dairy products, for example, went down from 1,244,000 litres in 1989 to 200,000 litres in 1995 (BoT, 1995, p. 50).

Only plantation land was distributed to peasants. Peasant areas were not touched. However it seems that there is agricultural stagnation and decline in both old peasant and old plantation land. In Unguja the 40,050 acres (16,224 ha.) distributed consisted of only 15.3 per cent of the 174,426 acres (70,642 ha.) of fertile land with farms (Shao, 1992, p. 53). Such data from Shao are not conclusive, but do suggest that it is not the land reform which led to the stagnation and decline in farming. For example, rice was basically untouched but rice production in Unguja was 5,000 tons in 1963 and only 4,334 tons in 1975. In Pemba rice production was 15,166 tons in 1963 and 13,416 tons in 1975 (Shao, 1992, p. 84).

**Conclusion**

Peasant production never died in Zanzibar but plantation agriculture had the upper hand. Peasant resistance to the plantation economy did not lead to capitalist farming among the peasants. The agrarian question in Zanzibar could not be resolved via plantation farming and such an economy and its semi-feudalism were abolished in 1964. Peasant agriculture can be advanced through technological and social innovations as has been evident from the green revolution in India and recent successes in Taiwan and South Korea. In these countries land reform removed the burden of rent but peasants were then subjected to ruthless state taxation directed to primary accumulation for industrialization (Bernstein, 1966-7, p. 27). The success of peasant farming in South Korea and Taiwan thus depended much on rapid technological advancement. The problem with Zanzibar (and Tanzanian agriculture generally) is failure to applying existing technological innovations. The peasant produces so little and there is failure to accumulate capital for investment even when prices are good. This is the fundamental problem in agriculture.

The wild fluctuations in crop output in Zanzibar indicate that the potential for increased output and productivity of land and labour is there. For instance the following data from the Zanzibar Ministry of Agriculture show rice output for the period 1975-92:

**Table 6.2 Rice output in Zanzibar (tons)**

| Year | Tons |
|------|------|
| 1975 | 10,028 |
| 1976 | 20,874 |
| 1977 | 10,820 |
| 1978 | 5,947 |
| 1979 | 6,166 |
| 1980 | 7,844 |
| 1981 | 18,051 |
| 1982 | 18,358 |
| 1983 | 7,130 |
| 1984 | 14,471 |
| 1985 | 11,525 |
| 1986 | 13,795 |
| 1987 | 17,306 |
| 1988 | 17,358 |
| 1989 | 22,573 |
| 1990 | 19,790 |
| 1991 | 22,660 |
| 1992 | 15,580 |

The fluctuations here are wild (5,947 to 22,660) and have no direction. Thus it is not possible to predict the performance of Zanzibar's agriculture. High output is not a consequence of a well-organized farming system, but rather chance such as a variation in the weather or a sudden adequate supply of affordable labour. The Ministry of Agriculture in Zanzibar has much work to do in helping peasants to apply 'green revolution' types of innovations. A community development campaign to convince potential peasant entrepreneurs that farming is a good profession and will pay well in the near but not immediate future will also help competent peasant farmers to put more effort into agriculture.

## Note

1. The *kipande* or 'ticket' system involved full payment of a worker only after the task was completed. A worker would sign up to complete a certain number of *kipandes*.

## References

Babu, A.M. (1991), 'The 1964 Revolution: Lumpen or Vanguard?, in Sheriff and Ferguson (eds.), pp. 220-48.

Bader, Z. (1991), 'The Contradictions of Merchant Capital, 1840-1939', in Sheriff and Ferguson (eds.), pp. 163-87.

Bank of Tanzania (BoT), *Economic Bulletin for the Quarter ended 31 December 1995* (vo. 24, no. 4).

Bernstein, H. (1996-7), 'Agrarian Questions then and now', *Journal of Peasant Studies*, 24, 22-59.

Clayton, A. (1981), *The Zanzibar Revolution and its Aftermath*, Archon Books, Hamden CT.

Cooper, F. (1980), *From Slaves to Squatters: Plantation Labour and Agriculture in Zanzibar and Coastal Kenya 1890-1925*, Yale University Press, New Haven CT.

Mlahagwa, J. R. and Temu, A.J. (1991), 'The Decline of the Landlords, 1873-1963', in Sheriff and Ferguson (eds.), pp. 141-62.

Shao, I.F. (1992), *The Political Economy of Land Reform in Zanzibar*, Dar es Salaam University Press, Dar es Salaam.

Sheriff, A. (1991), 'The Peasantry under Imperialism', in Sheriff and Ferguson (eds.), pp. 109-140.

Sheriff, A. and Ferguson, E. (eds.) (1991), *Zanzibar under Colonial Rule*, James Currey, London.

URT (1991), *1988 Population Census: Preliminary Report*, Bureau of Statistics, Ministry of Finance, Economic Affairs and Planning, Dar es Salaam.

# Part II

# INDIGENOUS TECHNICAL KNOWLEDGE

# 7 Linking Institutional Research and Extension to Indigenous Knowledge Systems: Experience from the UMADEP Project at Sokoine University of Agriculture (SUA)

A. Z. MATTEE AND T. LASSALLE

## Introduction

Much criticism has been levelled against institutional research and extension, as having had little success in generating and disseminating agricultural technologies for small-scale, resource-poor farmers. It is argued that many 'improved' technologies, although technically sound, are not even appropriate to the agro-climatic conditions. According to Byerelee and his colleagues (1980), farmers reject technologies not because they are conservative or ignorant, but because they rationally weigh the changes in incomes and risk associated with the given technologies under their natural and economic circumstances. They then decide that for them the technology does not work.

One of the solutions which has been proposed to redress this weakness is for institutional research and extension to work more closely with farmers. This is based on the acknowledgement of the central role of the farmer in the whole process of technology generation, dissemination and adoption. Thus, approaches like Farming Systems Research (Collinson, 1984) and its variants, Farmer Participatory Research (Farrington and Martin, 1988) and Participatory Technology Development (Waters-Bayer, 1989) have been developed as a way of involving the farmers more closely in the whole process. But despite the recognition of the critical role of the farmers in the agricultural development process and despite various approaches which have evolved, there still exists a lot of scepticism about the role farmers can play in the research and extension process: and much ignorance about how farmers may actually participate in this process.

This paper seeks to describe ways in which the power, resources and expertise of agricultural research and extension institutions can be complemented with the wisdom, resourcefulness and determination of small-scale farmers in order to improve their socio-economic conditions. These suggestions are based on the experiences of the Uluguru Mountains

Agricultural Development Project (UMADEP) which is a research and extension project based in the Faculty of Agriculture at Sokoine University of Agriculture (SUA) and implemented in collaboration with the government extension system and the farmers in Mgeta and Mkuyuni Divisions.

## Why should Farmers be Involved?

There are several reasons why farmers should be involved in the technology generation and dissemination process. Among them are the following:

(a) Farmers are the final decision-makers, as to whether to adopt or reject a technology. Involving them will improve the chances of the technologies being adopted.
(b) Farmers are the ones who bear the risk of any new technology: thus, they should have a 'voice' in the development of the technology.
(c) Farmers are much more likely to pay attention to a new technology if they see that their fellow-farmers are actively involved, somehow. Such a technology is less likely to be seen as alien to the farmers and as such, it is likely to diffuse faster within the community and even to other communities.
(d) A fundamental reason for farmers' involvement is that it offers an opportunity for co-operation in the mobilization of indigenous knowledge. Farmers have superior knowledge in matters like

- the complexity of their farming systems and the rationale for this complexity
- the socio-cultural milieu, including available resources and expertise in local agricultural production
- the physical environment, including climate, soils, water and vegetation under which agricultural production has to take place.

(Richards, 1985; Chambers, 1983)

## Why is Indigenous Knowledge Important for Institutional Research and Extension?

Originally indigenous knowledge was equated with 'local' or 'traditional' knowledge, implying a static pool of knowledge which has been handed down from generation to generation. But it is now realized that farmers are constantly engaged in the process of active innovation and invention, and are constantly reworking and updating their knowledge in the light of new challenges, and encounters with new forms of knowledge (Richards, 1986, 1985). This implies that:

(a) Farmers have the capacity to take actions to improve their farming system, with or without the assistance of institutional research and extension.

106

(b) Farmers' indigenous knowledge is dynamic and ever-changing, something created by farmers as part of their changing local environments. Farmers will therefore always fall back on their indigenous knowledge whenever the merits of new technologies are not obvious.

(c) Farmers will accept new knowledge, and modify their indigenous knowledge, where new challenges or conditions render their indigenous knowledge irrelevant or inadequate. Farmers are thus open to changes, and are not as conservative as they are sometimes made out to be by institutional researchers and extension workers.

It is obvious therefore, that farmers will place any new knowledge within the context of their indigenous knowledge, in deciding whether or not to adopt an innovation. Ki-Zerbo (1992) uses the term 'exogenous' and 'endogenous' to describe modern scientific and indigenous knowledge respectively and argues that only when farmers are able to combine 'exogenous' and 'endogenous' knowledge can permanent change take place in the society. According to him, any development effort must start from and recognize the local capacities of the local people, rather than relying exclusively on modern scientific knowledge. In order to have any impact, institutional research and extension must therefore start from and build upon the indigenous knowledge of the farmers.

## How can Farmers' Input into the Research and Process be Ensured?

The experiences of the Uluguru Mountain Agricultural Development Project UMADEP) serve to illustrate some of the techniques which can be used to ensure farmers' input into the research and extension process. The farmers in Mgeta ward of Morogoro Region, where this project initially started, have grown and depended on horticultural products for several decades. They have developed a fairly complex farming system adapted to the mountainous terrain they farm, including an elaborate system of terracing and furrow irrigation. However, despite the high degree of intensification of the agricultural system, farmers are faced with a number of important constraints which have limited the possibilities for an improvement in the productivity of the system, and which have even threatened the sustainability of the system (Lassalle and Mattee, 1994). The UMADEP project sought to build on the farmers' knowledge and skills based on their long experience in mountain agriculture, in developing appropriate innovations which can improve the agricultural productivity of the Mgeta farming systems.

The approach of the project is to link together researchers based at SUA, government extension workers in the Ministry of Agriculture, and farmers; in a common endeavour of identifying priority problems and seeking solutions to those problems. A number of strategies were used in this approach.

## Participatory Rural Appraisal (PRA)

PRA was one of the initial activities which were undertaken in the project villages. This had three basic aims.

(i)   To create cohesiveness between the SUA researchers, government extension workers and farmers,
(ii)  To involve farmers in the process of internal reflection so as to analyse their reality in terms of the existing socio-economic conditions and the underlying factors.
(iii) To identify priorities and problems which need attention from the researchers, extension workers and the farmers themselves.

Although the technique has succeeded in achieving all the three objectives, it has also presented a number of lessons (Chonya, 1996):

*   It is necessary to be clear from the beginning about the objectives of carrying out the PRA. Farmers in particular must be made to understand that the PRA is only the beginning of a long-term collaborative process whereby after identifying priority problems, they must continue to participate to work for the solutions.
*   The technique demands the right skills and attitudes on the part of institutional researchers and extension workers, who must be able and willing to use various ways of tapping the knowledge and experience of farmers concerning the local environment.
*   Results of PRA are very location-specific, and are hardly transferable to other places. There must be adequate time and resources to carry out PRAs in the various locations where intervention is intended.
*   In order to have maximum input from the farmers, the media to be used are critical. Farmers must be allowed to express themselves in the various ways in which they feel comfortable. For example, in the UMADEP project, roleplay, drama, pictures, drawing, comics and sketches are used to facilitate access to information by both the literate and illiterate.
*   PRA is one of the most effective techniques to build team spirit amongst professionals of different disciplines, and to establish rapport with farmers of a particular location.


## The Use of Farmers' Groups

Farmers' groups have been used in various areas to facilitate research/extension worker/farmer interaction (Norman, Baker, Heinrich and Worman, 1988; Masihara, Worman and Heinrich, 1988; Norman and Modiakgotla, 1990). Within the UMADEP project, farmers' groups are instrumental in facilitating dialogue between farmers and professionals, in the process of articulating farmers' needs, problems and interest and in designing programmes to solve problems (Mattee and Lassalle, 1994). Once the village situation has been analysed and described, and priorities set, the researchers and extension workers operate with existing and emergent co-operatives to undertake various activities which will solve their priority problems. So far, more than 15 farmers' groups have been formed, based on different interests of the farmers. These include vegetable growers' co-operative societies, a fruit tree nursery owners association, a dairy goat-keepers' association, and savings and credit societies.

In order to further the sharing of experiences amongst farmers, and to increase their collective capacities, farmers' groups have formed networks amongst themselves. These are at the local level (e.g. Mgeta Division) as well as on a national basis, where the various local networks have federated themselves into the Farmers' Groups Network in Tanzania or *Mtandao wa Vikundi vya Wakulima Tanzania* (MVIWATA) in Kiswahili: with the objectives of exchanging ideas and experiences, and disseminating solutions, reports and recommendations about those ideas and experiences to all concerned (Gilla, 1993).

Experiences of the project with farmers' groups and their networks have proved to be very effective in:

(a) Facilitating communication between institutional researchers and extension workers on one side, and farmers on the other,
(b) Facilitating communication amongst farmers themselves, including within communities, as well as between communities. A process of sharing knowledge and experiences is thus created.
(c) Facilitating the creation of dynamism and a momentum for action on those programmes which have been agreed upon by group consensus. As such this has resulted in concrete actions being taken by farmers.

However, to work effectively with farmers' groups, professionals need to:

(a) Establish mutual respect and confidence between farmers and themselves. Experience has shown that this relationship will be built over a period of time, through regular contacts with farmers, and engaging in certain concrete activities which demonstrate the professionals' ability and concern for the farmers (Lassalle, Kamuzora and Shekilango, 1990).
(b) Play a facilitating rather than a leadership role in working with these groups. In order to facilitate the emergence of genuine farmers' groups, the independence of these groups must be respected, and the professionals must recognize these groups as independent centres of decision-making. The role of the professionals in training and guidance of the group members is crucial. Training is always based on the actual situation, and so is conducted in the village, on farmers' or demonstration plots, and the farmers are encouraged to share their experiences in various ways such as role playing, drama, farmers' exchanges and group discussions (Noy, 1990).
(c) Accept the increase in farmers' power which will be brought by strengthening and networking of farmers' groups. By acting together, farmers are likely to be more confident in influencing the decisions of professionals on matters which have a bearing on their welfare. Local

groups will be more concerned with practical matters related to agricultural production, for example, the availability of inputs, and agricultural technologies; but the national network is likely to look more at policy issues of marketing, pricing and land tenure.

## Trial and Demonstration Plots

One of the decisions which have been made by some of the farmers' groups together with the researchers and extension workers is on the type of technologies to be tested for subsequent adoption on farmers' fields. A trial and demonstration plot was therefore established in one of the villages. It reflected the natural conditions of the area, and the management of the plot was undertaken jointly by farmers and the extension workers. Some of the technologies which were tested include the proper husbandry practices for tomatoes and a local vegetable (commonly known as *mnavu*), appropriate fruit tree propagation techniques, progressive terracing with the establishment of sugar cane strips (Mgumia, 1993) and other soil conservation techniques.

On the trial and demonstration plot, farmers are continuously involved in assessing the technologies at all stages. The role of the researchers is to provide information and the necessary inputs, to assist in the design, monitoring and evaluation of the results. Thus, the primary objective for the researchers is not to generate statistical data *per se*, but to assist farmers and the extension workers in evaluating the potential of technologies.

It is important to note that in the process of technology evaluation, the inputs of the professional and of the farmers are equally important, and must be given equal weight. Two examples may help to illustrate this. In one of the instances, the researchers tried to introduce wheat as a possible replacement crop for maize, which takes a very long time to mature because of the cool environment. While this made technical sense, the idea had to be abandoned after a few seasons because the farmers were not willing to substitute maize for wheat in their diets. However, in another case, farmers had been very sceptical of trying tomatoes, because according to their experiences they always succumbed to late blight, and so they believed that tomatoes could not be grown in Mgeta area. The researchers were able to demonstrate that through appropriate timing and proper management practices, tomatoes could be profitably grown in the area. Eventually, the farmers were convinced, and tomatoes are now being widely grown, and in fact they are about to become the second most important cash crop in the area after cabbages.

The trail and demonstration plot serves as a place for joint experimentation by researchers, extension workers and farmers. It is used not only as a technique to generate information, but also to draw the farmers into the process of knowledge creation, control and utilization.

## Strengthening Communication between Professionals, Farmers and Policy-makers

In order to increase the capacities of the institutions to work more closely with small farmers, a group of researchers within SUA started working together as a think tank to try to monitor, systematize and further refine the various techniques of linking researchers, extension workers and farmers. The motto of the group is 'Universities and rural communities: let us learn from each other' (SCOM, 1991).

As part of its activities, the group has organized a number of meetings and workshops which brought together representatives of farmers' groups, SUA academics and government policy-makers to discuss ways and means of forging a closer working relationship. Through such meetings and workshops, the farmers' voice is better heard, and researchers and extension workers become more sensitive to the needs and concerns of the farmers in their professional activities. Also, through participation in such workshops, farmers' self-confidence and astuteness in dealing with professionals is increased.

The experiences of the Strengthening Communication group so far indicate that, in general, the internal structure and the reward system in the university are such that they do not facilitate or encourage researchers to work more closely with rural communities (Mattee, 1993).


## Students' Field Practicals

Students have been involved in the UMADEP project by undertaking their field practical training in the project area. Their participation consisted of each student being hosted by a farm family for one month, during which time the student participates in all the agricultural activities in the family. Through participant observation and constant dialogue with the farm family, the student is able to analyse the situation of the farmer, including describing the system, identifying its strengths and weaknesses, and proposing solutions to improve the farm. The student prepares a detailed report in Kiswahili which is reviewed and discussed with the family, in order to come to an agreement.

This technique has helped very much in:

(a) Bringing the students and farmers physically and psychologically closer.
(b) Enabling the students to learn directly from farmers based on their long experiences with the local farming system, and likewise enabling the farmers to learn some modern knowledge from the students.
(c) Giving the students a practical and realistic perspective on smallholder agriculture.
(d) Giving an opportunity to the students to improve on their classroom learning in light of practical experiences.

However, where many students are involved, practical difficulties of assigning them to farm families will arise, especially if they all have to go to the same location.

## Establishment of Outreach Stations

Traditionally, outreach stations have been established by major research centres to facilitate research in different agro-ecological zones: particularly adaptive, on-farm type of research. However, such stations have not necessarily resulted in higher involvement of farmers in the research process. In the UMADEP project an attempt is being made to establish an outreach station which will not only facilitate research and extension, but will also facilitate the participation of farmers in this process. Facilities are therefore being established in Mgeta with the following purposes:

(a) To provide accommodation to SUA staff, students and government officials whenever they need to go and work in the villages, as well as whenever they need a place for quiet reflection;
(b) To provide accommodation to those farmers who will be visiting the area from other distant places;
(c) To provide facilities for holding meetings, workshops, seminars or cultural programmes either by SUA staff and students or any other outside group, as well as by the local farmers themselves, and;
(d) To provide office facilities to facilitate co-ordination between and amongst the different farmers' groups, SUA researchers, government extension workers and other interested parties.

The facilities, which will be called the Mgeta House of Agriculture, will be owned by SUA, but will be managed jointly by SUA and the farmers in the area. It is hoped that through such facilities, SUA researchers and students will be closer to the farmers, while farmers will find it easier to participate in the various research and extension activities. The psychological barriers between professionals on the one hand and farmers on the other are also likely to be reduced. Nevertheless, the issues of how to sustain the activities of such an outreach station and how to take care of other agroecological zones will need to be addressed sooner rather than later.

## Conclusion

It would seem logical to link institutional and indigenous knowledge systems, since institutional research and extension are supposed to be getting closer to the users' concrete applications, while indigenous knowledge is becoming more universal and transmittable. However, resistance from both sides is not easy to overcome. Conservative behaviour can be observed from both sides and the conditions upon which to merge the two systems are still vague.

The actors in the process, researchers, extension workers and farmers, must first of all be convinced of the necessity of a communication channel

112

among them. This will have to be as a result of regular and sustained contact and collaboration. However, such contact should avoid the romance of a lonely researcher gleaning here and there for indigenous knowledge from some white-haired elders and publishing it in an obscure journal only read by its own editorial committee. Both institutional and indigenous knowledge are generated over a long period of time. The linkage between these two systems must therefore be based on long term relationships. The UMADEP project has tried to use different methods for creating and sustaining such long term relationships. Still there are some issues that need to be addressed in order to sustain and institutionalize the approach.

*What will Happen to 'Mainstream' Research?*

Institutional research is generally associated with the very noble aim of expanding the frontiers of knowledge and is characterized by a high degree of freedom to the researcher to determine the research agenda. On the other hand, this freedom is in reality defined by sponsors - governments, international research agencies, private companies, non-governmental organizations etc. Each of them sets conditions for financial support and therefore substantially influences the 'researchers' freedom'. One may therefore ask, should not farmers also influence the research agenda since this research is presumably aimed at solving their problems? Mainstream research cannot ignore the context in which it is funded and executed. So, how can researchers be more conscious of the farmers' needs and priorities when setting a research agenda?

*How to Synthesize, Systematize and Share Farmers' Indigenous Knowledge*

Most of the institutional researchers and extension workers lack the skills to synthesize, systematize and share indigenous knowledge. Interfaces between indigenous knowledge and institutional research include oral transmission such as roleplays and drama as well as visual media such as drawings, pictures and video. In every case, the interface aims at giving access to the same information to the different actors generally with different levels of education and at the same time. Perhaps these skills are best acquired through practical involvement.

Fora have to be created to share information gained from indigenous knowledge. Networks are effective tools which allow the flow of information amongst members. These are even more effective in sharing indigenous knowledge which is mostly undocumented. A network should link people from different spheres, professionals from different disciplines and farmers or farmers' leaders. In other words, such a network should give allowance for every member to communicate with people who are not of his/her kind. As in every human venture, such a network relies on the people's dedication at its creation but its efficiency should attract funds for its sustenance.

113

Whenever researchers and extension workers are seeking for the indigenous knowledge of a particular locality, they have to bear in mind the question of representativeness. In other words, who in the locality can give the most correct version. In many areas or sectors, there are no structures for communication flow amongst farmers. Who, therefore, can be a representative of the farmers? Who can be the bearer of the indigenous knowledge? Even where formal farmers' organizations exist, can these be viewed as the most representative sources of indigenous knowledge? These questions are open and remain a challenge for both professionals and farmers.

## References

Byerlee, D.K., Collinson, M, Winkelmann, D., Perrin, R., Biggs, S., Moscardi, E., Martinez, J., Harnington, L. and Benjamin A. (1980), *Planning Technologies Appropriate to Farmers' Concepts and Procedures*, CIMMYT, Mexico.

Chambers, R. (1983), *Rural Development 'Putting the First Last'*, Longman, Harlow.

Chonya, A.B.C. (1996), *Participatory Rural Development Appraisal in Tanda Village in the Uluguru Mountains*, SUA, Morogoro.

Collinson, M.P. (1984), 'On-Farm Research with a Systems-Perspective, as a Link between Farmers Technical Research and Extension', Paper presented at the Networkshop on Extension Methods and Research/Extension Linkage, Eldoret, Kenya, June, 1984.

Farrington, J. and Martin, A. (1988), *Farmers' Participation in Agricultural Research: A Review of Concepts and Practices*, ODI, London (Occasional Paper No. 9).

Gilla, A. (1993), *Uundaji wa Mtandao wa Vikundi vya Wakulima Tanzania (MVIWATA) Taarifa ya Mkutano*, MVIWATA, Morogoro.

Ki-Zerbo, J. (1992), 'Le développement clés en tête', in Ki-Zerbo (ed.), *La Natte des Autres: Pour un Développement Endogène en Afrique*, CODESRIA, Dakar, pp. 1-21.

Lassalle, T. and Mattee, A.Z. (1994), *Towards Sustainable Rural Development using the Participatory Approach: The Case of Mgeta Farmers*, SUA, Morogoro.

Lassalle, T., Kamuzora, F. and Shekilango, J. (1990), 'Getting Farmers' Confidence through Participatory Action in a Horticultural Development Programme in Upper Mgeta, Morogoro District', in Mattee, A.Z., Evers, G. and Mollel, N.M. (eds.), *The Role of Agricultural Institutions in the Advancement of Small Farmers in Developing Countries*, SUA, Morogoro, pp. 149-94.

Masihara, S., Worman, F. and Heinrich, G. (1988), 'The Role of Farming Testing Groups in Research and Extension: Some Experiences in Botswana', Paper presented at the 8th Annual Farming Systems Symposium at the University of Arkansas, October 1988.

Mattee, A.Z. (1993), 'Strengthening Communication between Academics and Rural Communities: The Experience of SUA'. Paper presented at the International Workshop on Improving the Level of Communication between Farmers, Professionals and Policy-makers, SUA, Morogoro, September 1993.

Mattee, A.Z. and Lassalle, T. (1994), *Diverse and Linked Farmers' Organisations in Tanzania*, ODI, London (Agricultural Administration Network Paper no. 50b).

Mgumia, A.H. (1993), *The Use of Sugar Cane Strips to Control Soil Erosion in Kikeo Ward*, UMADEP, SUA, Morogoro.

Norman, D. and Modiakgotla, E. (1990), *Ensuring Farmers' Input into the Research Process within an Institutional Setting*, ODI, London (Agricultural Administration Network Paper no. 16).

Norman, D., Baker, D., Heinrich, G. and Worman, F. (1988), 'Technology Development and Farmer Groups: Experience from Botswana', *Experimental Agriculture*, 24, pp. 321-31.

Noy, F. (1990), 'Shangila Matunda' [videofilm], Department of Agricultural Education and Extension, SUA, Morogoro.

Richards, P. (1985), *Indigenous Agricultural Revolution: Food and Ecology in West Africa*, Hutchinson, London.

Richards, P. (1986), *Coping with Hunger: Hazard and Experiment in an African Farming System*, Allen and Unwin, London.

SCOM (1991), *Strengthening Communication Programme* [brochure], SUA, Morogoro.

Waters-Bayer, A. (1989), *Participaory Technology Development in Ecologically Oriented Agriculture: Some Approaches and Tools*, ODI, London (Agricultural Administration Network Paper no. 7).

# 8 Indigenous Knowledge and Natural Resources Management

G. C. KAJEMBE AND D.F. RUTATORA

## Introduction

In June 1992, the United Nations Conference on Environment and Development (UNCED) held in Rio de Janeiro discussed the urgent need to develop mechanisms that would lead to the protection of the earth's biodiversity. Many of the documents signed at the UNCED reflect the need to conserve the indigenous knowledge that is being lost in many communities (Warren, Liebenstein and Slikkeveer, 1993).

Although indigenous knowledge (IK) has been the subject of academic concern ever since anthropologists started their work in tropical countries, it is only recently that its role in natural resource management has been acknowledged (Richards, 1980; Padoch and Vayda, 1983; FAO, 1990; Barrow, 1991; Kajembe, 1994). It should be noted that the survival of the local people has depended on their ecological awareness and adaptation. Much of the indigenous knowledge is based on accurate, detailed and thoughtful observations collected and passed over many generations (Chambers, Pacey and Thrupp, 1989).

Local communities in Tanzania are repositories of vast accumulations of indigenous knowledge and experience. The disappearance of this knowledge is a loss for the country and for the international community. It is a terrible irony that as formal development reaches deeply into the rural areas, it tends to destroy the only cultures that have proved to thrive in these environments (World Commission on Environment and Development, 1987).

Much can be learned from local people which may prove useful for natural resource management in Tanzania. Modern technologies usually come in bits and pieces, and in order to fit them effectively into and build upon the local systems, we need to have a thorough understanding of indigenous knowledge (Brokensha and Riley, 1980). Indeed, there is a wealth of useful information stored in indigenous knowledge, for example in respect of utilization of local plant species, ecological requirements of different plant species and possibilities for stimulating their regeneration.

## Underlying View of Indigenous Knowledge (IK)

The term 'indigenous knowledge' is used synonymously with 'traditional' and 'local' knowledge to differentiate  the knowledge developed by a given community from the international knowledge system, sometimes also called

116

'Western' system (Anon., 1993), generated through universities and research centres. Indigenous knowledge systems relate to the ways members of a given community define and classify phenomena in physical/natural, social and ideational environments.

There are six underlying views of indigenous knowledge. These are not mutually exclusive; they overlap to some degree. Some people lean towards one view without necessarily rejecting the validity of the others. The six views might be conveniently labelled as those of the scientist, the development agent, the facilitator, the conservationist, the political advocate and the capitalist (Anon., 1993).

Parallel to and intertwined with the rapidly advancing body of international, scientific knowledge are bodies of local knowledge derived from the empirical trial-and-error of people struggling to survive over centuries. Little of this knowledge has been recorded or validated by the scientific methods. Most is localized, transmitted orally, and typically not codified. The scientist recognizes this and wishes to understand and incorporate the indigenous knowledge in the scientific corpus (Mgeni, 1993). Part of this desire is to understand the basis for indigenous knowledge systems as, for instance, in anthropological research. Part is the wish to validate and use the information, for instance, in identifying plants that may contain hitherto unknown active ingredients for drugs.

A second source of the interest in IK comes from the development community. Farmers are acutely attuned to their natural and social environment such as soils, climates, and markets. Natural resource management recommendations derived from international knowledge systems seldom fully fit local needs and often prescribe practices that are costly to maintain. The international system has shown little appreciation of this local environment. Farmers steeped in a different system of knowledge and beliefs find recommendations couched in scientific language difficult to understand. Many in the development community have come to accept the likelihood of frequent failures in their work if it does not incorporate indigenous needs, concepts and resources. So the development community needs to understand local systems, especially the local communication process. The goal is to identify, verify, and adapt IK and to promote it in areas where conditions are similar (Mgeni, 1993).

A third underlying school of thought hold the view of IK as a resource that local people can use to further their own development. Such a view sees the role of an extension agent as facilitating and stimulating farmers' indigenous practices (Kajembe, 1994, p. 137), and encouraging the interchange of information among them (Richards, 1975). This contrasts with the nearly universal (and often unsuccessful) current role of the extension agent, which is to try to persuade farmers to adopt technologies developed elsewhere. The role of the researcher is also transformed into one that responds to and supports the farmers' research agenda, rather than being independent of it.

A fourth view comes from the emphasis on environment and conservation that is now widespread in the world. The disappearance of forests and other natural resources, and the disruption of nature's self-regulating ability, parallel the disruption of traditional societies. The perspective focuses somewhat more heavily on minor, traditional groups such as the Dorobo of northern Tanzania. But there is also a concern for the disappearance of the knowledge base of all societies, under the onslaughts of urbanization, industrialization and Western culture. Support remains for the pursuit of knowledge per se, but normative judgements are also made, and there is an interest in preserving knowledge, in situ, for its own sake. The isolation of the indigenous system, so that it will remain unspoiled, is felt to be of value. Thus, there is potential conflict between intervention to determine knowledge, and isolation to prevent the introduction of change. Rather than the 'neutral' scientific interest in knowledge, the conservationist will add an element of advocacy for retention.

A fifth source of interest in IK derives from North-South conflict and tensions. The South's often expressed frustration with, and feelings of, exploitation by the North are translated into a perception of local people being suppressed by the wealthy, developed nations. Political advocates espouse the protection of rights, the end of exploitation, and exploiters' obligation to pay for past transgressions (Kihiyo and Senkondo, 1994). The advocate denies the scientist's ideal of sharing knowledge for mutual betterment, instead seeing the North-South relationship as having potential for exploitation. Sanctions are advocated in order to protect the weaker against the intrusions of the stronger: for instance by introducing patent rights for indigenous knowledge in order to prevent uncompensated exploitation by outsiders (Kaoneka and Ngaga, 1994).

Last but not least is the capitalist view of IK. The capitalist sees IK as a resource to be tapped by outsiders in pursuit of profit. Examples of this are the 'chemical prospecting' of tropical plants by Western drug companies and germplasm collection by crop breeding firms. Both may draw on the knowledge of local people to identify promising sites, species, and uses. The capitalist makes a large investment in developing, say, a new drug or crop variety from such germplasms. This, it is argued, dwarfs the original local contribution and justifies the high prices that the new products command.

Aspiring to the scientist's quest for knowledge and free access to information, universities and herbariums are often unwitting partners to the capitalist. The political advocate's contrasting position is essentially a reaction against the activities of the capitalists and their scientist partners.

Key to the capitalist's success is the potential for developing a commodity that can be bought and sold. Some types of knowledge are more readily commodified than others; hybrid seeds and drugs are two examples. Other forms of IK, such as planting techniques and soil classifications, are less easy to convert into cash, and so are of less interest to the capitalist.


**Indigenous Knowledge and Sustainable Natural Resource Management in Tanzania**

Tanzania has over 120 ethnic groups engaged in cultivation/farming, agro-pastoralism and nomadic pastoralism. Hunting, fishing and gathering are equally important in rural Tanzania (Mgeni, 1993). Many of these activities have a link with natural resource management. Indigenous knowledge has evolved in each of these ethnic groups. As a result, the amount and types of indigenous knowledge existing in Tanzania on the subject of natural resources are large, diversified and still largely undocumented. Kajembe (1994, p. 15) underscored this fact by pointing out that analysis of indigenous natural resource management systems has barely started in Tanzania and that much of the literature is anecdotal or depends on secondary sources.

Besides the limited work so far done in Tanzania, the potential of indigenous knowledge in managing natural resources is widely acknowledged. For example, Kajembe in his 1994 study, carried out in Dodoma and Lushoto districts, identified two categories of indigenous forest management systems: household-based and supra-household or communally based. Unlike forest management systems at the household level, those which operated at the communal level were found to be rather passive. They consisted mainly of the regulation of who had the right of access to particular forest/tree resources and who were excluded. In other words, they were more protection-oriented than use-oriented. In short, their intentions were not to achieve biological goals such as tree/forest regeneration. In such cases, limiting the number of people who take the product from the forest may reduce overall demands and will have biological consequences, but this is an accidental outcome. In the same study, the Sambaa of Lushoto district were found to have elaborate indigenous/traditional forest management systems. One finds that, although their reasoning was different from scientific thought, the consequences were frequently the same. It was for example traditionally forbidden to clear forests on hilltops and along watercourses as these clusters of trees were thought to attract water. Traditional forest reserves are accordingly often found high up on the hill slopes or along watercourses.

Kajembe also found that both the Gogo of Dodoma and Sambaa of Lushoto had sacred tree species (Table 8.1). Nobody was allowed to feel these trees or even cut branches without first having sacrificed an animal. In Lushoto district, only one sacred tree species (*Ficus thonningii*) was mentioned by farmers but a number of ritual forests were identified.

Certain forests have an important religious function. Nobody is allowed to take away trees or branches from such forests. To the people these forest groves are animated with power and may, if managed and treated properly, bring well-being to the people and livestock. By conducting their rituals and ceremonies in the forest, people domesticate it and transform the inauspicious and wild into a human, culture world. By using the products of the forest and by approaching it through their rituals, the Sambaa of Lushoto extend their culture into the 'empty' forest lands, filling it with social and religious significance.

## Table 8.1 Traditionally protected tree species in Dodoma Urban and Lushoto Districts

| District | Species | Sacrifice required |
|---|---|---|
| Dodoma | *Acacia tortilis* | goat or bull |
| | *Adansonia digitata* | goat or bull |
| | *Calyptroothea taitensis* | goat or bull |
| | *Combretum speicatum* | bull |
| | *Commiphora mollis* | bull |
| | *Cordia gharaf* | bull or goat |
| | *Faidherbia albida* | bull or black sheep |
| | *Ficus allis choudae* | goat or bull |
| | *Lannea stuhlmanii* | bull or goat |
| | *Vitex iringensis* | bull or black sheep |
| Lushoto | *Ficus thonningii* | bull or goat |

*Source:* Kajembe, 1994, p. 115.

As discussed in this paper, indigenous forest management systems at the suprahousehold level consist mainly of sets of use-rights. Therefore it needs no emphasis to say that the existence of a group of people with recognized use-rights is an essential feature of these systems. Indigenous use right exists outside the national legal system. Use-rights are claims to the right to use specified resources, such rights being regarded as legitimate by people in the same area. In many cases, secondary or residual rights are also recognized for people outside the primary user group (Kajembe, 1994, p. 125). The secondary rights may involve restricted access to products available to primary users or a restricted time framework for collection of the products. The rationale for the recognition of use-rights may vary. In some cases, but not in others, rights are inherited by members of a particular clan or lineage. In Dodoma urban district for example, every case of indigenous use-rights to common forest resources appeared to be based on residence rather than on membership of a kin group. In Lushoto district however, kin group membership was the factor determining use-rights to ritual forests.

Another study, conducted by Barrow, Lugeye and Fry (1992) showed that the Sukuma of Mwanza and Shinyanga regions used to have traditional grazing reserves called *ngitiri*, in order to have access to pasture during the dry season. The *ngitiri* areas within the village borders are closed at the beginning of the wet season. During scarcity of pasture, the *ngitiri* is opened for grazing. There are two types of *ngitiri* : family (household), and communally owned. The opening of *ngitiri* is done by sections, that is, one section is completely grazed before the next section is opened. The village maintains strict control over the communal *ngitiri* and severe sanctions are imposed for trespassing herders. Although the *ngitiri* system has been under pressure and it is disappearing, there is still some scope for promoting it and making it more effective for sustainable natural resource management.

# Rural People's Experiments

Perhaps the least recognized aspect of rural people's knowledge in Tanzania is its experimental nature. In fact the use of the word 'indigenous knowledge' itself may create an impression of knowledge that is static, after it has proved to be useful through countless generations (Kajembe, 1990). However, in reality this knowledge is constantly evolving and being updated with new information.

Rhodes and Bebbington (1988) identify three kinds of farmer experiments: curiosity experiments; problem solving experiments; and adaptation experiments. They give an example of a Peruvian farmer who simply out of curiosity did an experiment to test whether apical dominance would affect the number and size of potato tubers; the results might some day have been useful but that was not the motivation. The propensity to experiment to solve problems, they argue, may be pronounced in areas of diversified agriculture and poor extension services.

Two kinds of adaptation experiments are recognized: testing an unknown technology in a known environment; and testing a known technology in a new environment. Studying experiments as undertaken by rural people gives understanding of their 'sense making' activities (Brouwers, 1993).

Scientists tend to regard an experiment as an inquiry during which all the variables are highly controlled except those under study. Farmers differ from the scientists' way of experimenting in the sense that the experiment in question has to be included in daily circumstances (Kajembe, 1994, p. 14). Richards (1988) concludes that in recent literature the experimenting, innovative, adaptive peasant farmer is now accepted as a norm rather than as the exception. His own pioneering work has made a substantial contribution to this change of attitude. He has given numerous examples from West Africa including innovations in labour organization, rice variety selection, integration of tree-crop and rice cultivation, and intercropping in swamps (Richards, 1985).

However, besides all the available evidence, most scientists in Tanzania dealing with natural resource management are still sceptical about farmers' knowledge and experimentation, partly because farmers seldom record their discoveries and do not attach their names and patents to their invention. Chambers (1983) reports an anecdote that in Nigeria, a scientist made a breakthrough in yam propagation. Yam propagation is normally vegetative, but the scientist managed under experimental conditions to breed some yams from seeds, as he believed for the first time. However, by chance he encountered a farmer who claimed that he had himself succeeded in doing that and he had also discovered, as had the scientist, that although the first generation of tubers were small, second and subsequent generations were of normal size. Chambers concludes this anecdote by pointing out that the scientist just thanked God that farmers did not compete in writing scientific papers.

The readiness of small farmers to experiment and 'innovate' on their own has been obscured by the preoccupation with natural resource management which is normally conducted through official organizations. The fact is that experiments that farmers manage themselves with regard to natural resources are normally very successful. In Kakamega district in Kenya, several experiments were initiated by farmers in response to a fuelwood project. *Sesbania sesban* trees were planted within a field of napier grass to find out the effects of trees on grass production. The results showed that the trees do not affect grass production significantly. In fact fodder production was very much increased (Van Gelder, Enyola and Mung'ala, 1986).

### Dynamics of Indigenous Natural Resource Management Systems

Communities and individual households in Tanzania differ in the extent to which they practice natural resource management. Depending on the management strategy, they have sometimes been actively involved, for instance in seedling propagation and in intercropping trees between agricultural crops (Kajembe, 1994, p. 52). Other groups have been much more passive about their management practices; for instance, by limiting the number of livestock grazing in a given area. These indigenous/traditional practices have developed as responses to particular situations, reflecting a variety of cultural, social, economic, political, ecological and demographic factors. These practices are often historically and situationally dynamic rather than static. They evolve through time as a result of adaptive strategies of farmers. In such strategies the farmers strive to adjust the use of their household resources to changed conditions. The latter may take several forms: changed ecological conditions, such as soil degradation or other forms of environmental decline; or changed technological conditions caused by the introduction of new technologies in the form of new species, or improved tools and machinery; changed economic conditions such as development of new markets and increased commercialization: changed price relations of natural resource products and their needed inputs; and changed socio-political conditions, for example changed labour or land tenure arrangements including gradual privatization of land, population growth, and greater involvement of government in rural development.

In such adaptive strategies, farmers will normally adopt a 'micro-economic' orientation. They will adjust the use of their household resources in a way which they perceive as resulting in their best possible welfare. Such changes may involve moving into or out of, or intensifying or improving certain land use systems. Such changes in land use practices will also be reflected in changes in methods and/or intensity of natural resource management.

In some parts of Tanzania, the effectiveness of indigenous management systems has been undermined by intense, complex and interrelated changes. Pressures on natural resources have been building up gradually and almost imperceptibly because of these changes. But again in other cases, the changed rural conditions resulted in an intensification of natural resource management. It is clear from this discussion that rural people can respond quickly and appropriately not only to the stresses which their environments periodically offer, but to new opportunities as well (Vayda, 1979). In adapting to changes in their environments, local people will of course not only vary the products that they use, but also the subsistence techniques they employ, the amount of labour they expend, and other relevant socio-economic factors.

## Conclusion

To insist on the indigenous 'science' of farmers is not to revive the eighteenth century European idea of the 'noble savage' or in the words of Chambers (1983) to reincarnate him as a rational peasant whose actions are perfectly judged exercises in optimization that even well-informed computers can only struggle to simulate.

Local people have much to learn from scientists, but so do scientists have much to learn from farmers. Lines of communication have not been effectively opened in either direction. Mnzava (1983) underscored this fact by pointing out that professionals are so busy trying to transfer ideas to farmers, that in the end they do not have energy left to hear what ideas farmers also want to put into their heads. In most cases, professionals have attempted to impose inappropriate solutions from outside with little knowledge of small-scale farmers' priorities or realities. The farmers have ignored such advice and, more often than not, have been right in doing so. Professionals should be aware not only that farmers are making decisions under the influence of different sets of priorities but that they have also to contend with tremendous uncertainly. To come up with a fixed package of technology is not only 'arrogance'; it is 'ignorance'.

In many cases it may be advisable to integrate indigenous management systems with new interventions rather than to introduce radically new measures (Wiersum, 1989). A basic principle for introducing interventions to rural communities is that they should be based on an understanding of existing systems, as well as on the understanding of what makes intervention necessary.

## References

Anon. (1993), 'Background to the International Symposium on Indigenous Knowledge and Sustainable Development', *Indigenous Knowledge and Development Monitor*, 1 (ii), pp. 2-10.

Barrow, E.G.C. (1991), *Trees and Pastoralists: The Case of Pokot and Turkana*, ODI, London (Forestry Network paper no. 6b).

Barrow, E.G.C., Lugeye, S.C., and Fry, P. (1992), *Hifadhi Ardhi Shinyanga (HASHI) Evaluation Report*, Ministry of Tourism, Natural Resources and Environment, NORAD, Dar es Salaam.

Brokensha, D. and Riley, B.W. (1980), 'Introduction to Cash Crops in Marginal Areas of Kenya', in Bates, H.H. and Lofchie, M.F. (eds.), *Indigenous Knowledge Systems and Development*, Univesity Press of America, Washington DC, pp. 244-74.

Brouwers, J.H.A.M. (1993), 'Rural People's Response to Soil Fertility Decline: The Adja Case', Agricultural University, Wageningen, PhD Dissertation.

Chambers, R. (1983), *Rural Development: Putting the Last First*, Longman, Harlow.

Chambers, R., Pacey, A. and Thrupp, L.A. (1989), *Farmer First: Farmer Innovation and Agricultural Research*, Intermediate Technology Publications, London.

FAO (1990), *Community Forestry: Headers' Decision-making in Natural Resource Management in Arid and Semi-Arid Africa*, FAO, Rome (Community Forestry Note no. 4).

Kajembe, G.C. (1990), 'Indigenous Management Systems as a Basis for Community Forestry in Tanzania: An Overview', Paper presented at the DSI/ICE Research Seminar on 11 April 1990, Morogoro.

Kajembe, G.C. (1994), 'Indigenous Management Systems as a Basis for Community Forestry in Tanzania: A Case Study of Dodoma Urban and Lushoto Districts', Agricultural University, Wageningen (Tropical Resource Management Papers no. 6).

Kaoneka, A.R.S. and Ngaga, Y.M. (1994), 'Environmental Pollution Policy and Equity Distribution Effects with Particular Reference to Natural Forest Resources Management in Tanzania', Paper presented at the First Convocation Workshop, SUA, Morogoro, 26-7 July 1994.

Kihiyo, V.B.M.S. and Senkondo, E.M. (1994), 'Agricultural Production, Deforestation and Environment: A Forester's Viewpoint from the South', Paper presented at the First Convocation Workshop, SUA, Morogoro, 26-7 July 1994.

Mgeni, A.S.M. (1993), 'Ethnoforestry and Sustainable Forest Management in Rural Tanzania Development', *Advancement in Forest Inventory and Forest Management Sciences*, Forestry Research Institute of the Republic of Korea, Seoul, pp. 495-512.

Mnzava, E.M. (1983), *Tree Planting in Tanzania: A Voice from Villagers*, Dar es Salaam.

Padoch, C. and Vayda, A.P. (1983), 'Patterns of Resource Use and Human Settlement in Tropical Forests', in Golley, F.B., Lieth, H. and Werger, A. (eds.), *Tropical Rain Forest Ecosystems, Structure and Function* (2 vols), Elsevier, Amsterdam, vol. 1, pp. 301-13.

Rhodes, R. and Bebbington, A. (1988), *Farmers Who Experiment: An Untapped Resource for Agricultural Research and Development?*, International Potato Center, Lima.

Richards, P. (1975), 'Alternative Strategies for the African Environment: Folk Ecology as a Basis for Community-oriented Agricultural Development', in Richards, P. (ed.), *African Environment: Problems and Prospective*, International African Institute, London, pp. 102-114.

Richards, P. (1980), 'Community Environmental Knowledge in African Rural Development', in Brokensha, D., Warren, D.M. and Werner, O. (eds.), *Indigenous Knowledge Systems and Development*, University Press of America, Washington DC, pp. 181-94.

Richards, P. (1985), *Indigenous Agricultural Revolution: Food and Ecology in West Africa*, Hutchinson, London.

Richards, P. (1988), 'Experimenting Farmers and Agricultural Research', Paper prepared for ILEIA Workshop on Participatory Technology Development, ILEIA, Leiden.

Van Gelder, B., Enyola, K.L. and Mung'ala, P.M. (1986), 'Developing Traditional Agroforestry Practices on Farms in Makamega District', Paper for Kenya Woodfuel Development Programme/Beyer Institute, Nairobi.

Vayda, A.P. (1979), 'Human Ecology and Economic Development in Kalimantan and Sumatra', *Borneo Research Bulletin*, 2, pp. 23-32.

Warren, D.M., Liebenstein, G.W. and Slikkerveer, I.J. (1993), 'Networking for Indigenous Knowledge', *Indigenous Knowledge and Development Monitor*, 1 (i), pp. 3-4.

Wiersum, K.F. (1989), 'Forestry and Rural Development', Lecture course F550-121, Department of Forestry, Agricultural University, Wageningen.

World Commission on Environment and Development (1987), *Our Common Future*, Oxford University Press, London.

# 9   The Implications of Farmers' Indigenous Knowledge for Sustainable Agricultural Production in Tanzania

SIZYA LUGEYE

## Introduction

In June 1992, the United Nations Conference on Environment and Development (UNCED) met in Rio de Janeiro and discussed the urgent need to develop mechanisms that would lead to protecting the earth's biodiversity. Many of the documents signed by the UNCED reflect the need to conserve the knowledge of the environment that is being lost in many communities. There has always been indigenous knowledge; proof of its existence and value lies in the fact that many millions of people in the developing countries continue to feed themselves by pursuing agriculture in a difficult environment. We now know and accept that the smallholder farmer and his farming system must be the centrepiece of the decision-maker as well as the operational focus of research scientists. We also acknowledge that these problems are probably the most daunting that the developed community has so far faced (Warren, Liebenstein and Slikkerveer, 1993).

The daunting nature of these problems is indicated by the fact that the overwhelming majority of the population in most developing countries (including Tanzania) are small-scale farmers working on less than two hectares each. In Tanzania for example the knowledge systems of the farmers have never been recorded systematically in written form, hence they are not easily accessible to researchers, extension workers, development practitioners and other farmers. Despite this seemingly gloomy situation, there is ample evidence that a growing number of planners, policymakers, extensionists and researchers are recognizing the fact that an understanding of indigenous knowledge can play an important facilitating role in establishing dialogue between the rural population and development workers.

## The Nature and Meaning of Indigenous Knowledge

'Indigenous knowledge' is the sum of experiences and knowledge of a given ethnic group that forms the basis for decision-making in the face of familiar problems. It is a mixture of knowledge created endogenously within the society and that which is acquired from outside but is then observed, and integrated within the society. The situation is not static but is continuously changing and there is an inherent capacity for absorbing relevant new knowledge.

The indigenous knowledge of farm families is more than just agricultural practices or even ethnoscience. It involves interaction with the priorities and values of the society and with the methods of coping in an uncertain and changing environment.

## Indigenous Knowledge and Extension

The use of indigenous knowledge in extension involves the recognition that this is partly indigenous, and partly of external origin. The outside knowledge is incorporated into the store of indigenous knowledge only if it is compatible and considered relevant by the traditional practitioners. For many centuries traditional farm families have been involved in experimenting and adapting existing practices. Furthermore, new crop varieties or ideas have been and still are borrowed from neighbouring groups. In more recent years the base of indigenous knowledge has been affected in varying degrees by formal scientific output, which is a product of distant cultures. The degree of assimilation has varied. It is however this input and interaction that forms the basis of using indigenous knowledge in extension (Sharland, 1991).

However, in order to understand these indigenous management systems and their effect on agriculture and the environment it is necessary to conduct an in-depth study; such a study is justified for the following reasons:

1. Indigenous knowledge is widely applied by the rural people as is considered appropriate in their ecological conditions; and it indicates their success in doing things (Brokensha, Warren and Werner, 1980).
2. Farmers have important information to communicate to scientists. Chambers (1983) observed that the scientific community normally takes issues to farmers but very little effort has been made to listen and learn from the farmers' innovations.
3. Extension packages and regional planning would be realistic if they were based on the understanding of peoples' way of doing things given the resources available to them.

## Farmers' Agricultural Practice and the Environment

Studies on agricultural practice from the Sokoine Extension Project revealed that most farmers in the Morogoro and Kilosa Districts were still following traditional agricultural practices (Ngetti, 1989; Flatley, 1980). Similarly a study by Lugeye (1991) revealed the same results. The main practices carried out by farmers in the study area are summarized in Table 9.1. The data on Table 9.1 show that over half of the farmers interviewed used a monocropping pattern for the main crops. These results were expected because extension workers are still recommending a monocropping pattern for growing maize, rice, cotton and sunflower. Similarly, the data show that

**Table 9.1    Practices used by farmers in Morogoro and Kilosa Districts**

**(n = 300)**

| Farm practice | Number | Per Cent |
|---|---|---|
| Monocropping | 165 | 55.0 |
| Intercropping | 127 | 42.3 |
| Hand hoe | 286 | 95.3 |
| Tractor | 150 | 50.0 |
| No fertilizer | 286 | 95.3 |
| No insecticide/pesticide | 186 | 62.0 |
| No use of sacks for storage | 180 | 60.0 |

*Source*: Lugeye, 1991, p. 165.

a large proportion of farmers in the Morogoro and Kilosa Districts use traditional farm practices including intercropping and cultivation by hand hoes. They mostly do not apply fertilizers, insecticides and pesticides, and do not store their produce in sacks. Despite the importance of these farm practices for environmental conservation, the extension service recommendations are not supportive.

Furthermore in a study by Lugeye, Shio and Haule (1992) on indigenous knowledge of farmers in Kilombero District, farmers were asked to identify the traditional methods used in growing the major crops. The results are presented in Table 9.2.

According to data in Table 9.2, a majority of farmers used traditional practices for growing paddy, maize, and cassava. Specific traditional practices were mentioned for each crop and agricultural activity. These include most of the crop husbandry practices.

In order to understand what agricultural practices were used, farmers were asked to indicate these for each crop. The data presented in Table 9.3 is a summary of the indigenous farm practices for paddy in the study area in Kilombero. Similar results were obtained for maize and cassava.

Further analysis of the data from this study indicated that most agricultural activities were evidently carried out using special traditional tools which were locally made. The data also revealed that most of the tools were still available and still used in farming.

128

**Table 9.2  Percentages of farmers who practised traditional methods for each major crop**

Agricultural Practices (% of farmers using)

| Crop | Land Preparat ion | Plant- ing | Weed- ing | Fertili- zer Appli- cation | Vermin- Pest Disease Control | Harvest -ing | Storage |
|---|---|---|---|---|---|---|---|
| Paddy | 91.4 | 91.4 | 91.4 | 28 | 82 | 91.4 | 91 |
| Maize | 98 | 98 | 98 | 25 | 98 | 98 | 98 |
| Cassava | 54 | 54 | 54 | 6 | 11.4 | 48 | 1 |
| Sweet Potatoes | 28 | 28 | 28 | 2 | 8 | 13.3 | 4 |
| Bananas | 24 | 24 | 24 | 2 | 18 | 21 | 4 |
| Simsim | 3 | 3 | 1 | - | - | - | 3 |
| Cotton | 11.4 | 11.4 | 11.4 | 2 | 95 | 11.4 | 11 |
| Sugar Cane | 7 | 7 | 3 | 1 | 1 | 11.4 | 7 |

*Source*: Lugeye, Haule and Shio, 1992, p. 15.

## The Use of Indigenous Seeds

Discussions with farmers in the study area revealed that there were many indigenous seeds which were collected and used. There were seeds available for almost all crops. For paddy alone more than 30 different names of

**Table 9.3  Indigenous agricultural practices for paddy - Kilombero District**

| Land Preparation | Planting | Weeding | Fertilizer Application | Vermin, Pest Disease Control | Harvesting | Storage |
|---|---|---|---|---|---|---|
| Use of machetes | Broad- casting | Hand | Burying crop residue | Traps | Hand | Local structure |
| (Chengo)[1] Burning | Dibbing | Hoe | Following | Hunting Fire | Shells Knives | Ngoko and kichanja[1] |
| Handhoe | Trans- planting | | shift Culti- vation | Dcaring Uprooting Burning | | |

*Source*: Lugeye, Haule and Shio, 1992, p. 29.

129

indigenous seeds were mentioned. The following is a list of indigenous paddy seeds found in Kilombero District.

**Table 9.4   List of paddy indigenous seeds (local names)**

| Joho | Buga,aga,a | Dunduli | Faya | Bungale |
|---|---|---|---|---|
| Jambo twende | Rangi | Rangimblili | Kihogo | Kihogo rangi |
|  | Mdala mpati | Kamecha | Kayuki | Myayanga |
| Kingoma | Sindano | Kikweta | Tule na Bwana | Usiniguse |
| Masagati | Kifuka | Kisaki | Nyumbu | Kikopa cha mbega |
| Nambani | Mosi Lingwaya | Koge kikalati | Kiwanja | Lingalangale |
|  |  |  |  | Maninembo |
| Msusi wa Nguku | Karafuu | Sira kanjunguu |  | Limunga |
| Meli | Faa Maria | Mbega | Mzinaga | Njakalo |

*Source:* Lugeye, Haule and Shio, 1992, p. 32.

### Farmers' Indigenous Knowledge on Meteorological Information

The data from the study in Itakara District by Lugeye, Haule and Shio (1992) shows that farmers used nine major ways of identifying and recording of meteorological information. These included:

Farmers' observation of changes in trees and plants
Signs and activities of specific insects
Signs, presence and activities of specific birds
Stars in the sky
Activities of ants
Fishing activities and availability of specific types of fish
Farmers' monthly local calendar
Occurrence of winds, thunderstorms and lightning
Traditional worship and prayers
Harvesting of paddy (periods or season)
Temperature changes and fluctuations

Farmers reported using these ways in combination or individually to identify and provide meteorological information.

### Findings from Agro-Pastoralists in Shinyanga Region

In Shinyanga, the rising number of livestock and of the human population exert increasing pressure on the land, and environmental conditions are steadily deteriorating. Shinyanga today is experiencing serious soil erosion, water shortage, and drought, and a serious shortage of grazing land (Barrow, Lugeye and Fry, 1992; Kilahama, 1994; Shao, Mboma and Semakafu, 1992). Dense woodlands have been cleared to eradicate tsetse flies and to enable additional farming and settlement needs to be met, resulting in a shortage of tree products. The Government of Tanzania is well aware of the increasing environmental problems facing the region and efforts are being made to contain the situation. This entails undertaking a catalytic role by working closely with the farmers and pastoralists to bring to their attention the extent of the overall problem of land degradation, and to involve them fully in formulating and implementing a solution right from the start. By understanding the features of the traditional farming systems, it is possible to obtain information that can help to develop appropriate land use strategies that are acceptable to the user. It follows, therefore, that working from within the community enables us to understand their basic needs, the problem faced, and limitations to their perception of the effects of land degradation. As a consequence the solutions designed become community-based, using low cost technologies. In order to address environmental problems, a land conservation project was started to initiate efforts to reclaim the seriously affected areas of Shinyanga Region.

On the other hand farmers and livestock keepers in Shinyanga have used some available arable and rangeland areas for farming and grazing cattle for many years. Some twenty years ago signs of soil erosion became apparent and while today there is some evidence of environmental degradation reflecting excessive stocking rates, the farmers know well how the system works. They have used it for centuries successfully, acquiring in the process ecological knowledge related to the use of soil, trees, livestock and rangeland to sustain their survival. However, external interventions, mainly through government extension packages, which for many years have taken a top-down approach, disrupted the traditional system with the introduction of new technologies to improve and sustain land productivity without taking into account the farmers' or pastoralists' knowledge of their environment, and their ways of doing things. Also, other factors such as population pressure have an impact. Before suggesting altered usage and management of the land resources to the farmers in Shinyanga it is appropriate that full attention be given to how the farmers and livestock keepers in Shinyanga have used them traditionally. This requires appraisal of their ecological knowledge about trees, soil, livestock and pasture (propagation, management and usage) within their environment, and further appreciation of how such knowledge is disseminated in the entire community.

According to the study by Barrow, Lugeye and Fry (1992), it appears that there is abundant indigenous ecological knowledge about trees, soil, livestock and pasture in Shinyanga Region. This was revealed by:

1. The use and management of *ngitiris*. These are areas set aside enclosed during the rainy season, but opened for grazing during the dry season. This system allows for the sustainable use of land. The *ngitiri* system can also be recognized as in-situ conservation of pastures and shrubs. A *ngitiri* is an area reserved to provide fodder and thatch for housing. The use of *ngitiri* in Sukumaland is of long standing. The areas intended for establishment of *ngitiri* were initially reserved for very old cattle and for young calves, which were unable to travel long distances. Similarly sick animals were kept on these lands so that they could be given better care (pasture, water and treatment) and also be kept isolated from other animals, hence controlling the spread of disease.

131

*Ngitiris* are also used for draught animals and lactating cows, especially in times of critical grass shortage. These areas are managed in a way that allows tree species to mature and later to become sources of forage and fodder. Grasses are allowed to grow to maturity to produce sufficient seeds for regeneration. *Ngitiris* are usually established in areas with Mbuga or Malango soils[2] because of their high water retention capacity. Herders avoided grazing cattle on these soils during the wet season because they became muddy and restricted cattle movement.

There are two types of reserves: family and village-communal *ngitiris*. Family reserves are made on arable land in fallow. Those established and managed by individual households are often closed for grazing between February and October. They are usually about one to two hectares each and are exclusively for private use; and no-one is allowed to graze the *ngitiri* without the owner's permission.

The village or communal *ngitiris* (now known as *hazina*) are much larger (about 200 ha.). Their use is regulated by the village headman with assistance from other village leaders. These areas are divided into sectors, and grazing is permitted in one section at a time. When grass is finished in one section the herd is allowed to move on to the next.

Herders in Sukumaland understand their environment and use the resources available to sustain their animals. However, with the expansion of cotton acreage, and after villagization, it was no longer possible to practice this system. In many parts of Sukumaland where the *ngitiri* system was in operation, it resulted in greater pressure on land and forests, contributing significantly to environmental degradation.

2. The practice of agroforestry. This is a collective name for land use systems and practices, where woody perennials are deliberately integrated with crops and/or animals on the same land management unit. The integration can be either by spatial mixture or in temporal sequence. There are normally both ecological and economic interventions between the woody and non-woody components in agroforestry (ICRAF, 1992).

In Sungamile Village in Isagehe Division of Kahama District a unique and interesting example of in-situ conservation and sustainable management of widely spaced indigenous trees on farm and grazing land in the village was found to be practised. The experience of this village provides lessons on the conservation process, in that there is recognition of the importance and value of indigenous tree species in various combinations, on agricultural and grazing land and around the homestead. In other parts of the village, agroforestry was practised through (1) planting trees along borders and around homesteads, (2) a silvo-pastoral system such as *ngitiri*, (3) a system of leaving widely-spaced indigenous trees on cropped land, and (4) hedgerow intercropping.

**Farmers' Use of Trees for Medicine**

In Shinyanga and many other rural communities, trees form a major source of traditional medicines for both humans and animals. Farmers were found to use leaves, tree barks, roots, and stems of specific tree species for medicines. The following is an example of local names for trees, and their usage:

**Table 9.5   Trees and their local uses in Shinyanga**

| Local name of trees | Local use |
| --- | --- |
| Misubala | Chewed for cleaning teeth, tongue |
| Misambila | Stomach troubles |
| Mwarobaini | Malaria etc. |
| Ngagani | Eye and ear |
| Mipelemese | Sweetener |
| Lumhamba | Udder washing for milk let down during milking a cow |
| Misungululu | Stomach troubles |
| Makale | To induce vomiting |
| Ndago | Perfume, applied on children's skin |
| Malumba | To kill mosquitoes, snakes |

**Findings from Farmers in Iringa Region**

In the training needs study carried out in Iringa, Lugeye and Muturi (1993) found that farmers were involved in a number of conservation and afforestation activities. The ranking of farmers according to the extent to which they used conservation practices is shown in Table 9.6.

**Table 9.6   Farmers' ranking of conservation practices**

| Planted area activity | Ranking |
| --- | --- |
| Around home compound | 1 |
| In fallow land | 2 |
| Around the farm | 3 |
| In the farm/conserving existing trees | 4 |
| Around water services | 5 |

*Source*: Lugeye and Muturi, 1993, p. 26.

Furthermore, Kihwele, Lwoga and Sarakyam (1993) found that beekeeping was practised in many villages using traditional techniques. However the use of bark hives was discouraged because of its destructive nature with regard to the plant species which are good for bee forage. The use of other alternative hives such as pots and log hives is being encouraged. Other traditional agricultural practices used by farmers in Iringa include the use of ridges, ploughing across the hills, making contours, modes of utilization of the farmyard and the incorporation of crop residues.

## Conclusion

The complexity of rural people's knowledge of their environment has astounded many researchers, who have also documented many contrasting and fascinating elements of indigenous knowledge. Despite the growing interest it has not been easy to relate this indigenous knowledge to extension teaching within systems of directed change. Application of indigenous knowledge in agricultural extension research and training has been rare, leading to scepticism as to its real value by agricultural scientists.

It has been revealed that there is a considerable body of indigenous knowledge among farmers. This includes:

Agricultural practices (e.g. seed collection, selection, ridging, intercropping cultivation, harvesting, storage)
Tree planting activities (selection of tree species, local uses of trees, planting trees in specific areas)
Agroforestry activities
Beekeeping
Livestock keeping
Pasture and grazing systems (*ngitiri* system)
Farmers' own research
Medicinal use (livestock and humans)

It is therefore recommended that extension training and research strategies be sensitized to identify and incorporate farmers' indigenous knowledge in preparing and communicating scientific recommendations. The training curricula in our institutions need to be revised to incorporate and to be sensitive to farmers' indigenous knowledge.

## Notes

1. *Chengo* is a traditional knife for cutting trees or grass. *Ngoko* is a raised bed or platform made of trees, used to store or pile unthreshed paddy.
2. *Mbuga* are black cotton soils. *Malango* are soils in lowlands, valleys of rivers or swampy farm land.

# References

Barrow, E. (1991), 'Building on Local Knowledge: The Challenge of Agroforestry for Pastoralists', *Today* 3(4), pp. 4-7.

Barrow, E., Lugeye, S. and Fry, P. (1992), 'Hifadhi Ardhi Sinyanga (HASHI) Evaluation Report', Ministry of Tourism, Natural Resources and Environment and NORAD, September 1992.

Brokensha, D., Warren, D.M. and Werner, O. (eds) (1980), *Indigenous Knowledge Systems and Development*, University Press of America, Washington DC.

Chambers, R. (1983), *Rural Development: Putting the Last First* , Longman, London.

Chambers, R., Pacey, A. and Thrupp, L.A. (1989), *Farmers First: Farmer Innovation and Agricultural Research*, Intermediate Technology Publications, London.

Flatley, M.J. (1980), 'An Analysis of Farm Family Households in the Transition from Subsistence Agriculture: Towards a Cash Economy in the Morogoro Region of Tanzania', MSc thesis, University College, Dublin.

ICRAF (1992), *ICRAF: The Way Ahead. Strategic Plan*, Nairobi.

Kihwele, D.V.N., Lwoga, P.D. and Sarakyam, E.W. (1993), 'Beekeeping is for Socio-economic Development and Environment Conservation. A Feasibility Study: Report on Involving Women in Beekeeping in Iringa Region, January 1992, HIMA, Iringa.

Kilahama, F.B. (1994), 'Indigenous Technical Knowledge - A Vital Tool for Rural Extension Strategies: A Case Study from Shinyanga Region, Tanzania', *Forests, Trees and People Newsletter*, 24 June 1994, pp. 30-35.

Lugeye, S. (1991), 'A Study of the Sokoine University Extension Project and its Impact on Extension Work at the Village Level in Tanzania', PhD thesis, University College, Dublin.

Lugeye, S. (1992a), 'Some Lessons from Hifadhi ya Mazingira Shinyanga (HASHI)', HIMA, Iringa.

Lugeye, S. (1992b), *The Training Programme for Shinyanga Soil Conservation and Afforestation Programme (SHISCAP), A  Research Report*, ICE, Morogoro.

Lugeye, S. and Muturi, S.N. (1993), 'Training Needs Assessment for HIMA'. A Consultancy Report submitted to HIMA Project, Iringa, September 1993', HIMA, Iringa.

Lugeye, S. C., Haule, M.D. and Shio, L.B. (1992), 'A Study of Farmers' Indigenous Knowledge in Agriculture in Kilombero District. A Research Report', ICE, Morogoro.

Ngetti, M.M.S. (1989), 'A Study of Agriculture Production Practices in the Morogoro Region in Tanzania', MSc (Agric.) thesis, University College, Dublin.

Shao, I.R., Mboma, L.M.R. and Semakafu, A.M. (1992), 'Traditional Management of Natural Resources with Emphasis on Women: The Case Study of Shinyanga Rural District', ITK, Dar es Salaam.

Sharland, R. (1991), 'ITK and Extension', in Best, J. and Sharland, R. (eds), *Bulletin 31, Agricultural Extension and Rural Development Department*, University of Reading, Reading.

Warren, D.M., Liebenstein, G.W. and Slikkerveer, L. (1993), 'Networking for Indigenous Knowledge', *Indigenous Knowledge and Development Monitor*, 1, pp. 3-4.

# 10 The Matengo Pit System of Farming and its Sustainability in the Matengo Highlands of Mbinga District, Tanzania

D. F. RUTATORA

## Introduction

Mbinga district, one of the districts of Ruvuma region, is divided into four distinct agro-ecological zones namely the Matengo Highlands (mountainous area), Lowland or Rolling Hills, the Hagati Plateau, and the Lakeshore zone (the Coastal strip along Lake Nyasa). The district is situated within latitudes 10°17'(S) and 11°3'(S) and longitudes 34°38' and 35°15'(E). Its altitude ranges between 500 and 2000m above sea level.

In general the district is mainly dominated by three ethnic groups, namely the Ngoni, Nyasa and Matengo. The Ngoni occupy mainly the northeastern lowlands while the Nyasa occupy the Coastal strip of Lake Nyasa. The Matengo occupy the mountainous area to the east of Lake Nyasa on the escarpment extending south of the Ruhuhu Trough to the border of Mozambique. The Matengo people, who are Bantu speakers, are commonly referred to as 'the people of the woods' as derived from the Matengo word *itengo* meaning forest. The Matengo people migrated into the area about 150 years ago.

The mountainous area is characterized by strongly dissected mountains and narrow valleys where elevation ranges from 1400 metres to over 2000 metres above sea level. The original vegetation is most probably montane forest, but has almost been completely destroyed except for a small forest reserve. It is the most densely populated area in Mbinga district. Some studies (Schmied, 1989) show that a number of villages have population densities ranging between 150 and 300 persons per square kilometre which far exceeds the average population density of Mbinga district of 24 persons per square kilometre, according to the 1988 census.

The highland zone is an area of high agricultural productivity characterized by the utilization of the indigenous farming system commonly referred to as *ngoro* (Matengo pit) on which food crops such as maize, beans and wheat are grown, while coffee (which was introduced in 1939, and is the major cash crop of the area) is grown on bench terraces.

136

The chapter is essentially based on the study which was carried out in 1994 (Rutarora, Rugambisa, Mwaseba and Mattee, 1995) and relevant literature.

## Description of the Matengo Pit System of Farming

The Matengo pit system of farming, commonly known as the *ingoro* in Matengo dialect (*ngoro* in Kiswahili), is a unique indigenous cultivation technique used in all Matengo Highlands to conserve soil moisture and minimize soil erosion. It is described as a grass fallow tied ridge system characterized by crop rotation and maintenance of soil fertility by composting grass, weeds and crop residues. It is an intensive system of cultivation of the steep mountain slopes. The normal practice is the digging of pits which extend from the bottom of the hillsides to within a short distance of the top. It is a system of land preparation not found elsewhere in Tanzania. The system was once described by Basehart (1973) as an unusual indigenous system of intensive agriculture.

The Matengo people of Litembo are believed to be the first people to have developed this valuable technique (Pike, 1938). According to Pike the system came into being after the invention of the hand hoe by the Pangwa smiths. Before that the Matengo people used to cultivate the land by using the digging stick. At first the Matengo people adopted a system of cultivation known as *liande*, which is slash and burn with minimum cultivation. This system followed ordinary principles of shifting cultivation, something which led to early deforestation and soil degradation. However, this system did not produce substantial yields from it because of the nature of the land (steep mountainous slopes). With the invention of the hand-hoe, the Matengo adopted the *ngoro* system and this continues to be honoured in all Matengo land. The *ngoro* system of farming later spread to other areas of Mbinga as people began to migrate in search of arable land, a process which was propelled by dramatic increase in population.

Tools such as sickles (*nyengo*), hoe (*ligera*) and an axe (*liwago*) are used when preparing the *ngoro*. Clearing (*kukesa*) and laying of the cleared (dry) grass into square formation (*kubhunga*) are the initial activities performed by males. After this activity, there follows the job of women of removing top soil (*kujalila*) in the square and covering the grass. After lightly covering the grass with soil, women broadcast the bean/wheat seeds (*kulekalila*) and then cover the seed with the soil (*kukulila*) removed from the square. The soil used in covering the seeds is greater in amount than that used to cover the grass initially. Women's activities are performed on the same day and may consume 9 to 10 hours a day. If a labourer is involved in the preparation and construction of the pits the charge for the work done is TSh. 5 per pit (during 1994-95 farming season). From a distance fields with *ngoro* resemble honeycombs with crops on the ridges. The dimensions of the pits are about 1 metre by 1 metre and 0.3 metres deep. A quick count and calculation would indicate that in every field under *ngoro*, approximately half the area is occupied by pits and the other half by ridges on which crops are planted.

During the growing season the pits are gradually tilled by silt and weeds. When one season is over, the fields are prepared for the following crop.

Matengo pit system is not only a sophisticated technique but also represents an elaborate crop rotation system. Matengo pits are usually prepared from late February to early March in high altitude areas and in April in low altitude areas. At this time beans and/or wheat are planted. After harvesting the beans or wheat, a farmer later on lightly scratches the soil to remove weeds and crop residues in readiness for planting maize or an intercrop of maize and beans. Maize is planted in November/December where beans were harvested while maize/beans intercropping is practiced where wheat is planted. The two-year rotation of cereal and leguminous crops ends up as follows: At the end of the season, when the last crop is harvested, the earth banks or ridges are split and the soil is turned over to make new banks or ridges in which all the collected grass and crop residues are incorporated. This process could go on for a period of 8 to 10 years, after which the field would be allowed to revert to natural grass fallow. However, nowadays the duration of continuous cultivation and fallow period is different for different areas. The length of the fallow period depends on the population pressure of the area, land availability and utilization. While farmers (especially those with average farm sizes) in the Matengo Highlands leave their farms under fallow for an average period of one year, farmers in lowlands (less populated areas) can leave their farms under fallow for a period of about three to five years.

## The Strengths of the Matengo Pit System of Farming

This ingenious system of farming has made the Matengo people distinct from other tribes with whom they lived together and practiced common ways of life. That is why previous researchers such as Pike (1938), Stenhouse (1944) and Basehart (1973) have described the Matengo people as a unique ethnic group in the southern highlands of Tanzania and almost the only tribe practising such an indigenous system of farming in the mountainous areas. The following section describes the advantages of the Matengo pit system of farming.

The *ngoro* is believed to have sustained land productivity for over 100 years and all farmer-originated knowledge and technology revolves around this system. Traditionally, the *ngoro* system of farming has helped in conserving the fertility of the mountainsides. The major strengths of the system are that:

1.  Erosion of the hillside is checked very effectively. Any soil that may be swept down is caught by the ridge or trapped in the pit. Even if the field is left under fallow, the old pits and ridges continue to maintain this function. According to Pike (1938, p. 80):

    Even when the garden is lying fallow, the old ridges and pits still function and prevent the surface water from rushing down the hillside, instead of which it sinks into the ground. This may be the reason why often little streams do not fail at the end of the dry season ... So far it would appear as if the system were a cure for many of the ills that Africa has suffered from erosion due to cultivation but it has its doubtful features.

2. Organic matter is regularly returned into the soil by burying weeds and crop residues in the pits.
3. The layer of topsoil is gradually being deepened by exposing the subsoil in the pits.
4. Moisture or rain water is conserved in the pits for later use by the crops.

The effectiveness of the *ngoro* in reducing the loss of soil is clearly indicated in Table 10.1.

**Table 10.1 Effect of conservation practices and slope on seasonal soil loss**

| Site | Conservation practice | Soil loss (metric tons/ha) |
|------|----------------------|----------------------------|
| A | Bare | 39.0 |
| Slope 8.9° (metric) | Ridge | 7.3 |
| | *Ngoro* | 2.4 |
| B | Bare | 5.7 |
| Slope 20.5° (metric) | Ridge | 14.3 |
| | *Ngoro* | 5.8 |

*Source*: The Miombo Woodland Agro-Ecological Research Project Report No. 1 (1995, p. 35).

The main advantage of the Matengo pit, as pointed out elsewhere (Rutatora, Rugambisa, Mwaseba and Mattee, 1995), is that it does not involve the initial labour of terracing. Furthermore, the effectiveness of the Matengo pit in terms of crop yields (that is, when compared to other cultivation systems such as flat and ridge cultivation) has been proved to be higher (Rutatora, Rugambisa, Mwaseba and Mattee, 1995; Schmied, 1989; Allan, 1965). For example, farmers in Lupilo village reported that in 1993/94 growing season they were able to harvest 37 bags of maize (each bag is equivalent to 100kg) from one hectare under *ngoro* while those who grew maize on ridges could harvest 25 bags of maize per hectare. The system underscores the utilization of low external inputs and utilizes locally available materials. It is here that the indigenous technical knowledge becomes a valuable tool, and especially when farmers and the government at large cannot afford the utilization of external inputs which are dependent on foreign exchange.

## The Weaknesses of the Matengo Pit System of Farming

Having discussed the main strengths of the *ngoro* system of farming, it is appropriate to speak of its weaknesses or limitations. The main weaknesses of this system are:

(1) it is labour intensive and generally requires a good deal of cooperation on the part of more than one family household.
According to Allan (1965, p. 197) 'The work is cooperative, all the men of the village working together, stimulated by the prospect of the traditional beer party'. However, reciprocal labour (commonly referred to as *ngokela* in Matengo dialect) which was the most common activity in the past now appears to be disintegrating as explained in the following paragraph. In addition, most of the work pertaining to this system is still done by women while men value and spend most of their time looking after coffee or any other business.

(2) Mechanization within the *ngoro* system is difficult, hence the hand hoe will continue to be used for years to come.

(3) Root crops, especially cassava, seem to suffer from excessive soil moisture, while the root system of coffee trees appear to become too cramped (Pike, 1938). This might be an interesting issue for further investigation.

The following section presents issues related to the sustainability of the Matengo system of farming, namely the *ngoro*.


## The Sustainability of the Matengo Pit System of Farming in the Matengo Highlands

Although the *ngoro* system of farming has, over years, proved to be effective in controlling soil erosion and improving soil fertility, the productivity of the pits has been declining for the following reasons.
Firstly, reduced fallow period due to reduced farm sizes, as propelled by increase in population, has made people continue cropping their farm plots without a good period of rest; something which, among other things, has led to the decline in soil fertility. For example, in such villages as Litembo and Ngima the fallow period has been reduced from three or five years to less than one year (Rutatora, Rugambisa, Mwaseba and Mattee, 1995).
Secondly, from the socio-economic survey which was conducted by Rutatora and his colleagues sometime in 1994 it was found out that the *ngoro* of today is poorly executed when compared to previous years (for example, reduction in depth and width of the *ngoro*): something which is threatening its sustainability and ability to perform the functions it is supposed to play. The following quotation gives the reasons which were pointed out by the farmers themselves:

(i) Hired labourers although continue to be used they do not do a good job as they want to make as many pits as possible so that they can get much more money. When asked why they should pay labourers for the work poorly done, they responded that nothing much could be done as during that time they (farmers) are rushing to have their crop fields planted on time. Also, it should be remembered that most of the labourers come from outside Matengoland, thus they are new to the practice - which is essentially culture-bound. In addition, we were informed that some of the farmers (because of one reason or the other) do not supervise the labourers very closely (ii) Some farmers (of today) are born lazy hence do not put much effort in constructing effective pits (iii) Some farmers let their children (who do not have much knowledge about this tradition) do the job without close supervision (iv) In the past, this job was done on a cooperative basis (*ngokela*) but now this tradition is being phased out due to the fact that farmers of today have a wide choice of crops to be grown, unlike in the past. For example, while somebody is preferring to grow wheat for a particular season the other fellow may be preferring to grow beans. Shortage of seeds may also make somebody not grow a certain crop for that season and hence one sees no reason for joining the '*ngokela*' groups (v) In the past, nearly everybody followed the informal type of education (something which was transmitted from one generation to the next and this was the only type of education at that time) while today most people do not pay much attention to it due to availability of schools where formal education is being provided ... (Rutatora, Rugambisa, Mwaseba and Mattee, 1995, p. 21).

The type of informal education mentioned above was provided through a system known as *sengo* in Matengo dialect. This was a system whereby related people used to come and eat together. It was regarded as a basic socio-political unit, and it ended during the time of British rule. Under *sengo* we are told that elders used to provide advice on several aspects pertaining to their social well-being and farming at large. They decided when to begin clearing, when to plant and even when to harvest. That is, farming was done collectively and there was no chance for one to be lazy or make individual decisions regarding farming. With regard to labour availability and the interest of the young generation (who are attracted to easier ways of making a living elsewhere in the country), both Pike (1938) and Stenhouse (1944) had earlier deplored the fact that the *ngoro* system was disintegrating, among other things because of loss of labour.

Thirdly, introduction of more profitable crops such as coffee has resulted in reduction of individual farm sizes to the extent that farmers have either been forced to continuously crop the same areas year in and year out without rest or to go out of Matengoland and look for another area for growing food crops. As revealed in an ICRA report (1991) a good portion of the farmer's holding is under coffee, and, as observed during this study, a plot nearest to the homestead is planted with coffee, and plots farther away with food crops. For example, many farmers of Litembo, where land shortage is acute, have food crop fields at Kikolo, Lipilipili, Mateka and other villages in Mbinga and Mpepai divisions. That is, they have now to travel for more than 30km away from their homesteads. If the price of coffee continues to go up the chances are that even the small parcels of land which were left for food crops might be utilized for coffee production (depending on each individual's perception of life): something which might threaten the sustainability of the system. It will not disappear completely, as indicated in the report of Rutatora and his colleagues (1995). On the other hand, continuous cropping of the areas has led to poor preparation of the *ngoro* as not much of the grass necessary for its formation can be found in large quantities, in contrast to fields which are left under fallow. In addition, because most farmers (especially men, who are responsibile for the initial two stages of *ngoro* construction) are, during the months of January to March, busy with the management of coffee (pruning, spraying and fertilizer application), they do not have enough time for clearing and laying grass into squares. This tendency has led farmers to employ labourers or skip some essential stages of *ngoro* construction - such as failure to lay grass into square formation and hence rendering the *ngoro* prone to soil erosion. Clear cases were observed in Kitanda, one of the lowland areas.

Fourthly, migratory trends of the Matengo people are relevant. Because farmers continue to migrate (whether on a permanent or temporary basis) and continue to operate food farms far away from their homesteads (especially those who migrate on a temporary basis), this makes them pay less attention to *ngoro* farms left behind, because of lack of sufficient time. In addition, the Matengo people who move to the lowlands prefer to adopt the farming practice of the people found in those areas, namely ridging. Thus with time younger generations, depending on the level of exposure, might forget the *ngoro* system of farming. Ridging is suitable in the lowlands as the land is relatively flat and all the operations pertaining to it are performed by both men and women.

Despite the above-mentioned problems and men's continued dislike of working the system, farmers in Mbinga contended that the *ngoro* farming system, especially in the Matengo highlands, would never be abandoned even if soil fertility of the area were completely exhausted (Akitsu, 1995; Rutatora, Rugambisa, Mwaseba and Mattee, 1995; ICRA, 1991). According to Rutatora and his colleagues (1995, p. 22):

> Farmers who had practiced other farming systems (within the same area) such as ridging pointed out that the *ngoro* system is the only practice which has proved effective in as far as control of soil erosion and improvement of soil fertility are concerned. According to farmers what is required is provision of education through farm families, farmer groups and village committees so that people could realize the importance of revitalizing the system.

## Conclusion

The paper besides providing a description of the Matengo pit system of farming has dealt with the strengths of the system and the factors which are weakening it. The author contends that although the Matengo pit system (*ngoro*) has sustained land productivity for many years, its sustainability now appears to be threatened by the following factors (i) increase in population, which has resulted in intensification of human activities on the land with the

142

consequent decline in soil fertility (ii) competition of the system with the production of a lucrative crop namely, coffee (this having resulted in reduction of farm sizes under *ngoro*) (iii) poor construction of the *ngoro* and less attention paid to it by the male farmers as a consequence of increased interest in coffee production (and unfortunately labour peak periods for both crops [coffee and beans/wheat] appear at the same time) (iv) migratory trends of the Matengo people and adoption of other systems of farming, particularly in the case of those people who migrate to the lowlands. In summary, the author is of the opinion that if the *ngoro* is to be sustained in the mountainous areas for many years to come the following issues should be investigated further in order to be able to understand this indigenous system and be able to develop strategies for improving it:

(1) The whole system of Matengo agriculture and its rotation.
(2) Mechanisms of imiroving soil fertility within the *ngoro*.
(3) Optimal sizes of *ngoro*, their depth and distance apart.
(4) Reasons for decline in utilization of reciprocal labour (*ngokela*) while it is a recognized fact that the system is very labour intensive and generally requires a good deal of cooperation.
(5) Gender division of labour in the household.
(6) Coping strategies for farmers in view of the increased shoretge of land and increasing population.

# References

Akitsu, M. (1995), *Problems and Future of Agriculture in the Miombo Woodlands from the Socio-economic Viewpoint: Miombo Woodland Research Report*, Faculty of Agriculture, SUA, Morogoro.

Allan, W. (1965), *The African Husbansman*, Oliver and Boyd, Edinburgh.

Basehart, H.W. (1973), 'Cultivation Intensity, Settlement Patterns, and Homestead Forms among the Matengo of Tanzania', *Ethnology*, 7, pp. 57-73.

International Centre for Development-Oriented Research in Agriculture (ICRA) (1991), *Analysis of the Coffee-Based Farming System in the Matengo Highlands, Mbinga District, Tanzania*, ICRA, Wageningen (Working Document Series no. 15).

Miombo Woodland Agro-Ecological Research Project (1995), Project Report no. 1, Faculty of Agriculture, SUA, Morogoro.

Pike, A.I. (1938), 'Soil Conservation amongst the Matengo Tribe', *Tanganyika Notes and Records*, 6, pp. 79-81.

Rutatora, D.J., Rugambisa, J., Mwaseba, D., and Mattee, A.Z. (1995), *Socio-economic Issues arising around Indigenous Agricultural Knowledge Systems and Sustainable Development in the Miombo Woodlands of Mbinga District, Tanzania: A Preliminary Report*, Faculty of Agriculture, SUA, Morogoro.

Schmied, D. (1989), *Subsistence Cultivation, Market Production and Agricultural Development in Ruvuma Region, Southern Tanzania*, Bayreuth University, Bayreuth.

Stenhouse, A.S. (1944), 'Agriculture in the Matengo Highlands', *East African Agriculture Journal*, 10, pp. 22-4.

# Part III

# CASE STUDIES

# 11 The Development Crisis of Peasant Agriculture in Tanzania in the 1980s and 1990s

FRANCIS F. LYIMO

## 1. Introduction

This chapter presents a sociological analysis of the development crisis of peasant agriculture in Tanzania in the 1980s and 1990s. It gives research findings from selected case studies of three villages to show the farm production resources which peasants in those villages used in 1988/89 which was one of the years in economic crisis in Tanzania.

The chapter deals with four issues. First, the chapter argues that peasant agriculture in Tanzania has experienced government intervention mostly through policies and programmes. Yet this intervention has not succeeded in improving the peasant economy. The failure of government intervention to bring significant improvement on peasant agriculture together with other emerging problems which were caused by both internal and external factors led to the development crisis in peasant agriculture. This crisis is part and parcel of the general development crisis of the economy of Tanzania in the last fifteen years. Efforts to modernize peasant agriculture are an issue which must be addressed in order to raise the level of farm production and subsequently increase peasant household farm income.

Second, the crisis conditions are analysed to assess the impact on peasant farming. Third, research findings from selected villages in Kilimanjaro, Dar es Salaam and Tabora regions are presented to show the farm production resources which peasants used in a given year during the crisis. It is argued that the modernization of peasant agriculture requires appropriate and adequate production resources. Capitalist agriculture conditions in Tanzania have not touched many people in the agriculture sector. Many farm households lack adequate capital, modern technology and large farms to operate capitalist farming. The agriculture sector in Tanzania is dominated by peasant farming. About 85 per cent of the adult population are peasants. These devote their land and labour power to produce farm products for household consumption and for sale in the market. Production and marketing conditions and services must be improved in order to improve peasant farming. Finally, suggestions are made on institutional changes as well as modernization strategies to be implemented to enable peasants to improve their agriculture.

## 2. Failure of Government Intervention to Improve Peasant Agriculture

In this section we briefly discuss the government intervention in peasant agriculture through policies and programmes. Government intervention in peasant agriculture since the 1960s has been persistent. Such intervention has operated at the levels of production, marketing and distribution of farm products.

The government has imposed through bureaucratic means rural institutions and structures to improve peasant agriculture. Attempts were made during the early years of independence of Tanganyika. These attempts involved 'improvement' and 'transformation' approaches to agriculture modernization. Bureaucratic decisions were made and peasants were required to implement these approaches. These approaches did not succeed and these failures have been documented (Lyimo, 1983; Cliffe, 1977; Hyden, 1980; Kjekshus, 1977; McHenry, 1978; Raikes, 1978; and Coulson, 1981).

These approaches were abandoned and the *ujamaa* villages programme was adopted in 1967. In this programme attempts were made to change settlement patterns by moving the rural population into villages and then creating new rural structures and socializing the relations of production in the villages (Nyerere, 1968; Lyimo, 1975, 1983; Coulson, 1977; and Raikes, 1986). From 1967 to 1973 people were persuaded to come together and live in villages. Persuasion was thought to be a gradual process which would eventually culminate into voluntary cooperation in peasant farming. Persuasion also included government efforts to provide basic services such as health, education and water to peasants who had moved and settled into new villages.

The provision of services to lure peasants to move into new villages was faced with problems. First, some peasants from densely populated areas were also attracted by the services to move and open new villages in the less densely populated areas. Sometimes they grabbed other people's land. A research on the establishment of Shirimatunda Village in Hai District found that peasants from the densely populated Kibosho area on the slopes of mountain Kilimanjaro confiscated part of Kiyungi sisal estate on which they had been tenant farmers. The Kiyungi sisal plants had a government lease for the plantation yet the tenants were able to take part of the plantation on which they had cultivated as tenants on the ground that they were implementing the villagization programme (Lyimo, 1975). Second, as the number of *ujamaa* villages increased, the government ability to provide those services in the new villages could not cope with the rate of increase of the new villages. Third, because persuasion implied voluntary peasant movement into new villages, the entire populations of an area could not be moved at once into a new village. Thus the people left behind could not be incorporated into the programme of services and facilities which operated in the new villages.

The Tanzania government leadership was frustrated by the slow speed and unsystematic pattern with which the *ujamaa* villages were established. As a result, a change of policy in 1973 made the villagization programme a compulsory movement to be implemented systematically throughout the

148

country and the programme had to be completed in 1976.  Thus the villagization process was accelerated through government coercion.

Operations to form new villages were carried out and people were moved in large numbers at the same time without adequate and favourable communication.  Records exist about some villages which were formed with poor or no feasibility study or planning done on the new areas into which peasants were forced to move (Nyerere, 1977).

The forced villagization brought structural and psychological disturbance to the peasants.  This consequently had a negative impact on peasant agriculture.  Villagization changed settlement patterns and created new farming plots.  In many cases the homesteads and the farms were far apart and peasants needed more travelling time to and from the fields.  What was more serious was that for the newly established homes and farms, the peasants needed several years to build permanent houses and get the first harvests from the newly planted perennial crops.

Villagization policy was intended to facilitate egalitarian rural development.  This policy was expected to achieve the following objectives: first, to create collective and cooperative farms as socialist production units in the villages.  Second, to improve the social and economic infrastructure and provide basic services of education, health and water.  Third, to improve marketing and the distribution system of goods and promote rural development.  Finally, to create conditions and institutions which would mobilize the rural population for rural development and promote popular participation in rural development activities (Nyerere, 1968).

Contrary to these objectives, the villagization programme killed personal initiative and interfered with the free interplay of market forces.  Liberal critics accused the bureaucracy of being irrational and inefficient.  Its incessant desire for short term political pursuits and control have bred corruption and contempt for peasants as being irrational and inert (Coulson, 1981).  This has made peasants produce less agricultural products and they also prefer to sell a large proportion of their surplus farm products through unofficial marketing channels.

Another policy change which affected negatively peasant farming was the abolition of the Farmers' Cooperatives in 1976.  The cooperatives were replaced by statutory Crop Authorities which were made in overall charge of purchasing, processing and selling of crops.  They were also to provide credit and extension services, conduct innovation campaigns and invest in processing facilities.

The institutional changes of 1976 had serious problems.  The Crop Authorities did not get adequate preparation.  They did not have enough money to buy crops and they had inadequate transport to haul crops from the countryside to their marketing godowns.  They were also centralized, inefficient and corrupt.  Their costs were high and they ran up deficits.  The marketing margins swelled and the real producer prices especially for export crops fell.  Peasants were detached from the crop authorities.  The Crop Authorities were neither owned nor controlled by farmers.  These were institutions which were established to increase government involvement in the marketing of farm products.  But because the Crop Authorities were

149

ridden with many problems, they seriously disrupted the flow of farm produce and consequently affected negatively peasants income.

The government intervention in agriculture through villagization of peasants, nationalization of large capitalist farms and the unfavourable product producer prices in the 1970s affected the structure of agriculture, especially of wheat, maize and rice zones.

In 1970 almost all wheat was produced on private farms of peasants and capitalist farmers. But in the 1980s wheat production in the Arusha region, for example, was dominated by a complex of large State Farms. Wheat production from private farms in the Arusha region had almost stopped because of low crop prices, nationalization of capitalist farms in the 1970s and the villagization of rich peasants. The private wheat farms of the 1970s had been highly mechanized but owing to the conditions of the economic crisis in the 1970s/80s there was a general absence of equipment and spare parts.

For rice production, mechanization had been less widespread. But in the 1980s and 1990s production of rice had shifted from the official marketing channels to unofficial markets. Low prices on the official market and the unnecessary delays in paying farmers for their rice deliveries to the National Milling Corporation made peasants shift to unofficial marketing channels for rice.

Peasants produced the major portion of the maize deliveries but there has been emphasis on regional competence for maize production. During the period 1980-1985, Iringa, Mbeya, Ruvuma and Rukwa regions were the so-called 'Big Four' maize producing regions. Records in the Ministry of Agriculture showed that these regions were the 'traditional' maize surplus regions during that period. These are southern border regions and peasants access to attractive unofficial channels for marketing maize in Dar es Salaam, Tanga or into Kenya was limited. This was so because while Dar es Salaam could provide an attractive unofficial market for maize, the transport road link between Dar es Salaam and the southern regions was very bad, especially during the rainy season. As a result it was in these regions that official marketing of maize was most active.

In the Northern regions of Arusha and Kilimanjaro and the central region of Dodoma peasants avoided the official market channels for their maize crop. But the non-availability of maize crop marketing statistics in the Ministry of Agriculture appeared to indicate low crop production in these regions. In actual fact, there were unofficial channels for marketing maize in Tanga, Dar es Salaam and even across the border into Kenya where farm crops were sold at higher prices than those offered by the National Milling Corporation in Tanzania. At Taveta market on the Kenya-Tanzania border, for example, farm crops such as maize from the Kilimanjaro region were sold and industrial products such as domestic appliances, clothing, bedding, beer, cosmetics, soap, etc. were bought and sent to Tanzania where they were in big demand owing to commodity scarcity in the market in the 1980s.

Arusha region, for example, has always been a big maize grower. In 1979 Arusha delivered more maize to the National Milling Corporation than the 'Big Four' southern regions combined. But during the years which followed maize from Arusha region was sneaked into Kenya almost exclusively through the unofficial channels because the prices there were more attractive and the market for consumer items was plentiful relative to the situation in Tanzania (Raikes, 1986, pp. 118-119).

The above analysis has shown that government intervention in agriculture has been carried out through policies, programmes and crop pricing. But this intervention has not made a significant positive impact. Policy and programme changes have brought structural and institutional changes in peasant agriculture. And government prices on farm products have discouraged peasants or have not been attractive enough to the peasants. Thus government intervention in agriculture has partly explained the low level of production on peasant farms and consequently low peasant farm income in the 1980s.

Another factor which affected peasant agriculture, peasant farm income and the overall peasant life was the economic crisis of the country. Crisis in the peasant economy had been caused by internal as well as external factors. It was part of the general development crisis of the economy in Tanzania. In the following section, we analyse the crisis and assess its impact on peasant access to agriculture resources and their use in farm production.

3. **The Economic Crisis and its Impact on Peasants' Access to and Use of Agricultural Resources**

The 1980s were years in which Tanzania was experiencing serious economic crisis. This section outlines the manifestations of the crisis and discuss its causes. The impact of the crisis on peasants' access to agriculture resources and their use in farm production is examined.

This crisis manifested itself in deficits in government budget, imbalance in foreign exchange and in the fall of industrial and agricultural production. From early 1970s to the beginning of the 1980s, there was a fall in the volume of imports per capita of 40 per cent but at the same time there was an increase of deficit in the external trade balance. In terms of monetary Gross Domestic Product (GDP), the manufacturing sector declined at an average rate of 20 per cent per annum between 1978 and 1982 but the utilization capacity was as low as 20-30 per cent (Boesen, Havnevik, Koponen and Odgaard, 1986, p. 19). There was a decline or stagnation in agriculture production during the late 1970s and early 1980s especially in the export crops. Most crop sales also went through the unofficial marketing channels.

The crisis also manifested itself in declining domestic savings and poor provision of basic social services particularly water, health and education Legume, 1988, pp. 3-11). The crisis had manifestations in the real lives of the ordinary people. Imports of petroleum, spare parts, machinery, industrial and agricultural inputs were cut down because of shortage of foreign exchange. This resulted in low utilization of industrial and agricultural capacity. Transport problems also hit the movement of products of farm crops.

The manifestations of the crisis in the real lives of the ordinary people were seen in the context of severe shortages or non-availability of basic consumer items. People were frustrated and desperate as they failed to get their daily needs. Peasants failed to get the necessary farm inputs and implements.

The causes of the crisis have been serious issues of concern in Tanzania. This was a crisis involving severe shortages of foreign exchange, crisis in production sectors and in government budget, and the imbalance of trade. The national economic crisis was caused by both external and internal factors.

The external factors which caused the crisis included the breakdown of the East African Community in 1978, the Uganda-Tanzania war of 1979/80, the unmanageable oil prices which Tanzania found to be too high and the problem of the imbalance of trade in which Tanzania's exports of primary products were given low prices but her imports of industrial products were at high prices.

The internal factors which caused the crisis included natural calamities such as occasional floods which left damaged fields, roads and bridges. There were also severe droughts in 1973/74, 1981/82 and 1982/83 which affected crop yields (Boesen, Havnevik, Koponen and Odgaard, 1986a).

There were blunders committed in implementing government policies and programmes. The consequences of government intervention in agriculture have been discussed in the previous section. The major agricultural and industrial enterprises, commercial and financial institutions were nationalized in 1968-69. The district and regional administration were decentralized in 1972 and there was a deliberate government decision to expand the industrial sector through investment from 1975/76 onwards based on a policy of basic industries. The government intervened in all sectors in an attempt to control the economy. But there was stagnation or even decline in the output of the economy as a whole after 1981.

The impact of the crisis on the peasant and the nation as a whole was deeply felt. The government used taxation to squeeze money from agriculture by applying higher marketing margins. The surplus squeeze on peasant agriculture was a great disincentive for their increased farm production. In addition, the inflationary monetary and financial policies and pricing policies which were restrictive provided the basis for the emergence of unofficial marketing channels for farm products. In addition, the volume and value of the major cash crop exports declined during the crisis years. But the imports of both industrial products and foodstuffs to offset the shortages experienced by the rapidly growing urban population grew and caused serious imbalance of payments.

The crisis affected the marketing and transport systems for farm products, agricultural inputs and consumer items. The government prices for farm crops could not keep pace with the rising inflation. But farm inputs and imported foodstuffs and other basic goods were available with difficulty and at high prices. This discouraged peasants and affected their morale and capacity to increase farm production. By 1980 farm product deliveries had declined to a basic minimum and these came from areas which could not easily reach the unofficial markets because of their location and transport problems, such as the southern region. Deliveries also came from state farms.

In an attempt to bring the economic crisis under control, Tanzania has reacted in a number of ways since 1981. New policies and specific programmes to restructure and improve the economy have been attempted. In the agriculture sector, the cooperative movement was re-established in 1982 (URT, 1982) and a new agriculture policy was launched in 1983 (MoA, 1982).

The new agriculture policy emphasized individual peasant farms instead of village communal farms as the basis of future agriculture development (MoA, 1982). The government enacted legal security of tenure for farmers to protect private investment by farmers whether nationals or foreigners. The legal security of land tenure has encouraged private investors to enter into large-scale farming. The struggle over farm land has occurred in places which had land scarcity or in places where large farms have taken land which belonged to smallholders. For example, the large wheat farms which were established by the National Agriculture Food Corporation (NAFCO) in Mbulu district led to serious clashes and court action by the Barabaig villagers on the management of the NAFCO farms.

In response to this development crisis, Tanzania has launched new policies and plans which aimed at alleviating the crisis. The World Bank and the International Monetary Fund (IMF) have prescribed conditionalities for Tanzania to comply with in order to secure foreign aid. A National Economic Survival Plan (NESP) was launched in the beginning of the crisis but was replaced by Structural Adjustment Programmes (SAP) covering the period 1982/83 to 1985/86. The SAPs were aimed at correcting certain economic imbalance, and making the national economy more flexible, efficient and able to use local resources. SAP reforms included decreasing government control over prices, reducing budget deficit, devaluation of the Tanzania shilling, a wage freeze, reducing government expenditure, privatization and liberalization of trade (Kiamba and Kiamba, 1992, p. 1). SAP was to be achieved by using foreign aid.

An agreement between IMF and Tanzania was signed in August, 1986. Under this agreement Tanzania was obliged to surrender control over critical elements of the national economic policy to foreign donors. This affected public expenditure, wages, imports, exports, devaluation, external payments and the public sector (Sawyer, 1989, p. 13). The Economic Recovery Programme (ERP) for the period 1986/87 to 1988/89 was positively received by the IMF and the foreign donors.

Some of the objectives of the ERP included the increasing of production of material goods especially in agriculture and industry. Also ERP was to achieve great efficiency in allocation of resources in the service and production sectors. To achieve the ERP objective of increasing the material production in agriculture something had to be done to raise the agriculture production in state farms, capitalist private farms and peasant farms.

Peasant farming in Tanzania is small-scale farming. It operates in isolated small plots which have not applied science and technology. The next section will present research findings to show the agriculture production resources which peasants used in 1988/89.

## 4. Peasant Use of Farm Production Resources during the Crisis Period

One way of modernizing peasant agriculture is by the application of technological resources in the production process. These resources include high yield seeds, chemical fertilizers, pesticides, tractor or plough, good quality animal feed, hybrid animals and poultry and good transport of the farm products. Some peasants do not have the economic ability to buy these resources. Such peasants would need loans to pay for the farm inputs or they would need to be provided with these resources on credit.

A study of 341 peasants was conducted in three villages to find out the peasant use of farm production resources in 1988/89 farming season. The peasants studied were from Chekereni Village in Kilimanjaro Region, Chanika Village in Dar es Salaam Region and Ussoke Mlimani Village in Tabora Region. The study tried to find out the number of peasants who used these resources and if the resources were enough for their farm requirements. The study also tried to find out the number of peasants who receive agriculture inputs on credit.

Peasants generally depend on sources outside their villages for the supply of bio-chemical and technological farm production resources. The study found that the village retail shops had so little capital that they were not able to stock farm inputs which could easily be accessible to peasants. Farm production inputs were made available to peasants through the distribution system of the Ministry of Agriculture or through the more accessible farmers' cooperative societies which supplied their members with farm inputs on credit or on cash basis. Small farm implements such as hoes, axes and knives could be bought in the local shops on a cash basis (Coulson, 1977, pp. 86-90).

The analysis of the data collected from a sample of 341 respondents from the three villages in 1988/89 year showed that 157 peasants (46 per cent of the sample) did not use high yield seed. 12 peasants (3.5 per cent of the sample) did not get enough high yield seed while 172 peasants (50.5 per cent of the sample) got enough seeds. The research found that the Rural Cooperative Society in Ussoke Mlimani supplied tobacco seeds to farmers to improve crop production in that village. In Chekereni Village there was an irrigation project for rice cultivation and the Rural Cooperative Society in that village sold good quality rice seeds to farmers. Chanika Village did not have annual crops which received high yield seeds through the Rural Cooperative in that village: peasants had to buy high yield maize seeds from traders in Kariakoo market in the city.

The use of chemical fertilizers was recommended in order to improve the production of tobacco, rice and maize. The field assistants in the villages advised peasants on the type of fertilizers to be bought and the way of applying the fertilizers. The study found that 143 peasants (42 per cent of the sample) did not use fertilizers upon their crops. Nine peasants (2.6 per cent of the sample) did not get enough fertilizers and 189 peasants (55.4 per cent of the sample) got enough fertilizers. The agriculture extension assistants carried close supervision on putting fertilizers on the tobacco farms. This made tobacco farmers collect the fertilizers on credit, or pay cash from the

Cooperative Society in Ussoke Village. In Chekereni and Chanika Villages the field extension assistants were not fully carrying out campaigns to enforce the use of fertilizers on rice and maize farms. Many peasants also found the fertilizers to be rather expensive relative to their household incomes. The general complaint was that while prices for farm products were low, the fertilizer prices were high and there was no government subsidy on the prices of the fertilizers.

A similar situation was observed in connection with the peasants' use of pesticides on their crops. 188 peasants (55.1 per cent of the sample) did not use pesticides; 8 peasants (2.3 per cent of the sample) did not get enough pesticides and 145 peasants (42.6 per cent of the sample) got enough pesticides for their farms. Besides the complaints raised by peasants that the prices of pesticides were high, the study found that many peasants were not sensitive enough to the need to apply pesticides on their seasonal crops. Very few peasants talked about the need to use pesticides on the rice and maize farms. The study also showed that for the crops which were not marketed through the Rural Cooperative Society, the peasants found it difficult to get the fertilizers or pesticides on credit from the cooperative society. The tobacco crop was marketed through the Rural Cooperative Society and this organization ensured that pesticides for tobacco were brought to the village and were sold to peasants on credit or a cash basis.

Considering the situation of low economic conditions of many peasant households, the study tried to find out external sources for the funding of the purchase of farm production resources. The research found that three peasants (0.9 per cent) got loans from a bank. 338 peasants (99.1 per cent) did not get bank loans for agriculture activities. We found that many peasants were unaware of the possibility of applying for bank loans for farming. The study found a general complaint by peasants that the bank loan conditions were unfavourable to small peasants. We were informed by our respondents that only rich peasants could meet the bank loan conditions.

The study found that securing farm inputs on credit was practiced in the villages. 283 peasants (83 per cent of the sample) did not get agricultural inputs on credit; 58 peasants (17 per cent of the sample) got farm inputs on credit. The research found that all 58 peasants received farm inputs on credit through the Rural Cooperative Society. We found that the cooperatives recover the farm credit when peasants sell their crops through the cooperative society. All deductions for the farms inputs supplied on credit are made from the money for the crops sold through the cooperative.

The use of plough or tractors relieves peasants of the burden of hand hoe cultivation. Cultivation of peasant farms by plough or tractor is done quickly and large farms can be cultivated. The study found that 230 peasants (67.4 per cent of the sample) did not use tractor or plough in farming. 111 peasants (32.6 per cent of the sample) did use tractor or plough. The tractor cultivation was considered to be expensive for households which were poor. There was also a problem of non-availability of tractors during the farming season. In Ussoke Mlimani Village the tractor which belonged to the village had a trailer and it was mainly used to carry logs for smoking tobacco. In Chekereni Village there was a tractor for the village but many maize farmers complained that priority for using the village tractor was given to rice farmers because the tractors had been bought under the rice farming project.

Success in farming also needs efficient transport to carry the farm products to the households or to the market. The study found that 201 peasants (58.9 per cent of the sample) carried the crops on their heads. 140 peasants (41.1 per cent of the sample) did not carry their crops on their heads. Motor vehicles and bicycles were the most common forms of transport used in the villages. Lorries and pick-ups were used to carry crops from the farms to the peasant homes or to the market. We observed, however, that rural road conditions were bad and this affected the transport in the rural areas.

The study also tried to find out the number of peasants who kept hybrid animals and poultry. The research found that 330 peasants (96.8 per cent of the sample) did not keep such animals or poultry. 11 peasants (3.2 per cent of the sample) did keep them. Many peasants did not have enough money to invest in keeping hybrid animals and poultry. Such money was needed for the purchase of the animals or poultry and for building the animal house plus the medicines and the expenses for the daily upkeep of the animals.

Finally the study tried to find out the number of peasants who used purchased good quality animal feed. We found that 324 peasants (94 per cent of the sample) did not buy it, and only 17 peasants (5 per cent of the sample) did so. The purchase of animal feed was mainly done by peasants who kept hybrid animals and poultry.

## 5. Conclusions and Recommendations for Modernizing Peasant Agriculture

Efforts to improve peasant agriculture have been attempted in Tanzania since independence. The government has intervened in peasant agriculture but peasants have struggled against state subordination and extraction of surplus from peasant farming.

Previous bureaucratic government approaches to modernize peasant agriculture have become unacceptable and unsuccessful. This study on peasants' use of production resources in order to alleviate the economic crisis among themselves shows that we need a different approach to peasant agriculture modernization in Tanzania. The peasant-centred development approach has to be adopted in the agriculture policies. The peasant has to be made to occupy the key position in the planning and programmes geared to modernize peasant farming. That means policies should focus on creating rural institutions which are controlled and owned by peasants to serve the interest of the peasants.

The study in the three villages revealed that farmers' cooperatives were viable institutions which could be organized by peasants to serve them in modernizing their agriculture by providing production, processing, distribution, marketing and farm credit services. The bureaucratic government policy formulation from the top must be changed to the two-way communication between peasants and government so as to facilitate planning from the top as well as from below. This can be achieved by involving farmers in their cooperatives. But the most crucial problem facing farmers' cooperatives in Tanzania is the problem of the economic viability of these organizations. The situation is even more serious because there is the overall crisis of the economy of Tanzania. As Tanzania struggles to overcome the crisis, farmers' cooperatives must strive to become economically viable. By doing so the cooperatives would become credit worthy, so as to be able to borrow money from banks and provide farm credit to peasants. The farmers' cooperatives must also overcome the problem of financial mismangement, poor account procedures and corruption that are known to have crippled the credit worthiness of farmers' cooperatives in Tanzania and causing problems in raising the marketing margins (Widstrand, 1970; Cliffe, Lawrence, Luttrell, Migot-Adholla and Saul, 1975).

The village government is another local institution which must undergo changes in order to make it serve its members. Democratic machinery must be instituted in the village government in order to make it a government of villagers by the villagers for the villagers. These institutional changes will help to enhance citizen participation in the decision-making process and the peasants' participation in implementing their programmes such as those on peasant farming in the villages. The village government, for example, can help to ensure that farm production resources and extension services flow into peasant farms.

Finally the study on peasants' use of resources on agriculture production revealed two issues. First there is the problem of peasant access to the technological resources of farm production and their application on farming. This problem emanates from the individual peasants' unawareness about the resources as well as their economic inability to purchase the farm inputs. Second, improving peasant agriculture involves many factors and issues and the application of the technological resources is one of the factors which could help to improve peasant agriculture in Tanzania

## References

Bernstein, H., Crow, B. and Johnson, H. (1992), *Rural Livelihoods: Crises and Responses*, London, Oxford University Press.

Boesen, J., and Mohele, A.T. (1979), *The 'Success Story' of Peasant Tobacco Production in Tanzania*, SIAS, Uppsala (CDR Publication no. 2).

Boesen, J., Havenvik, K.J., Koponen, J., and Odgaard, R. (1986a), 'Introduction' to Boesen, Havnevik, Koponen and Odgaard (eds) (1986b), p.p 19-29.

Boesen, J., Havenvik, K.J., Koponen, J., and Odgaard, R. (1986b), *Tanzania: Crisis and Struggle for Survival*, SIAS, Uppsala.

Cliffe, L. (1977), 'Rural Class Formation in East Africa', *Journal of Peasant Studies*, 4, pp. 195-224.

Cliffe, L., Lawrence, P., Luttrell, W., Migot-Adholla, S., and Saul, J. (eds) (1975), *Rural Cooperation in Tanzania*, TPH, Dar es Salaam.

Coulson, A. (1977), 'Agricultural Policies in Mainland Tanzania', *Review of African Political Economy*, 10, pp. 74-100.

Coulson, A. (1981), 'Agricultural Policies in Mainland Tanzania', in Heyer, J., Roberts, P., and Williams, G. (eds), *Rural Development in Tropical Africa*, London, Macmillan, pp. 52-89.

157

Grabowski, R. (1990), 'Agriculture, Mechanisation and Land Tenure', *Journal of Development Studies*, 27, pp. 43-53.

Hyden, G. (1980), *Beyong Ujamaa in Tanzania: Underdevelopment and an Uncaptured Peasantry*, Heinemann, London.

Kiamba, J., and Kiamba, J.M. (1992), 'The Effects of SAPs on Rural Health Development in Kenya', Paper presented at International Conference of Social Sciences and Medicine, Nairobi.

Kjekshus, H. (1977), *Ecology Control and Economic Development in East African History*, Heinemann, London.

Legum, C. (1988), 'The Nyerere Years:. A Preliminary Balance Sheet', in Hodd, M. (ed), *Tanzania after Nyerere*, Pinter, London, pp. 3-11.

Lyimo, F.F. (1975), 'Problems and Prospects of Ujamaa Development in Moshi District', MA thesis, University of Dar es Salaam.

Lyimo, F.F. (1983), 'Peasant Production and Cooperative Experiences in Tanzania: Case Studies in Villages in Moshi (Rural) and Urambo Districts', PhD thesis, University of Madison-Wisconsin.

McHenry, D.E. (1978), 'Peasant Participations in Communal Farming: The Tanzanian Experience', *African Studies Review*, 20, pp. 43-63.

Ministry of Agriculture (MoA) (1982), *The Tanzania National Agricultural Policy (Final Report)*, Task Force on National Agricultural Policy, Printpak, Dar es Salaam.

Mlawa, H.M. (1995), *Perspectives about Structural Adjustment and Transformation in Sub-Saharan Africa*, Dar es Salaam University Press, Dar es Salaam.

Msambichaka, K.A. (1995), *Beyond Structural Adjustment Programmes in Tanzania: Success, Failures and New Perspectives*, ERB, University of Dar es Salaam.

Nelson, J.M. (ed) (1990), *Economic Crisis and Policy Choice: The Politics of Adjustment in the Third World*, Princeton NJ, Princeton University Press.

Nindi, B.C. (1988), 'Issues in Agricultural Change: Case Study from Isimani, Iringa Region, Tanzania', in Brokensha, D.W., and Little, P.D. (eds) (1988), *Anthropology of Development and Change in East Africa*, Westview Press, Boulder, pp. 161-82.

Nyerere, J.K. (1968), 'Socialism and Rural Development', in Nyerere, *Freedom and Socialism*, Oxford University Press, Dar es Salaam, pp. 337-366.

Nyerere, J.K. (1977), *The Years after the Arusha Declaration*, Government Printer, Dar es Salaam.

O'Neill, N., and Mustafa, K. (eds) (1990), *Capitalism, Socialism and the Development Crisis in Tanzania*, Avebury, Aldershot.

Onimode, B. (1969), *The IMF, the World Bank and the African Debt: The Economic Impact*, Zed Books, London.

Raikes, P. (1978), 'Rural Differentiation and Class Formation in Tanzania', *Journal of Peasant Studies*, 5, pp. 285-325.

Raikes, P. (1986), 'Eating the Carrot and Wielding the Stick: The Agricultural Sector in Tanzania', in Boesen, Havnevik, Koponen and Odgaard (eds), pp. 105-41.

Redclift, M. (1984), *Development and Environmental Crisis*, London, Methuen.

Sawyer, A. (1989), 'The Politics of Adjustment Policy', *African Journal of Political Economy*, 2 (iv).

Shanin, T. (ed) (1971), *Peasants and Peasant Societies*, Penguin, Harmondsworth.

United Republic of Tanzania (URT) (1982), *Cooperative Societies Act 1982*, Government Printer, Dar es Salaam.

Widstrand, C.G. (ed) (1970), *Cooperatives and Rural Development in East Africa*, Africa Publishing Corporation, New York NY.

# 12 Peasant Agriculture in Tanzania: Access to and Use of Resources to Improve Agricultural Production

FRANCIS F. LYIMO

## Introduction

Agriculture is the backbone of the economy of Tanzania. More than 80 per cent of the economically active adult population is engaged in the agricultural sector. But in terms of the contribution of agriculture to the total GDP, the sector showed a decline between 1980 (40.2 per cent) and 1984 (39.5 per cent). But there was an increase in this contribution since 1985. This is explained partly by higher rates of growth during the period in real terms - 39.9 per cent in 1985, 58.9 per cent in 1986 and 61.1 per cent in 1987 - and partly by the drop in the growth rates of the industrial sector output. Industrial production has mainly been affected by high costs of raw materials, machinery and other imported inputs.

There is an increasing demand placed on the agricultural sector by the economy as a whole in terms of three factors:

(a) Surplus generation for investment purposes and recurrent expenditure for non-agricultural sectors.
(b) Supplying adequate quantities of food to achieve self sufficiency accompanied by targeted improved nutritional standards.
(c) The growing foreign exchange requirements to support all sectors, largely through agricultural exports (MoA, 1982, pp. 21-22).

Against these demands, the overall performance of the agriculture sector has been inadequate. After 1970/71 food production registered a low growth rate of 2.9 per cent which could not support fully the population which was increasing at 3.3 per cent annually. As indicated in Table 12.1 Tanzania changed from net exporter position prior to 1970/71 to a large net importer in the 1980s. In the case of foreign exchange earning, the real value of Tanzania's agricultural exports in 1980 was less than 60 per cent of the 1977 peak.

The poor performance in the export sector is a major concern. The dependence on foreign grants and loans to finance imports cannot be indefinitely sustained and is unpredictable and subject to political whims of donor countries and international financial institutions (Onimode, 1989).

**Table 12.1 Tanzania exports and imports (US dollar in millions)**

|          | 1981/82 | 1982/83 | 1983/84 | 1984/85 | 1985/86 |
|----------|---------|---------|---------|---------|---------|
| Exports  | 16.38   | 19.88   | 22.29   | 21.71   | 49.53   |
| Imports  | 44.52   | 45.56   | 56.35   | 75.96   | 149.25  |

Converted from Tanzanian Shillings to US dollars at exchange rate of Tsh. 230 = 1 US$ in June, 1991.

*Source*: The United Republic of Tanzania (URT), 1990, p. 13.

Tanzania has the potential to improve peasant agriculture by using production resources. This chapter presents the research findings on the ways and extent to which peasants in Tanzania get resources and use them to improve their agriculture performance in villages.

We focused on smallholder farms in villages because these are numerically predominant in the countryside and they constitute the focal point for bringing about rural development.[1] But village farming is traditional and it needs to be modernized. Village farming varies from household farms with an average size of 0.4 hectares, communal or cooperative farms; and in a few cases block farms.

Large-scale farming includes both state farms and capitalist private farms. These are numerically fewer than peasant farms but they contribute substantially to the agricultural output. They are modernized farms using science and technology in production.

**Approaches to Modernizing Peasant Farming**

Tanzania has attempted different approaches to the modernization of peasant farming. During the period 1961-1967, government agricultural policy focused on the 'improvement approach' and the 'transformation approach'. Both were recommended by the World Bank but they failed to modernize peasant farming.

The 'improvement approach' was expected to facilitate the provision of agricultural credits, farm inputs and extension services to a small number of farmers who were considered to be relatively progressive. It was expected that the adoption of innovation by the progressive farmers would have a 'trickle down effect' on the larger population of backward peasants. It was envisaged that technical assistance to the few selected progressive farmers would make an impact in the community without changing settlement patterns, forms of land ownership or relations of production.

The progressive farmers benefited from the improvement approach but the trickle down effect did not come forth. The widely scattered household farms could not easily get adequate extension services, farm inputs or marketing services for their products. Thus the poor peasants remained poor while the few progessive farmers grew richer (Raikes, 1978; Awiti, 1973; Cliffe, 1977). This approach was mainly designed to engage progressive farmers in cash crop farming. Thus the period 1961 to 1968 had increased cash crop production as indicated in table 12.2.

**Table 12.2 Cash crop production in Tanzania**

| Crops | 1960-1962 average '000 British tons' | 1966-1968 average '000 British tons' | Growth rate per annum % |
|---|---|---|---|
| Coffee | 23.6 | 48.1 | 12.5 |
| Cotton | 33.5 | 70.0 | 13.0 |
| Cashewnuts | 45.1 | 74.3 | 9.0 |
| Tea | 4.0 | 6.4 | 8.0 |
| Tobacco | 2.2 | 3.8 | 10.0 |

*Source:* United Republic of Tanzania (URT),1967, p. 18.

The 'transformation approach' was expected to transform the peasantry through the establishment of settlement schemes. In this approach new farmers were recruited to join the settlements (Brain, 1977).

The settlement schemes had many bottlenecks. These were capital intensive projects involving utilization of farm machinery of which the farmers had little or no experience. The machines were expensive to buy and operate. Mechanization of the settlement schemes was not efficient but the farmers had to pay back the capital involved in establishing them.

There was little farmer involvement in making decisions on the activities of the settlement schemes. On the contrary, there was strict government control and supervision. The settlement schemes were designed to be very dependent on the government for initial capital investment. But the government had no money and the external financing was not available when it was needed. The government abandoned this approach in 1966.

The villagization approach was adopted in 1967 after the previous two approaches to rural development had failed to improve the level of agricultural production (Nyerere, 1968). One of the objectives of villagization was to move people into villages where they could be enabled through cooperative organization and/or government assistance to get and use resources to improve production (Lyimo, 1983). It was thought that eventually peasants would start cooperative farms. Some of the economic advantages of cooperative farming include the realization of the economies of scale and the possibility of channelling production resources through the cooperative organization.[2]

Tanzania has long had cooperatives which market the agricultural products. The first of these were started as early as 1933 and the cooperative movement expanded rapidly during the early years of independence of Tanzania (Widstrand, 1970; Cliffe, Lawrence, Luttrell, Migot-Adholla and Saul, 1975).

162

Policy and organizational changes in the cooperative movement have enabled the government to intervene more into cooperatives. Instead of members' control, the government exercised control through the parastatal Marketing Boards and Crop Authorities. But these government institutions for marketing farm products did not have good coordination with the farmers' marketing cooperatives. The government agricultural marketing institutions sold the farm products and the cooperatives and subsequently the farmers had to accept prices offered, and had no say in the matter (Hyden, 1976).

In attempting to establish villages as cooperative organizations, the government abolished all farmers' agricultural marketing cooperatives in May 1976. The villages were then made agents to collect agricultural commodities from growers to be sold by Marketing Boards and Crop Authorities. But the government agricultural marketing institutions had financial and operational problems which caused late crop collection from growers, late crop payment to farmers, and inadequate transport and storage facilities. These problems contributed to the general decline of crop production during the period (URT, 1975).

Cooperatives were re-established under the cooperative societies Act No. 4 of 1982. In 1985 Agricultural Producer Cooperatives were introduced. These cooperatives were new to both farmers and the officers. The producer cooperatives focused on cooperative production of goods and services as their primary task of economic activity. This form of cooperative organization tried to integrate the production and marketing of farm commodities (URT, 1982).

The producer cooperatives were expected to be multipurpose agricultural institutions which would transform the countryside and create self-reliant communities. This has not been achieved. Agriculture among the farmers is generally still engaged in individually and on a homestead basis. The Rural Cooperative Societies assist in channelling farm credit and agricultural inputs to farmers; and in marketing the farm products.

But the performance of the Rural Cooperative Societies during the last five years of the 1980s was generally bad. This was so because of the manner in which they were promoted and registered. There was little democratic and voluntary participation in the village cooperatives because of the provision of the Cooperative Act No. 4 of 1982 which prohibited formation of other cooperative societies within the areas of operation of the multipurpose village cooperative. This anomaly has been rectified by establishing farmers' cooperatives on a democratic and voluntary basis in accordance with 1991 Amendment of the Cooperative Act No. 4 of 1982.

In 1982 Tanzania had 8,174 registered villages. More than 13 million people or over 85 per cent of the population of Tanzania lived in them (Nyerere, 1982). But the level of production of farm products in these villages remained low.

A survey in 1986 (Collier, Radwan, Wangwe and Wagner, 1986) found the village agriculture production level to be low. The study found that in Tanzania, peasant agriculture used little modern technology and science and that the peasants lacked farm inputs, good extension services and good marketing services.

The Tanzanian economy had declined during the first half of the 1980s but during the second half of the decade the agriculture sector began to recover. Under the Structural Adjustment Programme (SAP) which was launched in 1982 important reforms were introduced to improve agriculture. During 1984/85, reforms were aimed at an increase in produce prices. The trend in production of farm crops was positive as shown in table 12.3.

**Table 12.3 Production of major grain crops in Tanzania 1982/83 - 1988/89 (in '000 metric tons)**

| Crops | 1982/83 | 1983/84 | 1984/85 | 1985/86 | 1986/87 | 1987/88 | 1988/89 |
|---|---|---|---|---|---|---|---|
| Maize | 1739.9 | 1711.7 | 2013.0 | 2670.8 | 2787.3 | 2429.4 | 2527.5 |
| Sorghum | 253.6 | 301.2 | 441.9 | 383.6 | 367.3 | 423.5 | 405.1 |
| Millet | 148.8 | 168.4 | 272.5 | 300.9 | 259.0 | 197.7 | 219.1 |
| Paddy | 254.8 | 328.3 | 275.6 | 417.8 | 565.8 | 782.3 | 768.3 |
| Wheat | 59.4 | 72.4 | 66.8 | 97.9 | 71.9 | 75.2 | 81.3 |

*Source*: United Republic of Tanzania (URT), 1987, p. 38 and URT, 1990, p.39.

The sources of increase after the reform years have not been fully established. We would suggest that as a result of reform measures and changes in agricultural policy which were coupled with incentive goods and a favourable climate, farmers expanded farm sizes and/or used more farm inputs such as fertilizers, improved seeds and insecticides. Research reported here studied the ways and extent to which peasants in Tanzania get resources and use them to improve agricultural performance in villages.

**The Study**

This study focused on the utilization of resources to improve agriculture performance in villages. The assumption is that peasants' access to resources and their use for agricultural production can improve the level of production. The study tried to find out how and the extent to which peasants obtain and use resources.

The following hypotheses are tested in this study.

1. Peasant access to resources for agriculture production varies within one village and across villages. That means some farmers in the villages tend to have more access to resources for agricultural production than do other farmers.

2. The availability of resources and their use for agricultural production on peasant farms varies between villages. It is assumed that there are historical, social, and geographical factors which explain the variations in the use of resources for agricultural production between villages.
3. The use of production resources on peasant agriculture is systematically associated with the peasant's household level of agricultural production activity. This means that the extent of the use of resources for agricultural production will tend to be systematically associated with the amount of farm produce from the peasant's farms and ultimately with the peasant's farm income.
4. The amount of farm production is systematically associated with the use of various types of appropriate resources in the production process and in the marketing of farm products. That means level of farm production is systematically associated with the application of various factors of production.

The study assumed that there were various factors associated with farmers' access to agricultural resources and the use of the resources in agricultural production. It was also assumed that the low agriculture production in the peasant farms was partly related to the failure by the farmers to use production resources in farming. Thus the dependent variable which we are studying is *The peasants' household level of income for agriculture production.* The assumption is that the peasants have to get and use agricultural production resources in order to improve farm production. These resources must also include the services in the marketing process for farm products.

This research studied *economic, technological, extension and marketing services* issues and their related independent variables of the *resources and services which peasants used in the 1988/89 farming season.* The study tried to find out whether or not the variables were systematically related to the level of agricultural income among farmers in villages. The following independent variables were tested.

*1. Economic Factors:*

(i)    Size  of peasant farm
(ii)   Labour input in peasant farming
(iii)  Prices of farm products

*2. Technological Factors:*

The research studied the use of high yield seed, chemical fertilizers, pesticides, tractor or plough in peasant farming. On improving livestock, the research studied the use of hybrid animals and animal feed by peasants.

## 3. Extension Services to Peasant Farming:

The research studied extension services on using modern farm implements, applying science in crop farming, modern animal husbandry and irrigation of peasant farms.

## 4. Marketing Services to Peasant Farming:

The research studied the marketing services which are transporting crops, crop storage, crop inspection and crop weighing.

The survey also collected data about the village cooperative/communal farm. The research tried to find out about the participation of peasants in making decisions on village cooperative farming and animal keeping. Labour input by household members on the village cooperative farm was studied; also whether or not peasants were satisfied with the amount of farm produce from the cooperative farm. The research also tried to find out the total amount of net income (in shillings) the household members received from the cooperative farming/animal keeping activities in 1988/89.

The study was concerned with how village political, historical, social and geographical conditions were related to the use of agricultural production resources. It was assumed that unique conditions operated which help to explain the variations of the use of agricultural resources between villages.

**Theory and Methods of the Study**

The study was guided by theoretical aspects of two major perspectives, namely: an individual level perspective and a political economy perspective. The individual level perspective focuses on the individual and changes in the individual. The individual modernity theories focuses on individual values, beliefs and motivations which are considered to be associated with modernization. This perspective was most popular in the 1950s and 1960s. Theorists of this perspective include Hagen (1962); Rogers (1968, 1962); Kunkel (1958); Banfield (1958); McClelland (1961); Lerner (1958); Forster (1965); Schultz (1964); and Inkeles and Smith (1974). Many individual modernity theorists saw the major impetus for change coming from forces external to a traditional society. Modernization of traditional society involved bringing new technologies, innovations and knowledge to be diffused eventually throughout the entire society (Rogers, 1962).

The individual modernity theorists have been criticized for failing to realize that individual behaviour and attitudes are often shaped or constrained by structural and environmental factors. Thus Portes (1973, 1976) criticized such theorists because they did not consider historical and structural factors in explaining socio-economic changes in developing societies.

The political economy perspective challenged the major premises of 'individual modernity' theories for failing to focus on historical, political and economic forces and their contribution to the problem of underdevelopment of poor nations. Theorists of the political economy perspective include

166

Baran (1957); Frank (1976); Szentes (1971); Amin (1974) and Wallerstein (1978).

Long and Robert (1978) suggest that the individual level perspective and the political economy perspective should be combined in order to obtain a more complete picture of the socio-economic processes taking place in a developing society. In this study I combined the two perspectives to enable me to focus on the individual peasant and the behaviour of the individual peasant (Portes, 1976) as well as on political, historical, economic, social and geographical factors which are systematically associated with peasant access to the resources of agriculture and their use to improve production (Rogers, 1976).

Field research was conducted to collect data on household farms and village cooperative/communal farms on peasant access to agricultural resources and their use to improve agricultural production. Villages in Kilimanjaro, Dar es Salaam and Tabora regions were selected as case studies; one village was selected for study from each region. The villages are Chekereni, Chanika and Ussoke Mlimani respectively.

In each village respondents were selected from the list of households using simple random sampling procedure. From each village I drew a systematic random sample. The first interviewee in each village was determined by a random number within an interval of integers 1 to 5. After picking the first number from the numerically ordered list of households, I continued to pick every fifth household until the whole list was finished. In this way I picked a random sample of 371 households which included 114 households from Chekereni Village, 122 households from Chanika Village and 135 households from Ussoke Mlimani Village.

Face to face interviews were used in this survey. The major problem encountered was non-availability of respondents when the interviewer came to the door. Because of this problem we interviewed 341 respondents distributed as follows: 102 respondents from Chekereni, 112 respondents from Chanika, and 127 respondents from Ussoke Mlimani.

A structured questionnaire design was used in this study. The questions were item analysed to see if each focused on a specific issue. The questionnaire was pretested on a small number of people in Chekereni Village.

Unstructured interviews with the leaders and officers in the villages, government and parastatal organizations were also conducted. I conducted library research and collected other secondary data from the files and records of villages and district offices.

The field research for data collection was done from May 1989 to March 1990. I visited and stayed in each of the three villages for a continuous period until the entire survey for that village was completed. I and my research assistants interviewed the respondents and filled in the questionnaire as the interview progressed. The interviews were conducted in Swahili in all villages. But in Ussoke Mlimani Village there were a few cases of respondents who could not respond well in Swahili language. In such cases my research assistants asked the questions in Nyamwezi. The time taken to complete a questionnaire varied from 30 minutes to one hour. Most

167

questionnaires were completed in about 45 minutes. The questionnaire was followed closely during interviewing.

**The Survey Sample**

Of the 341 peasant respondents 261 were male (76.5 per cent) and 80 were female (23.5 per cent). More males than females were picked from the list of peasants in each village because the registration of peasant households was made using the names of the head of each household. For married couples, the husband is usually the head of the family in these villages.

The level of formal education of the respondents was generally low. 127 respondents (37.2 per cent) did not attend formal schools. 204 respondents (59.8 per cent) had primary school level education; and only 10 respondents (3.0 per cent) received secondary school education. The theories of individual modernization suggest that formal education for farmers creates attributes which help them to adopt the innovations for modern agriculture. The villages studied here have historical, social, economic and geographical differences, which had to be taken into account during the process of analyzing the research data.

*Chekereni Village* is located in Mabogini Ward, Hai East Division in Moshi (Rural) District. It is about 14 km away from Moshi town. The village was formed in July 1970 by peasants on their own initiative. It has a communal farm, dairy cattle, poultry, a tractor, a butchery and a grain grinding mill. The village has a big irrigation project for peasant farms. It is in the low dry plains, and it is suitable for annual and seasonal crops like maize, beans, cotton, finger millet, groundnut and vegetables. Rice is grown on the irrigated plots. Chekereni Rural Cooperative Society buys crops from the peasants, and sells farm inputs.

*Ussoke Mlimani Village* is located in Uyumbu Ward, Ussoke Division in Urambo District. The village is 38 km from Urambo town. This is a traditional village which had dispersed homesteads; but during the villagization programme more people were moved in from other areas. The village lies in the Miombo woodland zone and it is suitable for the cultivation of tobacco, maize, groundnut, sorghum, simsim and vegetables. Ussoke Village has a communal farm, a butchery, a tractor, and a grain grinding mill. Ussoke Rural Cooperative Society buys crops from peasants and supplies farm inputs.

*Chanika Village* is located in Ilala District. It lies in the coastal zone where coconuts, cashew nuts and rice thrive well. Peasants grow cassava, sweet potatoes, fruits and vegetables and sell them at the Dar es Salaam city markets. Small traders come to the village from the city to buy cassava, sweet potatoes, fruits and vegetables from the peasants. Chanika Rural Cooperative Society buys cashew nuts from the peasants.

# Analysis of Data

## 1. Income from Village Communal Farms

The frequency distribution of the Total Net Income of the households from the village communal/cooperative farming and animal keeping indicated that it would be difficult for correlations and regressions to be computed for this dependent variable. Although each village had a communal farm, only Chekereni Village distributed the income from the village communal farm to peasants who worked there. Chanika Village had young coconut trees planted on the village communal farm. In Ussoke Mlimani Village, all income from the village communal farm was put into the account of the village agricultural fund instead of distributing the money to the peasants who worked there. In this survey 96 respondents (28.2 per cent) received income from the Chekereni Village communal farm products. 245 respondents (71.8 per cent) did not receive any income from the agricultural products which they produced on the village communal farms.

Of the respondents who received income from Chekereni communal farm, 91 (26.7 per cent) received less than 1,500 shillings; three (0.9 per cent) received from 1,501 to 3,000 shillings; and two (0.6 per cent) received from 6,001 to 12,000 shillings. No respondent received between 3,001 and 6,000 shillings; and no respondent received over 12,000 shillings (Exchange Rate was 1 US$ = Tsh. 230 in June, 1991).

Respondents were asked to evaluate their participation in decision-making in village communal farming and animal keeping. Peasants usually participate in making such decisions during the village general meetings. They also participate through their elected representatives on the village council and committees. 37 respondents (10.9 per cent) said they participated more than most people in making decisions on the communal farming and animal keeping. 240 respondents (70.4 per cent) said they participated about the same as other people; and 37 respondents (10.9 per cent) said they participated less than most people in making such decisions. The research found that most decisions on communal farming and animal keeping were made by the village council and committees; such decisions were finally tabled in the village assembly meeting.

Results concerning the total number of days which adult members of the household worked on farming and keeping animals on the village communal farm in 1988/89 show that 54 respondents (15.8 per cent) did not work on the village communal farm; 218 respondents (63.9 per cent) worked for less than 45 days during the previous years; 41 respondents (12.0 per cent) worked between 45 days and 90 days; and 28 respondents (8.2 per cent) worked for more than 90 days. These findings suggest that adult members of these households did not have many man-days of labour input on the communal farms in the three villages.

Respondents were also asked to say how satisfied they were with the amount of agricultural products from the communal farm. 119 respondents (34.9 per cent) said they were generally satisfied. 97 respondents (28.4 per cent) said they were sometimes satisfied and sometimes not satisfied; 90 respondents (26.4 per cent) said they were generally unsatisfied.

169

If the respondents were generally satisfied with the amount of farm production from the village communal farms, that could be an indirect incentive for their household adult members to be involved in more man-days of labour input on working there. But for the respondents who said that they were generally unsatisfied with the amount of agricultural products from the village communal farm, a special attempt has to be made to motivate them.

## 2. Income from Family Farms

The peasant's income from the family farm is derived from farm crops and from animals and animal products. This study collected data on the following dependent variables of the peasant's income from agricultural products from the family farm in the year 1988/89:

(a) The estimated total value (in shillings) of all the crops harvested.
(b) The estimated total value (in shillings) of all the animals kept at the peasant's family farm.
(c) The total amount of money (in shillings) received from the sale of crops.
(d) The total amount of money (in shillings) received from the same of animals.
(e) The total amount of money (in shillings) received from the sale of animal products.

I subtracted the total amount of cash (in shillings) received from the crops sold from the estimated total value (in shillings) of all the crops harvested from the peasant's family farm in 1988/89 in order to obtain the total value (in shillings) of the crops not sold in that year. I also subtracted the total amount of cash (in shillings) received from the animals sold from the estimated total value (in shillings) of all animals kept at the peasant's family farm in 1988/89 in order to obtain the total value (in shillings) of all animals not sold in that year.

I computed the Pearson zero-order correlation coefficients between the dependent and the independent variables. I wanted to find out the size and the direction of the correlation coefficient between each pair of variables, and if that relationship was statistically significant. If a correlation coefficient was significant at .01 level I concluded that the relationship between the pair of variables was highly significant. If a correlation coefficient was significant at .05 level I concluded that the relationship between the pair of variables was significant.

The dependent variables in the peasants' income from crops of the family farm in the year 1988/89 were the following:

(a) The estimated total value (in shillings) of all crops harvested.
(b) The amount of money (in shillings) received from the crops sold.
(c) The total value (in shillings) of all the crops not sold in the household.

The independent variables which were correlated with the above dependent variables were the following:

170

(a) The size of the respondent's family farm.
(b) The use of household man-days of labour and hired man-days of labour on the family farm.
(c) The agricultural products price incentive to farmers.
(d) The use of high yield seeds, chemical fertilizers, pesticides, tractors and ploughs.
(e) The use of farm irrigation services, extension services, and scientific crop farming services. Other independent variables were the use of marketing services which include transporting crops, storage services, crop inspection and crop weighing services.

The correlations between the dependent and the independent variables for crops are shown in Table 12.4. The size of the respondent's family farm showed highly significant correlation with the three dependent variables. The correlations between all other independent variables and the estimated total value (in shillings) of all crops harvested from the peasant's family farm and the correlation between those independent variables and the total value (in shillings) of all the crops not sold from the household were not statistically significant.

The correlation between each independent variable and the total amount of money received from the sale of crops from the family farm was greater than .1 and was statistically significant. I then focused the regression analyses on these variables which had correlations which were statistically significant.

(a) The estimated total value (in shillings) of all the animals kept at the peasant's family farm.
(b) The total amount of money (in shillings) received from the animals sold.
(c) The total amount of money (in shillings) received from the animal products sold.
(d) The total value (in shillings) of all animals in the respondent's household which were not sold.

The independent variables which were correlated with the above dependent variables were the following:

(a) The use of household man-days of labour and hired man-days of labour for family farm animal keeping activities.
(b) The animal and animal products price incentive to farmers.
(c) The use of animal feed, hybrid animals and modern animal husbandry services in peasant livestock activities.

The correlations between the dependent and independent variables for animals and animal products are shown in Table 12.5.

The use of household man-days of labour input on the family animal keeping activities, and the animals and animal products price incentive to peasants had correlation coefficients which were less than .1 and were statistically not significant. There was correlation between the remaining independent variables and two dependent variables as follows: the estimated total value of all the animals kept at the peasant's family farm, and the total value of all animals not sold on the family farm had correlation coefficients which were greater than .1 and were statistically highly significant.

**Table 12.4 Correlations of crop-related variables**

|  | Total value of crops | Cash from crops sold | Value of crops not sold |
|---|---|---|---|
| **Economic** | | | |
| Farm size | .1375** | .2828** | .1203** |
| | (335) | (335) | (335) |
| Household labour | -.0128 | .1447** | -.022 |
| | (340) | (340) | (340) |
| Hired labour | .0086 | -.4947** | -.0229 |
| | (336) | (336) | (336) |
| Satisfied with | -.0582 | -.1307** | -.0377 |
| prices | (259) | (259) | (259) |
| **Technological** | | | |
| High-yield seeds | .0503 | .2688** | .0334 |
| | (341) | (341) | (341) |
| Fertilizer | .0306 | .1922** | .0334 |
| | (341) | (341) | (341) |
| Pesticides | -.0292 | .3252** | -.0501 |
| | (341) | (341) | (341) |
| Tractor/plough | .0107 | .3327** | -.0105 |
| | (341) | (341) | (341) |
| **Extension services** | | | |
| Irrigation | -.0259 | .2477** | -.0418 |
| | (341) | (341) | (341) |
| Modern | -.0346 | .2478** | -.0506 |
| implements | (341) | (341) | (341) |
| Scientific farming | -.0093 | .2881** | -.0277 |
| | (341) | (341) | (341) |
| **Marketing services** | | | |
| Transport | .00905 | .2190** | .0770 |
| | (341) | (341) | (341) |
| Storage | .0316 | .2441 | 0161 |
| | (341) | (341) | (341) |
| Inspection | .0351 | .2365** | .0202 |
| | (341) | (341) | (341) |
| Weighing | .0427 | .2447** | .0273 |
| | (341) | (341) | (341) |

\*   The total amount of money (in shillings) received from the animals sold.
\*\*  The estimated total value (in shillings) of all the animals kept at the peasant's family farm.

Number of cases shown in parentheses.

# Table 12.5 Correlations of variables relating to animals and animal products

| | Total Animal Value | Cash from Animals Sold | Cash from Animal Products Sold | Value of Animals Not Sold |
|---|---|---|---|---|
| **Economic** | | | | |
| Household | -.0042 | .0766 | .0675 | -.0140 |
| labour | (340) | (340) | (340) | (340) |
| Hired labour | -.1670** | .0986* | .2831** | .586** |
| | (336) | (336) | (336) | (336) |
| Satisfied with | -.0065 | .0459 | -.0534 | -.0126 |
| prices | (259) | (259) | (259) | (259) |
| **Technological** | | | | |
| Animal | .3332** | .1415** | .0915* | .3235* |
| Feed used | (341) | (341) | (341) | (341) |
| Hybrid | .2822** | .1667 | .0587 | .2742** |
| animals | (341) | (341) | (341) | (341) |
| **Extension** | | | | |
| **Services** | | | | |
| Modern | .4323** | .1526** | .1616** | .4236** |
| husbandry | (341) | (341) | (341) | (341) |

\*   Significant at $p \geq .05$ level
\*\* Significant at $p \geq .01$ level

Number of cases shown in parentheses.

In this survey, 65 respondents (19.1 per cent) sold animals and 275 respondents (80.9 per cent) did not sell animals in 1988/89. 313 respondents (91.8 per cent) did not sell animal products and only 28 respondents (8.2 per cent) sold animal products in that year. The findings on the animals and animal products sold suggest that animal keeping is not a commercialized economic activity. In view of this I decided that in the next section I should focus the regression analysis on explaining the value of animals not sold in 1988/89.

The level of the household farm income is explained by several predictor variables. That is why I decided to use multiple regression analyses to consider the relationship between more than two variables at a time. For each dependent variable, all related independent variables were entered into multiple regression analysis to test their relationship to the household farm income variable.

The multiple regressions could be expected to provide information on the presumed causal effect of the independent variables on the two dependent variables which are: (a) the peasant's household farm income from crops sold; and (b) the estimated total value (in shillings) of all animals not sold from the peasant's family farm. The test of significance was done for the whole sample in order to get analytical statistics which could be used to make inferences from the sample findings on the relationship between the predictor variables and the dependent variable. Because the three villages are categorical variables, we created dummy variables for the villages and included them in the overall regression model (Hanushek and Jackson, 1977, pp. 101-102). The village differences provide the environment in which the peasants perform farm activity and get income from that activity. The village dummy variables give the mean (intercept) for each village.

The regression analysis enables us to find out the following three things:

(a) Whether or not the villages differ from each other after the differences on the agricultural production resources are controlled.
(b) Whether or not the production resources variables make any difference to farm income when the village variables are controlled.
(c) What proportion of the total variation in the farm income variable can be explained by all the independent variables acting together.

In this research I tested the null hypothesis that the independent variables were not associated with the dependent variables. The alternative hypotheses are that the villages differ from each other and that there is a linear relationship between the production resources variables and the income level variables.

The F test statistic for significance was used to see how useful the regression model was. The multiple $R^2$ showed how successfully the regression model explains the variation (Lewis-Beck, 1980, p. 23). The $t$ test statistic for significance was used to test the hypothesis that there is no effect of an independent variable on a dependent variable (Blalock, 1979, p. 425).

To test the hypotheses, a confidence interval around the regression coefficient was predetermined. If the calculated $t$ statistic did not fall within the .05 or .01 intervals in a two tailed test, I rejected the null hypotheses with 95 per cent or 99 per cent confidence. I then concluded that the regression coefficient was significantly different from zero at 0.5 or 0.1 level (Blalock, 1979, pp. 154-166).

Two regression equations are analysed in this study:

## The First Regression Equation

The total amount of money (in shillings) received from the sale of crops from the family farm in the year 1988/89 (dependent variable) was regressed on the village dummy variables and the following interval scale independent variables:

(a) The size of the respondent's family farm.
(b) The agriculture products price incentive to farmers.
(c) The use of household man-days labour and hired man-days labour on the family farm.
(d) The use of high yield seeds, chemical fertilizers, pesticides and tractor or plough in peasant agriculture.
(e) The use of irrigation services, extension services or modern farm implements and scientific crop farming services in peasant agriculture.

(f) The use of transport services, crop storage services, crop inspection services and crop weighing services in marketing agricultural products.

The computer output of the regression analysis is shown on Table 12.6. The F 24.59 which was obtained for the model was significant at .01 level. 41.3 per cent of the variation in the total amount of money (in shillings) received from the sale of crops from the family farm in the year 1988/89 was explained by the regression model. I therefore rejected the null hypothesis which suggested that there was no systematic relationship between the household farm income from crops sold and the production and marketing resources independent variables.

212 respondents (62.2 per cent) said they sold crops in 1988/89. Out of these, 73 respondents (21.4 per cent) were from Chekereni Village, 68 respondents (19.9 per cent) were from Chanika Village; and 71 respondents (20.8 per cent) were from Ussoke Mlimani Village.

129 respondents (37.8 per cent) said they did not sell crops in 1988/89. Out of these households which did not sell crops, 29 respondents (8.5 per cent) were from Chekereni Village; 44 respondents (12.9 per cent) were from Chanika Village; and 56 respondents (16.4 per cent) were from Ussoke Mlimani Village.

Five independent variables had a significant relationship with the total amount of money (in shillings) the household received from selling crops from the family farm in the year 1988/89.

(a) The use of employed labour on the family farm had a (regression coefficient) B 9840 with $t$ 6.462, which was significant at .01 level (two tailed test).

250 respondents (73.3 per cent) did not employ labour on the family farm in 1988/89. 91 respondents (26.7 per cent) did employ farm labour. This finding could suggest that employment of farm labour was done by the higher income peasant households especially during the peak farming seasons of crop planting, weeding and harvesting. It is unlikely that the low farm income households could employ additional farm labour.

(b) The size of the respondent's family farm had a (regression coefficient) B 6633.42 with $t$ 3.652 which was significant at .01 level (two tailed test).

10 respondents (2.9 per cent) said they had less than one acre (0.4 ha) of family farm. 151 respondents had one to three acres (0.4 - 1.2 ha.) of family farm; 87 respondents (25.5 per cent) said they had from three acres to five acres (1.2 to 2.0 ha.) of family farm. 69 respondents (20.2 per cent) said they had five acres to ten acres (2.0 to 4.1 ha.) of family farm; and 18 respondents (5.3 per cent) said they had more than ten acres (4.1 ha.) of family farm. Six respondents (1.8 per cent of the sample) did not know the size of the family farm. These findings suggest that farm size has a systematic relationship with the amount of money the household received from selling farm products in 1988/89.

### Table 12.6 Multiple regression, income from crops sold (controlling for village)

| Variable | Regression Coefficient B | T | Significance of T | Multiple $R^2$ |
|---|---|---|---|---|
| Village 2: Chanika | -440.903 | -.103 | .918 | |
| Village 1: Chekereni | 6539.637 | 1.296 | .196 | .048 |
| Employed labour | 9840.200 | 6.462 | .000 | .255 |
| Farm size | 6633.420 | 3.652 | .000 | .328 |
| Used tractor/plough | 7372.286 | 3.615 | .000 | .364 |
| Crop weighing services | 5848.083 | 3.250 | .001 | .394 |
| Household labour | 2611.433 | 2.810 | .005 | .413 |
| Constant | -36712.499 | -5.932 | .000 | |

F entire equation = 24.590; significance = .000  N = 252

(c) The use of tractor or plough in peasant agriculture had a (regression coefficient) B 7372.29 with *t* 3.615 which was significant at the .01 level (two tailed test).

230 respondents (67.4 per cent) said they did not use tractor or plough on the family farm and 111 respondents (32.6 per cent) did use them in 1988/89.

These findings suggest that there is a systematic relationship between using tractor or plough on the family farming activity and the level of farm income which the household received. The research found that Chanika Village had no tractor and 106 peasants (31.1 per cent) cultivated their farms by hand hoes. Ussoke Mlimani Village had a tractor which cultivated 20 household farms (5.9 per cent). The tractor was mainly used to pull a trailer for transport purposes. Chekereni has a rice irrigation project which was established under the Japan and Tanzania governments' agreement on technical cooperation. Under this project 85 peasants (24.9 per cent) benefited from the use of tractor cultivation in 1988/89.

(d) The use of crop weighing services in marketing agriculture products had a (regression coefficient) B 5848.08 with *t* 3.250 which was significant at 0.1 (two tailed test).

(d) The use of crop weighing services in marketing agriculture products had a (regression coefficient) B 5848.08 with *t* 3.250 which was significant at 0.1 (two tailed test).

236 respondents (69.2 per cent) said they did not use crop weighing services in marketing family farm crops. 105 respondents (30.8 per cent) did make use of these.

These findings suggest that there is a systematic relationship between household farm income and the use of crop weighing services in marketing crops from the family farm. The tobacco farmers of Ussoke Mlimani sell through their Rural Cooperative Society where it is weighed. The rice farmers of Chekereni are required to bring a certain proportion of their farm produce to be sold through their cooperative society. Chanika Village peasants mostly sell their fruits and vegetables in the village to small traders who do not bring weighing machines with them. Even when the peasants sell their fruits and vegetables to consumers, they just estimate prices without weighing the crops.

(e) The use of household labour on the family farm had a (regression coefficient) B 2611.43 with *t* 2.810 which was significant at .01 level (two tailed test).

Two respondents (0.6 per cent) did not know the total number of days the adult members of the household worked on the family farm in 1988/89; 39 respondents (11.4 per cent) said their household adult members worked a total of less than 45 days on their family farm. 56 respondents (16.4 per cent) said they worked for between 45 and 90 days; 69 respondents (20.2 per cent) said they worked a total of 91 to 135 days. 32 respondents (9.4 per cent) said the adult household members worked a total of 136 to 180 days; 30 respondents (8.8 per cent) said they worked a total of 181 to 225 days, and 113 respondents (33.1 per cent) said the adults from their household worked a total of more than 225 days on their family farm. The research findings suggest a systematic relationship between the household farm income and the total number of days which the adult members of the household worked on the family farm. This conclusion coincided with the fact that many peasant households in Chanika and Ussoke Mlimani did not use tractor or plough to cultivate their farms.

The constant coefficients -30172.86 for Chekereni Village; and -37153.40 for Chanika Village were not significantly different from the constant coefficient - 36712.50 for Ussoke Mlimani Village. In this research there was insufficient evidence to reject the null hypothesis that the constant coefficients for the three villages were not significantly different. That means the impact of contextual factors such as political, historical, social and geographical factors was not significantly different among the three villages.

The geographical locations of the villages are: in the low dry plains for Chekereni; the Coastal Zone for Chanika; and the Miombo Woodland Zone for Ussoke Mlimani. Such geographical locations, together with the associated soil and climatic conditions, the infrastructure, culture and the history of the villages affect the life of the people including their agricultural activities. Analysis of the data suggested that impact of the village context factors on the total income which the household received was not significantly different when you compare that effect between the three villages.


**The Second Regression Equation**

In the second regression equation, the dependent variable was the estimated total value (in shillings) of all animals in the respondent's household which were not sold in 1988/89. This dependent variable was regressed on the village dummy variables and the following interval scale independent variables:

(a) The use of household man-days labour and hired man-days labour on the family farm animal keeping activities.
(b) The animal and animal products price incentive to farmers.
(c) The use of good quality animal feed by peasant's animals and the use of hybrid animals in the household.
(d) The use of modern animal husbandry services in peasant agriculture.

The computer output of the regression analysis is shown in Table 12.7. The F 19.278 which was obtained for the model was significant at 0.1 level of significance. 27.8 per cent of the variation in the total value (in shillings) for all animals in the respondent's household which were not sold in 1988/89 was explained by the regression model. I therefore rejected the null hypothesis which suggested that there was no systematic relationship between the value of the animals kept in the household and the production and marketing resources independent variables.

The animals kept in the peasant's family farms were cattle, goats, sheep and pigs; chickens and ducks were also included in this survey. The study showed that 85 respondents (24.9 per cent) said they did not keep animals on their family farms. 256 respondents (75.1 per cent) said they did keep animals.

The independent variables had significant relationship with the total value (in shillings) of all animals in the respondent's household which were not sold in 1988/89.

(a) The use of modern animal husbandry services in peasant agriculture had a (regression coefficient) B 22446.16 with $t$ 6.662 which was significant at .01 level (two tailed test). This finding suggests that there is a systematic relationship between the total value (in shillings) of all the animals in the respondent's household which were not sold and the use of modern animal husbandry services in peasant agriculture.
The survey showed that 258 respondents (75.7 per cent) did not get modern animal husbandry services on the animals kept on the family farm. 83 respondents (24.3 per cent) said they did obtain such services. The survey showed that many peasants who keep hybrid animals, good

178

**Table 12.7 Multiple regression, value of animals (controlling for village)**

| Variable | Regression Coefficient B | T | Significance | Multiple R² |
|---|---|---|---|---|
| Village 2: Chanika | 1457.265 | .225 | .822 | |
| Village 1: Chekereni | 7357.974 | 1.207 | 1.207 | .064 |
| Modern husbandry | 22446.164 | 6.662 | .000 | .211 |
| Used animal feeds | 15795.965 | 4.206 | .000 | .262 |
| Employed farm labour | 5793.279 | 2.348 | .020 | .278 |
| Constant | -3563.033 | -.665 | .507 | |

F Entire Equation = 19.278;  Signficance = .00   N = 256

quality chicken layers and broilers were the peasants whom the field veterinary assistants visited most often.  The survey also showed that many peasants who kept local breed animals and fowls did not receive or use modern animal husbandry services.

(b) The use of animal feed by the peasant's animals had a (regression coefficient) B 15795.97 with $t$ 4.206 which was significant at .01 level (two tailed test).  This finding suggests that the use of animal feed by the animals kept on the family farm had a systematic relationship with the total value of all animals in the respondent's household which were not sold in 1988/89.
17 respondents (5.0 per cent) said the animals in their households used good animal feed and 324 respondents (95.0 per cent) said that this was not the case.  Good animal feed is not easily available in the village for peasants to buy for their animals.  Animal and chicken feed were prepared by special grain mills which were located away form the villages.  Because there were few peasants who kept hybrid cattle and good quality chicken layers and broilers, the villages did not provide a big enough market to attract businessmen to bring manufactured animal feed into the villages.  Peasants who wanted this good quality animal feed had to search for it away from the villages and in most cases in the urban shops.

(c) The use of hired labour on the family farm animal keeping activities has a (regression coefficient) B 5793.28 with $t$ 2.348 which was significant at .05 level (two tailed test).  The survey showed that 245 respondents (71.8

per cent of the sample) said that their households did not employ people to work on the family farm in 1988/89. 91 respondents (26.7 per cent) said their households employed additional people to work on the family farm in that year. Five respondents (1.4 percent) did not indicate whether or not their households employed farm labour in 1988/89. The survey showed that the richer peasants tended to employ people to tend their animals when they were pre-occupied with some other activities on the farm or when they were away from the family farm.

The constant coefficients -2105.77 for Chanika Village; and 3794.941 for Chekereni village were not significantly different from the constant coefficient -3563.03 for Ussoke Mlimani Village. There was insufficient evidence to reject the null hypothesis that the constant coefficients for the three villages were not significantly different. The impact of the village context, controlling for the other explanatory variables, was not significantly different in the three villages. This means that if we control for the other explanatory variable, the mean for each village on the total value (in shillings) of all animals in the respondent's household which were not sold in 1988/89 in the three villages would not be significantly different from each other.

## Conclusions and Implications

i)  The importance of agriculture and the contribution of the agricultural sector in the economy of Tanzania are the considerations which underline the need for research to find ways to improve agricultural production. The concern for research to modernize agriculture in the peasant sector was based on the evidence that Tanzanian agricultural policy has placed emphasis on the farmers in the villages; yet existing records show that agriculture production in the peasant farming is low.

ii)  This study examined selected factors which are considered to be the resources for agricultural production. I wanted to find out whether or not peasant access to resources for agriculture production varied among peasants within one village and across villages; whether or not the availability of agricultural production resources and their use on peasant farms varied between villages; and whether or not the use of agricultural production resources on the peasant's farms was systematically associated with the level of farm income. Finally, I wanted to identify by using regression analysis the combination of the production resources to be used in order to get a certain level of agricultural production.

iii)  The study demonstrated statistically that access to and the use of agricultural production resources on peasant farms varied significantly among peasants within one village and across villages. There was variation between villages in the availability and use of agricultural resources. The use of agricultural production resources on peasant farms was shown to be systematically associated with the level of agricultural production. The study also indicated that the level of agricultural

180

production was to be explained by the application of a combination of several production resources on the farm unit level and at the marketing process level. The multiple regression analysis showed that five production resources were significant in helping to account for the level of agricultural production on the peasant household farm.

iv) The survey showed that little had been achieved in developing communal or cooperative agriculture in the three villages. People's participation in communal farming in the villages and the household income from the village communal farming activity have not registered any success in the three villages. The free market economy which is practised in Tanzania has adversely affected cooperative or communal farming in Tanzania.

v) The survey showed that few peasants used production resources on their household farms. Some peasants seemed not to be informed about the type and amount of farm inputs. Others did not know the place to get the inputs or they did not have the money to pay for the resources. Peasants did not get loans from banks because they had difficulty in meeting the conditions required.

vi) The research found that the agricultural cooperative society and the village government were important local institutions which could be mobilized successfully to help peasants to get and use resources for agricultural production. The agricultural cooperative societies could be strengthened financially and in management to enable them to mobilize resources from financial credit institutions and to channel such credit to the peasants. The agricultural cooperative society should also provide the marketing resources for the peasants' farm products.

The village government has to oversee the smooth provision of all the production and marketing services to the farmers. The village government should liaise with the district administration to make sure that field agricultural and veterinary assistants are available in the village.

vii) Success in modernizing peasant agriculture in Tanzania largely depends on the peasants' access to modern agricultural production resources and the use of such resources at the farm production unit as well as in the marketing process. The research indicated that there were problems in the crop marketing institutions because of failure to buy agricultural crops on time and to pay the farmers good prices. If good marketing of farm products is not there, the peasants tend to switch to producing for home consumption or move to alternative economic activity such as petty trading, work for wages, or other activities within or even outside the village. The central government has the role of ensuring that there is good coordination and cooperation between the institutions which deal with agricultural production and marketing of farm products in the entire chain that affects peasant agriculture in Tanzania.

## Notes

1. Peasant household farms in 1971/72 constituted 97.4 per cent of all cultivated land in Tanzania. Communal or cooperative farming was 0.8 per cent while the remaining 1.8 per cent of the cultivated land was for large-scale farming in public and private ownership.
2. Extensive literature on the reasons for adopting villagization and the implementation of the villagization programme is cited in Lyimo, 1983, p. 72.

## References

Amin, S. (1974), *Accumulation on a World Scale: A Critique of the Theory of Underdevelopment*, Monthly Review, New York, NY.

Awiti, A. (1973), 'Economic Differentiation in Isimani, Iringa Region: A Critical Assessment of Peasants' Response to Ujamaa Vijijini Programme', *African Review*, 3, 209-39.

Banfield, E.C. (1958), *The Moral Basis of Backward Society*, Free Press, New York, NY, NY.

Baran, P.A. (1957), *The Political Economy of Growth*, Modern Reader, New York, NY.

Blalock, H.M. Jr. (1979), *Social Statistics*, McGraw Hill, New York.

Brain, J.L. (1977), 'Is Transformation Possible? Style of Settlement in Post-Independence Tanzania', *African Affairs*, 76, 231-45.

Cliffe, L. (1977), 'Rural Class Formation in East Africa', *Journal of Peasant Studies*, 4, 195-224.

Cliffe, L., Lawrence, P., Luttrell, W., Migot-Adholla, S. and Saul, J. (eds) (1975), *Rural Cooperation in Tanzania*, TPH, Dar es Salaam.

Collier, P., Radwan, S., Wangwe, S. and Wagner, A. (1986), *Labour and Poverty in Rural Tanzania: Ujamaa and Rural Development in the United Republic of Tanzanai*, Clarendon Press, Oxford.

Forster, G.M. (1965), 'Peasant Society and the Image of Limited Good', *Americcan Anthropologist*, 67, 293-315.

Frank, A.G. (1976), *Capitalism and World Underdevelopment*, Monthly Review Press, New York, NY.

Hagen, E.E. (1962), *On the Theory of Social Change: How Economic Growth Begins*, Dorsey Press, Homewood, IL.

Hanushek, E.A. and Jackson, J.E. (1977), *Statistical Methods for Social Scientists*, Academic Press, New York, NY.

Hyden, G. (ed) (1976), *Cooperation in Tanzania: Problems of Organisation Building*, TPH, Dar es Salaam.

Inkeles, A. and Smith, D.B. (1974), *Becoming Modern: Individual Change in Six Developing Countries*, Harvard University Press, Cambridge, MA.

Kunkel, J.H. (1958), *Society and Economic Growth: A Behavioural Perspective on Social Change*, Oxford University Press, New York, NY.

Lerner, D.M. (1958), *The Passing of Traditional Society: Modernizing the Middle East*, Free Press, Glencoe, IL.

Lewis-Beck, M.S. (1980), *Applied Regression: An Introduction*, Sage, London.

Long, N. and Robert, R.B. (1978), *Peasant Cooperation and Capitalist Expansion in Central Peru*, Institute of Latin American Studies, University of Texas Press, Austin, TX.

Lyimo, F.F. (1983), 'Peasant Production and Cooperative Experiences in Tanzania: Case Studies in Villages in Moshi (Rural) and Urambo Districts', PhD thesis, University of Wisconsin-Madison.

McClelland, D.C. (1961), *The Achieving Society*, Van Nostrand, New York, NY.

Ministry of Agriculture (MoA) (1982), *The National Agriculture Policy (Final Report)*, Task Force on National Agriculture Policy, Printpak, Dar es Salaam.

Nyerere, J.K. (1968), 'Socialism and Rural Development', in Nyerere, *Freedom and Socialism* Oxford University Press, Dar es Salaam, pp. 337-66.

Nyerere, J.K. (1982), 'Five Years of CCM Government', Address given to the National Conference of CCM on 20 October 1982, Government Printer, Dar es Salaam.

Onimode, B. (1989), *The IMF, the World Bank and African Debt: The Economic Impact*, Zed Books, London.

Portes, A. (1973), 'The Factorial Structure of Modernity: Empirical Replications and a Critique', *American Journal of Sociology*, 79, pp. 15-44.

Portes, A. (1976), 'On the Sociology of National Development: Theories and Issues', *American Journal of Sociology*, 82, pp. 55-85.

Raikes, P. (1978), 'Rural Differentiation and Class Formation in Tanzania', *Journal of Peasant Studies*, 5, pp. 285-325.

Rogers, E.M. (1962), *Diffusion of Innovations*, Free Press, New York, NY.

Rogers, E.M. (1968), 'Motivations, Values and Attitues of Subsistence Farmers: Towards a Subculture of Peasantry', in C.R. Wharton Jr (ed), *Subsistence Agriculture and Economic Development*, Aldine, Chicago, IL, pp. 111-35.

Rogers, E.M. (1976), 'Communication and Development: The Passing of the Dominant Paradigm', in Rogers (ed), *Communication and Development: Critical Perspectives*, Sage, New York, NY, pp. 121-48.

Rogers, E.M. and Svenning, L. (1969), *Modernization among Peasants: The Impact of Communcation*, Holt, Rinehart and Winston, New York, NY.

Schultz, T.W. (1964), *Transforming Traditional Agriculture*, Yale University Press, New Haven, CT.

Szentes, T. (1971), *The Political Economy of Underdevelopment*, Akadeia Kiada, Budapest.

United Republic of Tanzania (URT) (1967), *Background to Budget, 1967/68*, Dar es Salaam.

URT (1968), *Cooperative Societies Act, 1968,* Government Printer, Dar es Salaam.

URT (1975), *The Village and Ujamaa Villages (Registration, Designation and Administration Act, 1975*, Dar es Salaam.

URT (1982), *Cooperative Societies Act, 1982*, Government Printer, Dar es Salaam.

URT (1987), *Basic Data: Agriculture and Livestock Sector 1981/2 - 1985/6*, National Printing Company, Dar es Salaam.

URT (1990), *Basic Data: Agriculture and Livestock Sector, 1984/5 - 1988/9*, National Printing Company, Dar es Salaam.

Wallerstein, I. (1978), *The Capitalist World Economy*, Cambridge University Press, New York, NY.

Widstrand, C.G. (ed) (1970), *Cooperatives and Rural Development in East Africa*, Africa Publishing Corporation, New York, NY.

# 13 Urban Agriculture and its Damaging Effects on the Urban Environment: The Case of Tanzania

MALONGO R. S. MLOZI

## Introduction

Urban agriculture is a global phenomenon that involves the raising of livestock (dairy cattle, chicken, pigs) and food crops (vegetables, field crops, fruit trees, ornamental trees, flowers and shrubs). In some places it also involves the raising of bees and fish. The type and intensity of urban agriculture that people conduct in many cities and towns in the world depends on the governments' policies towards urban agriculture and the inhabitants' socioeconomic status (SES). Other factors are the presence of the infrastructure, land ownership and availability of capital and markets for the products. Urban agriculture, therefore, is a diverse, omnipresent, thriving, and profitable activity in towns and cities all over the low-income and high-income world (Smit and Ratta, 1992).

There are studies of people who engage in urban agriculture in the United States, in the metropolis of Greater Vancouver in Canada, in Asia, in Holland, Italy, the United Kingdom, Russia, Poland, China, and Nepal. Many Asian countries such as Japan, Philippines, South Korea, Malaysia, Indonesia, Thailand, Sri Lanka and Bangladesh, among others, promote home gardening and success varies. People in South American towns and cities are also doing urban agriculture such as in Brazil, Chile, Bolivia, and Colombia.

In African towns and cities, most people are engaged in urban agriculture for food and economic survival. There are studies of urban agriculture in North Africa (Khouri-Dagher, 1986), West Africa (Manshard, 1992; Diallo, 1993; Gbadegesin, 1991; Gefu, 1992), Central Africa (Streiffeller, 1987), East Africa (Mlozi, 1995; Mvena, Lupanga and Mlozi, 1991; Mlozi, 1994; Sawio, 1993; Freeman, 1991; Maxwell and Zziwa, 1992) and Southern Africa (Mbiba, 1994; May and Rogerson, 1995; Potts, 1989; Drakakis-Smith, Bowyer-Bower and Tevera, 1995; Byerley, 1996). Most people are involved in urban agriculture because of its enormous benefits. It provides food: for income generation or poverty alleviaton, for waste management, and for conversion into other preferred food products (for example, eggs, milk, meat). In Tanzania, urban agriculture is the rearing of animals (dairy cattle, chicken, goats, pigs) and the growing of vegetables and field crops (maize, cassava, legumes, plantains) in urban areas. People of high SES do

184

most urban agriculture (dairy cattle, chicken, goats and pigs) of a kind that damages the urban environment (Mlozi, 1996; Mosha, 1991; Sawio, 1993). Contemporary urban agriculture, however, has evolved tremendously and has become intensive. But there are disadvantages, chief among which is environmental degradation that concerns the public, city councils, and the government.

## Environmental Degradation

### Degradation due to Animals

Urban agriculture has two impacts that pertain to environmental degradation: risks to health, and aesthetic and social concerns.

*Risks to health:* Urban agriculture has negative impacts for the population and the urban environment and poses new problems for planning (Rogerson, 1993). In Tanzanian towns, evidence suggests that these negative impacts will increase because of the increasing economic severity that forces urban dwellers to intensify urban agriculture activities. It is also possible that the global ubiquity of urban agriculture in most developing countries causes environmental degradation. Domestic animals transmit zoonoses or animal diseases that can afflict humans and circulate among other animals (Acha and Szyfres, 1987; Satterthwaite, 1993; Phillips and Sorensen, 1993; Wathes, 1994; Bradley, 1993).

In most Tanzanian towns and cities, people raise domestic animals (dairy cattle, chickens and goats) in the households' compounds in circumstances that could easily transmit zoonotic diseases. Acha and Syzfres (1987) give an exhaustive list of zoonotic diseases that include brucellosis, tuberculosis, leptospirosis, psittacosis, q-fever, schistosomiasis, trypanosomiasis, shigellosis, taenisis and cysticerocosis, tetanus, trichinosis, tularemia, pasteurellosis, and yesimiosis. Animals can transmit most of these diseases to humans either directly (animals to human and vice versa), or indirectly through milk, meat, food pollution, water, and soil. Since the 1970s, in most Tanzanian towns, people have increased their livestock; and given the poor husbandry, it is possible that the incidence of zoonotic diseases has also increased. The probability of animals transmitting diseases increases when large groups of people are in contact with large groups of animals, and are exposed to a full range of excretions and fluids regularly (Cohen, 1992).

People who raise livestock in the city are liable to dispose of animal dung haphazardly. This dung decomposes and produces odour and acts as a breeding ground for harmful bacteria and flies. Animal dung is a source of tetanus (Ellner and Neu, 1992; Rosen, 1975), especially if animals are left out to graze, a common practice in most Tanzanian urban centres. Clostridium tetani causes tetanus and kills about 500,000 people in the world annually and is more serious in the developing countries (Acha and Szyfres, 1987). Studies conducted in other parts of the world (Phillips and Piggins, 1992; Wathes, 1994) show that there are harmful pathogens in domestic animal wastes. These pathogens include brucella abortus, clostridium perfringes, escherichia coli, mycobacterium bovis, pasteurella, salmonella dublin, and staphylococcus aureus.

People also improperly dispose of slurry containing animal dung, urine, and waste water from the dairy cattle shed, the chicken shed, and pig pens. Slurry pollutes the surroundings and attracts harmful pathogens and disease causing vectors such as the culex species of mosquitoes. Mosquitoes are probably the most important insect vectors, even in the urban areas; they bear malaria; also yellow fever and denge (aedes mosquitoes). They also cause bancroftian filariasis - elephantiasis and lymphatic filariasis (culex quinquefasciatus), along with several less known diseases (McGranahan, 1993; Satterthwaite, 1993; Bradley, 1993). In many cities in the developing countries malaria is a main cause of illness and death (Bradley, 1993), and Tanzanian towns are no exception. Here the *culex* mosquito also causes a male conspicuous socially stigmatized disease called *busha* (lymphatic filariasis) in Swahili where the scrotum swells because of the infection of the lymph nodes. Although the disease is common among some people of low SES, some people of high SES could in the future have the disease because of the presence of *culex* mosquitoes in slurry that comes out of the animal shed.

Urban agriculture also pollutes drinking water through the waste run-off from households that raise livestock. Also animals' organic manure goes into underground drinking water that is enriched with nitrates. People drinking water containing high levels of nitrates could develop methaemoglobinaemia (blue baby syndrome) and gastric cancer (Archer and Nicholson, 1992; Morse, 1995). In the city of Dar es Salaam, for example, this is perhaps apparent to most people of low SES in the suburbs of Buguruni, Mabibo, Magomeni, Mbagara, Mtoni, and Vingunguti - most of whom drink water from the wells. The allowable nitrate content in drinking water is 50 milligrams per litre (Archer and Nicholson, 1992), and evidence suggests that well water has higher levels of nitrates in urban areas that raise livestock. Nitrates in drinking water are potentially dangerous, especially to newborn infants and young animals (Morse, 1995).

In Tanzania's towns and cities, other health problems that are due to raising livestock include chemical contamination such as the use of insecticides, acaricides, antibiotics, and other animal medications. In the city of Dar es Salaam, most people do not often seek veterinarians' advice when treating their animals, because of the consultation fees. Other urban agriculture problems include air pollution. In most towns, gaseous pollutants are on the increase because livestock production creates unavoidable and undesirable waste products. For example, the degradation of nitrogen-containing compounds leads to the impairment of the ozone layer (Tamminga, 1992; Crutzen, Axelmann and Seller, 1986; Tarcher, 1992). In most towns, cattle feed consists of forage containing high fibre contents. This means that there is more methane gas ($CH_4$) emitted by the methanogenic flora bacteria as they digest in the animals' rumen. Methane and other reactive organic compounds that include ethane, acetone, isopropyl, alcohol, propyl acetate, ethylamine, and trimethyl amine are precursors to the ground level ozone. People claim that these chemicals also irritate respiratory tissues, especially in elderly adults, very young children, and asthmatics. Methane is also repulsive to neighbours. In most households where zero-grazing is practised, people burn wet and dry animal wastes because of the paucity of municipal disposal vehicles. Such waste consists of dung, urine and forage leftovers that upon burning smell and produce smoke that can impede the vision of motorists and pedestrians.

Yet another health problem includes the production of obnoxious odours. There are over 60 volatile compounds in animal wastes and a dozen of them are contributors to malodour. These include carbolic acids (acetic acid, butylic acid), phenolics (p-cresol, phenol) aliphatic and nitrogen-containing compounds (ammonia) or sulphur-containing compounds (hydrogen sulphide, dimenthyl sulphide, ethyl mercaptan) (Tamminga, 1992). In the urban centres, these compounds originate from chicken deep litter systems, dairy cattle sheds, pig pens, and the outside dumped animal wastes whose fumes and odours disturb most urban dwellers. People's health is also at risk from the dust, smoke, and noise which are due to raising livestock in the urban centres.

*Aesthetic and social concerns due to livestock*: Raising livestock in the urban centres engenders the destruction of ornamental plants, flowers, grass, parks, and live hedges. Cattle and goats also hamper urban afforestation efforts and destroy roads. Likewise, some government officers house livestock in servant quarters and damage them. Dairy cattle also damage water lines, telephone installations, recreational areas, and traffic lights. Livestock also destroys the cities' and towns' beauty, obstruct traffic, disturb urban dwellers and cause soil erosion (i.e. through grazing animals, gathering forage, and tilling the soil to grow forage).

*Degradation due to Plants*

*Risks to health:* Environmental degradation due to plants is less serious than that caused by animals. Health and medical personnel claim that watering of vegetables in the urban centres creates moist conditions underneath the plants providing suitable conditions for malarial mosquitoes to breed. They also claim that field crops (maize, plantains, cassava, sweet potatoes, yams, pigeon peas and beans) act as resting places for malaria-causing mosquitoes. In the mid-1980s, for example, most city authorities used this as a reason for slashing urban dwellers' maize. Several agronomic practices such as making ridges, planting holes and furrows, are claimed to hold rain water in which mosquitoes breed. Environmental degradation is increasing as a consequence of the use of organic manure of cattle, chicken and pigs. The latter, for example, can spread harmful disease pathogens and parasites (i.e. worm cysts of taenia solium). Another health risk is the use of polluted water to raise vegetables. About 70 percent of all African spinach raised in the city of Dar es Salaam uses polluted water from the broken household sewerage system, and from industrial effluents.

*Aesthetic and social concerns due to uncontrolled growing of crops*: In Tanzanian towns, people are growing different species of plants haphazardly thus destroying the towns' beauty. Crops that are one metre high (i.e.

187

plantains, maize, cassava, and pigeon peas) are believed to hide bandits and other undesirable elements in the urban communities. Sometimes crops planted at sharp corners can obstruct the vision of motorists and pedestrians and can cause accidents. In some areas, highly valued land grows vegetables and field crops instead of being used for building expensive structures for apartments, hotels, markets, and shops. In the Tanzanian towns urban agriculture seriously damages the urban environment thus destroying public property such as open spaces which could be used for recreational pruposes. This desperate ecocide of the urban centres leads to health risks and destruction from an aesthetic and social viewpoint. This thinking further attests to views held by Hardin (1968) concerning the apparent inability of humans to administer limited resources in an equitable way.

## The Present Research

This study was conducted in 1993 with people over eighteen years of age in two Dar es Salaam urban districts (Kinondoni and Ilala) (Map 13.1). The people engaged in mixed urban agriculture in five areas. The areas have different plot sizes and population densities. Two areas were in Ilala district: Kalenga and Shabani Robert (all quasi-medium density areas with house-plots sizes between 1,750 and 2,400 square metres). Three areas were in the district of Kinondoni: Oysterbay (a low density area with house plots whose sizes are of 3,640 square metres); Kinondoni Block 41 (a medium-density areas with house-plot sizes of 896 square metres); and Kinondoni Block A (a high density area with house-plot sizes of 300 square metres).

The researcher selected the areas so as to have representation of people from different densities, and adopted a multistage random selection that involved wards, areas within wards, and house-plot size or numbers. This study sought to include the views of those engaged in or connected with urban agriculture. The concern was to try to unravel the perception, experiences, and actions of 29 urban agriculturalists about five issues which related to the damaging of the environment by animals: these were (i) psycho-social, (ii) socio-politico-legal, (iii) disease-related, (iv) accident-related and (v) landscape-related. This chapter presents a summary of quantitative data collected.

## Respondents' Characteristics and What they Did

Of the 29 urban agriculturalists interviewed, 19 were females and 10 were males. Their age range was between 20 and 60 years with a mean of 43. Their general education range was between 7 and 18 years with a mean of 11.6. Of the 29 urban agriculturalists, 17 kept dairy cattle. Most interviewees raised cattle of crossbreeds between Ayrshires, Boran, Friesian, Guernsey, and Jersey cattle, to sell milk. All commercial chicken raised in Dar es Salaam are for eggs and broiler meat, and consist mainly of the exotic

# Map 13.1  Location of study areas in the City of Dar es Salaam

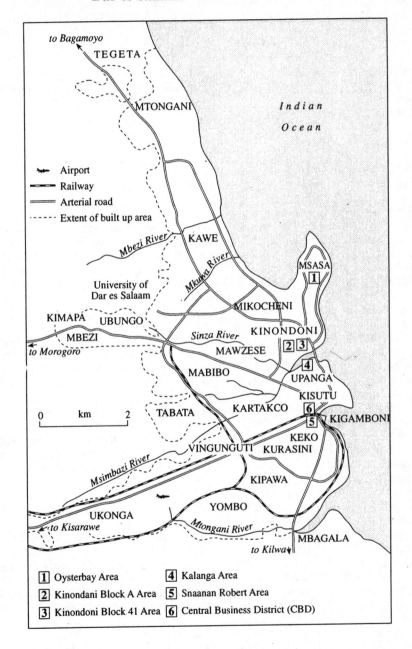

1  Oysterbay Area                4  Kalanga Area

2  Kinondani Block A Area        5  Snaanan Robert Area

3  Kinondoni Block 41 Area       6  Central Business District (CBD)

crossbreeds. The study found that 16 people raised from 100 to 400 chicken of the Arbor acres, Starbro, and Shaver Star crosses. Respondents raised few ducks, goats, local fowls, rabbits, and sheep. The study found that an interviewee who raised a combination of cows and chicken for eggs (layers) earned an average annual net profit of Tsh 2.3 million (US$4,792). The annual net profit per person who raised layers alone was Tsh 1.6 (US$ 3,333), for broiler chickens alone was Tsh 946,000 (US$ 1,971), and for cows was Tsh 450,000 (US$ 938). On average, these earnings were 10.8 times the total net annual salary of Tsh 64,800 (US$ 135) of a low income worker. Such earnings were 4.2 times the total net annual salary of Tsh 168,000 (US$ 350) of a senior official.

*Respondents' Opinions*

Urban agriculturalists gave their opinions about five issues of environmental damage due to keeping livestock. The next section looks at them.

*Psycho-social issues:* Most urban agriculturalists (n=23) agreed that livestock in the city caused noise and odour, and disturbed urban dwellers. About half the respondents (n=15) concurred with the statement that raising pigs in areas inhabited by Muslims was not ideal. However, less than half the interviewees (n=12) agreed with the statement that animals scared children in the city. For all four statements, the respondents' main bases for their beliefs were personal experience. Other bases for their beliefs mentioned included 'everyone knows' and 'complaints from neighbours'.

*Socio-political-legal issues:* The researcher asked interviewees about three statements on socio-politico-legal issues. Most respondents (n=24) agreed with the statement that urban agriculture persisted in the city because the city council did not enforce its bylaws. More than half the interviewees (n=18) expressed agreement with the statement that some livestock owners used official time to look after their animals. Fewer than half the respondents (n=14) concurred with the statement that some politicians had condemned urban agriculture in the city. For these issues, the respondents' major bases for their beliefs were personal experience, and minor bases included 'every knows', complaints from neighbours, city council staff, and hearing it through the radio.

*Disease-related issues:* Over half the respondents (n=19) agreed with the statements that animal dung in the city was unhealthy. Eleven interviewees concurred with the statement that animals can transmit diseases such as anthrax, brucellosis and tuberculosis to humans. Fewer than half the interviewees agreed with the statements that animals caused pollution of ground water or that livestock increased malaria in the city. Here, the respondents' main bases for their beliefs concerning most issues of damage were personal experience, 'other people say', and occasionally the radio.

*Accident-related issues:* Most interviewees (n=24-27) expressed agreement with statements about accident-related issues. These included statements such as animals in the city caused traffic jams, or caused accidents, and that animals could sometimes harm human beings, particularly children, the old and the sick. However, fewer than half the respondents (n=5) agreed with the statement that animals could rub themselves against electricity poles and make these fall, thereby causing electric hazards. The most frequently given basis for their beliefs was personal experiences. Besides these, other bases included 'everyone knows', and 'other people say'.

*Landscape-related issues*: Most respondents agreed with all the four statements related to environmental damage affecting the city landscape. Interviewees agreed particularly with two statements: that livestock destroys city hedges, streams, ornamental trees, flowers and parks (n=28); and that the presence of livestock in the city had destroyed its beauty (n=26). Most respondents (n=24) also expressed agreement with the statement that livestock cause damage to the government houses, water pipes, telephone installations, and roads. Similarly, most interviewees (n=24) agreed with the statement that the poorly designed and built sheds that house animals cause the city to look ugly. The most frequently given basis for their beliefs was personal experience.

## Explanations on why People Continue to Engage in Urban Agriculture in spite of its Damaging Effects

It is clear from the examination of the literature on urban agriculture world-wide and from the presentation of field data of this study that the persistence of urban agriculture is a complex phenomenon. In Tanzanian towns, people engage in urban agriculture as a way of life, and most sections of the urban centres look similar to parts of rural areas, except for the infrastructure that symbolizes urbanity. Figure 13.1 portrays a model that assists in the understanding of such complexity. The figure shows socioeconomic and political factors at four levels: Government, Ministry, City Council, and the Individual. Factors at these four levels interact with each other and beyond their boundaries. Figure 13.1 shows a theoretical model of the four levels.

*Government Level*

There are four factors at the government level that encourage people to persist in urban agriculture in spite of its damaging effects. These include the national economic climate, government policies, problems of coordination, and the culture of status and rewards of senior officials and the elite. First, since the 1970s, the Tanzanian economy has experienced a decline. Because of this, people's real income has been eroded tremendously and urban dwellers have been hard hit (Maliyamkono and Bagachwa, 1990; Bukuku, 1993; Sarris and Van den Brink, 1994; Mans, 1994; IBRD, 1995). To

191

**Figure 13.1  Model showing factors nested at four contextual levels to explain people's persistence in performing urban agriculture in spite of its damaging effects**

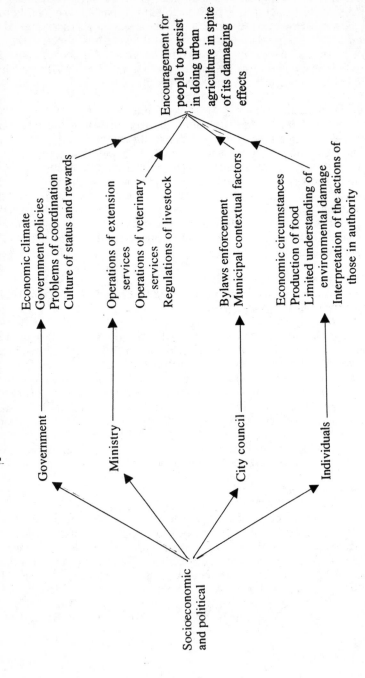

mitigate the economic crises, most people in the urban centres started to engage in activity within the informal sector including urban agriculture, to get food and to supplement their incomes. Data collected from this study show that people who raised cows and chicken earned higher average total annual net profits than those growing vegetables. Similarly, people with formal employment earned higher annual incomes from urban agriculture than from regular wages. Also, since the 1970s, the government has pursued policies that have in practice encouraged urban agriculture.

There is, however, a lack of coordination among some government ministries, departments, public institutions, the public, and the private sector so as to lessen urban environmental damage due to urban agriculture. There is rather a particular culture of status and rewards among the elite and senior officials of the government, public institutions, the ruling party, and those in private companies. People of high SES and political clout enjoy several privileges that the government provides. They have often used these to pursue urban agriculture, most of which damages the urban environment. For example, the study found that such people live in high quality housing areas in which they raise dairy cattle, chickens and goats. Despite the damage that livestock causes to the infrastructure and the environment, the government does not prohibit officials from raising livestock in its premises, e.g. servants' quarters.

**Ministerial Level**

This concerns the Ministry of Agriculture, Livestock and Cooperative Development (MALCD), and there are three factors at this level. In the first place, there are the haphazard operations of urban extension services that appear to encourage urban agriculture that damages the urban environment. This study found that the MALCD extension agents were not effective in educating agriculturalists in proportion to their numbers. For example, most respondents relied on personal experience and not on information from agents as the bases for most of their beliefs about environmental damage. Second, the three MALCD district offices in the city sell animals, medications, drugs, supplies, and offer information to people raising livestock. Because the government and municipal authorities neither supervise nor coordinate livestock activities in the cities, they often contribute to environmental damage (i.e., bringing in cows, unsupervised use of antibiotics to treat mastitis, and use of acaricides). Third, MALCD extension agents do not enforce the bylaws for lessening environmental damage that livestock causes. This study found that extension agents often issued annual permits to agriculturalists to obtain licences from the City Council to do urban agriculture without thoroughly inspecting their compounds and premises.

## City Council Level

People partly engaged in urban agriculture in spite of its damaging effects because the city did not enforce its by-laws and because of the existence of several municipal contextual factors. The study found that most interviewees agreed that most people persisted in doing urban agriculture because the City Council did not enforce its by-laws. The inability of the City Council to enforce its by-laws stems from a moral and humanitarian dilemma: in general, most people involved in urban agriculture are poor, and they do it to meet their basic food needs for survival. On the other hand, however, the elite and senior government and the ruling party officials also engage in urban agriculture for profit maximization. However, the damage to the urban environment that these two groups cause is equally significant. For the latter group their hegemony and economic considerations impede the ability of the City Council to enforce its by-laws. Another factor is the existence of municipal contextual factors that include the presence of several markets for urban agricultural products, and the infrastructure (open spaces, houses, water, and the road system).

## Individual Level

Here, there are four factors, and the first one is the economic climate. This study found that the primary reason for engaging in urban agriculture in spite of its damaging effects was economic. The high earnings that people obtained from their agricultural enterprises are illustrative of this aspect. Also, the harsh economic conditions force most people to resort to supplementary income generating activities, one of which is urban agriculture. Second, there was a limited understanding of environmental damage of urban agriculture among those who practised it. For example, on average less than half the respondents agreed with statements related to disease and health issues. Third, besides income generation, people partly persisted in performing urban agriculture in order to produce their own food. Fourth, low and medium income earners persisted in performing urban agriculture in spite of its damaging effects on the environment because they saw that government and ruling party bureaucrats who practised urban agriculture and caused damage to the urban environment were not punished by the City Council officers.

## Conclusion

This chapter has considered the practice of urban agriculture in the city of Dar es Salaam, Tanzania. In developing countries, the practice of urban agriculture appears to have four characteristics. First, it is seen as beneficial. Second, both the poor and well-to-do sections of the population practise it. Third, most people engage in it to obtain food. Fourth, it is part of the informal sector as distinct from the formal one. But although there are several benefits of urban agriculture, it also causes considerable

194

environmental damage. The issue that needs resolution is, first whether urban agriculture should continue, and second, if it should, how to continue it without damaging the urban environment. This study has shown that urban agriculture is here to stay because of the continuing economic austerity that is eroding urban dwellers' incomes, and for other reasons as discussed earlier.

For urban agriculture to continue without damaging the urban environment, three points are worth considering. First, the discussion should not only focus on the practitioners. Second, by-laws should be mandatory for all. This study has shown that agriculture/livestock extension agents offer education inequitably, favouring people of higher status. The education that agents offer is inadequate and emphasizes yield maximization rather than the means for lessening environmental damage. There is therefore a need to recognize the interdependence of government, MALCD, the City Council, and individual interests, in order to lessen environmental damage that urban agriculture is causing. All parties should aim for sustainable urban agriculture that encompasses three major points of view: economic, social, and ecological. This study shows that at the moment the economic point of view predominates. The thrust should be to arrest 'the tragedy of the commons' (Hardin, 1968) traced to selfish exploitation of the commons by using private capital for short term gains (Eckersley, 1993). By-laws in the city of Dar es Salaam do not work because some people who practise urban agriculture are senior government and party officials who impede efforts to enforce regulations. To curb this, the government should collaborate with the City Council to supplement existing regulations with taxation incentives e.g. by imposing high taxes upon people with more than four cattle. Besides, agriculturalists do not pay for the full range of social and environmental costs that they directly or indirectly generate.

**Recommendations for Policy, Practice and Research**

*Recommendations for policy and practice*

The study advances ten recommendations for policy and practice.

1. The government should formulate an Urban Agriculture Policy, clearly describing respective roles of the government, the MALCD, and city, municipal and town councils.
2. All levels of government should pledge to enhance coordination with respect to urban agriculture among various government ministries, departments, institutions, agencies and individuals.
3. Planners should re-examine their concepts with a view to incorporating urban agriculture in urban planning, thereby minimizing the environmental problems that accompany it.
4. The government should formulate a policy for developing peri-urban areas to which urban agriculturalists could move their activities.
5. There should be the development of non-agricultural small businesses such as transportation, manufacturing, retailing and hotel management.

6. The government should review the taxation system to see whether new or redesigned taxes on urban agricultural earnings or practices might serve as incentives for more sustainable practice.
7. The government, and MALCD in particular, should formulate a clear and firm policy for education of both the general public and urban agriculturalists in matters of environmental damage.
8. There should be a coordinated sharing of educational and bylaw enforcement duties of the two departments presently involved (City Council and MALCD).
9. MALCD should improve the coordination of its extension agents. It should review the hours of work of those involved in the city areas so that agents can be available when clients are able to see them.
10. MALCD and the City Council should jointly enforce and manage the city by-laws.

*Recommendations for Research*

The study offers four recommendations for further research:

1. Relevant researchers should coordinate their studies on urban agriculture.
2. Any future research on urban agriculture should include the poor section of the population in the squatter areas of the city.
3. There is a need to initiate action research to monitor the progress of new policy recommendations and chart alternative courses of action.
4. Experts should initiate adult education and extension research to determine how best to use education as a tool in lessening environmental damage that urban agriculture causes.

## References

Acha, P.N., and Szyfres, B. (1987), *Zoonoses and Communicable Diseases Common to Man and Animals* (2nd edition), Pan-American Health Organization, Washington DC.

Archer, J.R., and Nicholson, R.J. (1992), 'Liquid Wastes from Farm Animal Enterprises', in Phillips and Piggins, pp. 325-43.

Bills, N.J. (1991), 'Urban Agriculture in the United States', ms, Agricultural Economics Staff Paper no. 91-2, Department of Agricultural Economics, Cornell University, New York, NY.

Bohrt, J.P. (1993), 'Chasing away Hunger in Bolivia', *IDRC Reports*, 21 (iii), pp. 19-20.

Bradley, D.J. (1993), 'Human Tropical Diseases in a Changing Environment', in Lake, J.V., Bock, G.R., and Ackkrill, K. (eds), *Environmental Change and Human Health*, Wiley, Chichester, pp. 234-46.

Bukuku, E.S. (1993), *The Tanzania Economy: Income Distribution and Economic Growth*, Praeger, Westport CT.

Byerley, A. (1996), *Urban Agriculture in Botswana*, Working Paper no. 307, IRDC/Swedish University of Agricultural Sciences, Uppsala.

Cohen, M.N. (1992), 'The Epidemiology of Civilization', in Jacobsen, J.E., and Firror, J. (1992), *Human Impact on the Environment: Ancient Tools, Current Challenges*, Westview, Boulder CO, pp. 51-70.

Crutzen, P.J., Axelmann, I., and Seller, W. (1986), 'Methane Production by Domestic Animals, Wild Ruminants, other Herbivorous Fauna, and Humans', *Tellus*, 38 (viii), pp. 271-81.

Deelstra, T. (1987), 'Urban Agriculture and the Metabolism of Cities', *Food and Nutrition Bulletin*, 9 (ii), pp. 5-7.

Diallo, S. (1993), 'A Plot of One's Own in West African Cities', *IDRC Reports*, 21 (iii), pp. 8-9.

Drakakis-Smith, D., Bowyer-Bower, T., and Tevera, D. (1995), 'Urban Poverty and Urban Agriculture: An Overview of Linkage in Harare', *Habitat International*, 19, 165-81.

Eckersley, R. (1993), 'Free Market Environmentalism: Friend or Foe?', *Environmental Politics*, 2 (i), pp. 1-19.

Ellner, P.D., and Neu, H.C. (1992), *Understanding Infectious Diseases*, Mosby, St. Louis, MO.

Freeman, D.B. (1991), *A City of Farmers: Informal Agriculture in Open Spaces of Nairobi, Kenya*, McGill-Queen University Press, Montreal.

Gbadegesin, A. (1991), 'Farming in the Urban Environment of a Developing Nation: A Case Study from Ibadan Metropolis in Nigeria', *The Environmentalist*, 11 (ii), pp. 105-111.

Gefu, O. (1992), 'Part-time Farming as an Urban Agriculture Survival Strategy: A Nigerian Case Study', in Baker, J., and Pedersen, P.O. (eds), *The Rural-Urban Interface in Africa: Expansion and Adaptation*, SIAS, Uppsala, pp. 295-302.

Hardin, G. (1968), 'The Tragedy of the Commons', *Science*, 162, pp. 1243-8.

Hartvelt, F., and Gross, B. (1992), 'Urban Agriculture in Latin America, Africa and Asia', ms., UNDP/IBRD, Washington DC.

International Bank for Reconstruction and Development (IBRD) (1995), *African Development Indicators*, IBRD, Washington DC.

International Development Research Centre (IDRC) (ed) (1994), *Cities Feeding People: An Examination of Urban Agriculture in East Africa*, IDRC, Ottawa.

Khouri-Dagher, N. (1986), *Food and Energy in Cairo: Provisioning the Poor,* Food Energy Nexus Programme, United Nations University, Tokyo (Research Report no. 18).

Kleer, J. (1987), 'Small-scale Agricultural Production in Urban Areas in Poland', *Food and Nutrition Bulletin*, 9 (ii), pp. 24-8.

Latz, G. (1991), 'The Persistence of Urban Agriculture in Japan: An Analysis of the Tokyo Metropolitan Area', in Ginsburg, N., Kopel, B., and McGee, T.G. (eds), *The Extended Metropolis: Settlement Transition in Asia*, University of Honolulu Press, Honolulu, HI, pp. 217-38.

Lee-Smith, D., and Trujillo, C.H. (1992), 'The Struggle to Legitimize Subsistence: Women and Sustainable Development', *Environment and Urbanization*, 4 (i), pp. 77-84.

McGranahan, G. (1993), 'Household Environmental Problem in Low-Income Cities', *Habitat International*, 17, pp. 105-121.

Maliyamokono, T.L., and Bagachwa, M.S.D. (1990), *The Second Economy in Tanzania*, James Currey, London.

197

Mans, D. (1994), 'Tanzania: Resolute Action', in Husain, I. and Faruqee, R. (eds), *Adjustment in Africa: Lessons from Country Studies*, IBRD, Washington DC, pp. 352-426.

Manshard, W. (1992), 'Agricultural Change: Market Gardens in West African Urban Communities: The Case of Ougadougou (Burkina Faso)', in Raza, M. (ed), *Development and Ecology*, Rawat Publications, Jaipur, pp. 347-56.

Maxwell, D., and Zziwa, S. (1992), *Urban Agriculture in Africa: The Case of Kampala*, ACTS Press, Nairobi.

May, J., and Rogerson, C.M. (1995), 'Poverty and Sustainable Cities in South Africa: The Role of Urban Cultivation', *Habitat International*, 19, pp. 165-81.

Mbiba, B. (1994), *Urban Agriculture in Zimbabwe*, Avebury, Aldershot.

Mlozi, M.R.S. (1994), 'Inequitable Agricultural Extension Services in the Urban Context: The Case of Tanzania', in Stromquist, N.P. (ed), *Education in Urban Areas: Cross-National Dimensions*, Praeger, Westport, CT, pp. 105-28.

Mlozi, M.R.S. (1995), 'Child Labour in Urban Agriculture: The Case of Dar es Salaam, Tanzania', *Children's Environment*, 12, pp. 197-208.

Mlozi, M.R.S. (1995), 'Information and the Problems of Urban Agriculture in Tanzania: Intentions and Realizations', PhD dissertation, University of British Columbia.

Mlozi, M.R.S. (1996), 'Urban Agriculture in Tanzania and the Marketing of its Products', Research Paper, Department of Agricultural Education and Extension, SUA, Morogoro (ms).

Morse, D. (1995), 'Environmental Considerations of Livestock Producers', *Journal of Animal Science*, 73, pp. 2733-2740.

Mosha, A. (1991), 'Urban Farming Practices in Tanzania', *Review of Rural and Urban Planning in Southern and Eastern Africa*, 1, pp. 83-92.

Mougeot, J.A. (1994), 'African City Farming from a World Perspective', in IDRC (ed), pp. 1-24.

Mvena, Z.S.K., Lupanga, I.J., and Mlozi, M.R.S. (1991), 'Urban Agriculture in Tanzania: A Study of Six Towns', Research Report, Department of Agricultural Education and Extension, SUA, Morogoro.

Phillips, C., and Piggins, D. (eds) (1992), *Farm Animals and the Environment*, CAB International, Wallingford.

Phillips, C.J., and Sorensen, T. (1993), 'Sustainability in Cattle Productions Systems', *Journal of Agricultural and Environmental Ethics*, 6, pp. 61-73.

Potts, D. (1989), 'Urban Environment Control in Southern Africa with special reference to Lilongwe', *Resource Management and Optimization*, 6, pp. 321-34.

Rogerson, C.M. (1993), 'Urban Agriculture in South Africa: Policy Issues from the International Experience', *Development Southern Africa*, 10 (i), pp. 61-73.

Rosen, M.N. (1975), 'Clostridial Infections and Intoxication', in Hubbert, W.T., McCulloch, W.F., and Schnurrenberger, P.R. (eds), *Diseases Transmitted from Animals to Man*, C.C. Thomas, Springfield IL, pp. 251-62.

Sachs, I. (1987), 'Cultivating the Cities', *Development Forum*, 2(v) (February/March), p. 5.

Sarris, A.H., and Van den Brink, R. (1994), *Economic Policy and Household Welfare during Crisis and Adjustment in Tanzania*, New York University Press, New York NY.

Satterthwaite, D. (1993), 'The Impact of Health on Urban Environments', *Environment and Urbanization*, 5, pp. 87-111.

Sawio, C.J. (1993), 'Feeding the Urban Masses: Towards an Understanding of the Dynamics of Urban Agriculture and Land Use in Dar es Salaam, Tanzania', PhD dissertation, Clark University, Worcester MA.

Smit, J., and Ratta, A. (1992), 'Urban Agriculture in Sustainable Cities: Using Wastes and Idle Land and Water Bodies as Resources', *Environment and Urbanization*, 4, pp. 141-52.

Streiffeller, P. (1987), 'Improving Urban Agriculture in Africa: A Social Perspective', *Food and Nutrition Bulletin*, 7 (iii), pp. 15-24.

Tamminga, S. (1992), 'Gaseous Pollutants produced by Farm Animal Enterprises', in Phillips and Piggins, pp. 345-57.

Tarcher, A.B. (ed) (1992), *Principles and Practice of Environmental Medicine*, Plenum Medical Book Co., New York NY.

Wade, L. (1987), 'Community Food Production in Cities of the Developing Nations', *Food and Nutrition Bulletin*, 9 (ii), pp. 29-36.

Wathes, C.M. (1994), 'Animals in Man's Environment: A Question of Interest', *Outlook on Agriculture*, 23 (i), pp. 47-54.

Yeung, Y.M. (1988), 'Agricultural Land Use in Asian Cities', *Land Use Policies*, (5 (i), pp. 79-82.

Yeung, Y.M. (1993), 'New Challenges for China's Urban Farmers', *IDRC Reports*, 21 (iii), pp. 6-7.

Zurick, D. (1983), 'Food Production in the Urban Environment of Katmandu, Nepal', ms., Resource Systems Institute, East West Centre, Honolulu, HI.

# 14 Near and yet so Poor: Explaining Underdevelopment in the Coast Region of Tanzania

SIMEON MESAKI

This chapter is about the poor socio-economic status of Coast Region, in relation to Dar es Salaam (and the rest of Tanzania) and the ostensible reasons for such a pathetic situation. The argument is that though within a very dynamic 'growth centre', Coast Region has failed to benefit from such a unique and advantageous location. This is contrary to Perroux's theory on 'poles of growth' (Perroux, 1955) and instead bears witness to the thesis by Gould (1964, p. 124) that physical contiguity of induced growth is by no means certain. It also confirms the argument by Berry that growth impulses only rarely 'trickle down' to infuse dynamism into the most tradition-bound peripheries (Berry, 1972, p. 138). As pointed out by Datoo and Gray (1977), underdevelopment of a region is a consequence of a unique combination of natural and human factors considered both in qualitative and quantitative aspects. These will be presented in the third part of the chapter. The first section profiles the region and the second part demonstrates the state of backwardness of the area.

## Regional Profile

### Area

Coast Region (Pwani) (see Map 14.1) was created in 1974 to allow Dar es Salaam city and its environs to become a regional entity. It comprises five districts, namely Bagamoyo, Kibaha, Kisarawe, Mafia and Rufiji.[1] The headquarters are situated in Kibaha town, only fifty kilometres on the Dar es Salaam/Morogoro road (see map). Many civil servants live in Dar es Salaam and commute daily to and from Kibaha for work. The region has a total area of 33,800 square kilometres and each district's portion is as follows: Bagamoyo (9,842 sq.kms); Kibaha (1,630 sq.kms); Kisarawe (5,967 sq.kms); Mafia (518 sq. kms); and Rufiji (13,339 sq.kms).

**Map 14.1: Coast Region**

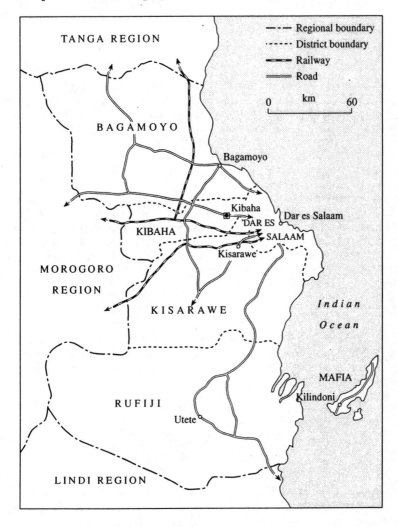

## Topography and Soils

Much of the region consists of low-lying plains with an altitude of around 150 metres above sea level. Behind the coastal plains, there is a central spine composed of a series of undulating hills running all the way from Kunduchi (in Dar es Salaam) towards the Rufiji river valley. The flood plain and delta of the Rufiji constitute distinctive agro-economic zones (Conyers, 1970; Havnevik, 1993). Other principal rivers are the Wami in the north and the Ruvu, which drains a smaller watershed in the Western and central areas of the region. The latter river is the main source of water for the city of Dar es Salaam, Bagamoyo and Kibaha towns.

The region has loamy and sandy soils but the Rufiji valley has alluvial and black cotton soils. Agriculture in the region depends practically on natural fertility of these soils which is very low.

## Climate

The climate in the region is typically tropical with average monthly temperatures of 24-28 degrees Centrigrade. Hot and humid conditions are the norm though the region has a relatively cooler dry season from June to October. Light rains (*vuli*) are experienced in November and December and the main rainy season (*masika*) is between March and May.

## Rainfall

Rainfall varies between 1000 mm along the coast to 600 mm in the West (Ruvu river drainage). Rain is the most important climatic factor in agriculture. Most of the agriculture in the region is rain-fed and therefore the behaviour of rainfall is a very critical factor in these areas. But it is not just the amount of rainfall that counts; other characteristics have to be considered, such as distribution, variability, dependability, and losses (e.g. evaporation).

## Population

With a population of 618,015 (1988 census) Coast Region is the least populated region of mainland Tanzania. Population density is around 19.6 per sq. km (Kamuzora, 1993, p. 133). The region's population is distributed in the five districts as follows:

| | |
|---|---|
| Bagamoyo | 173,918 |
| Kibaha | 83,018 |
| Kisarawe | 195,709 |
| Mafia | 33,056 |
| Rufiji | 152,316 |

Originally most of the Coastal inhabitants were matrilineal. but according to L. Swantz and M-L. Swantz the matrilineal social system has been undergoing modification due to the influence of Islam, as well as being affected by new forms of commodity production introduced under colonialism. Thus Islamic law has strengthened patrilineal inheritance and the general influence of the father in the total system (Lienhardt, 1968; L. Swantz 1970, p. 157; M-L. Swantz, 1986b, p. 111).

## Poverty in Plenteousness?

A former Prime Minister of Tanzania once proclaimed that '... almost all crops on earth can grow in the Coast Region' (J. Malecela, *Daily News*, February 7, 1993). In the same vein the immediate past president of the country, Ali Mwinyi, had occasion to speak of how Coast Region could join the 'Big Four' regions of Rukwa, Ruvuma, Iringa and Mbeya in abundant agricultural production (*Uhuru*, January 19, 1992). The proximity of the region to the biggest market in the country and to a sure outlet to the outside world in the form of an international airport, offers the region exceptional opportunities of being an economic giant. But this has not been the case as one newspaper headline recently declared 'Coast: the bread basket that is half empty' (*Daily News*, January 17, 1997). The plight of the region is vividly depicted in Tables 14.1 and 14.2.

**Table 14.1 Coast Region and its immediate neighbours**

| Region/ Years | 1990 | 1991 | 1992 | 1993 | 1994 |
|---|---|---|---|---|---|
| Coast | 6,637 | 8.372 | 10.504 | 13.312 | 17.033 |
| Dsm | 135.139 | 163.955 | 200.929 | 243.805 | 316.541 |
| Tz | 663.770 | 834.730 | 1,030.955 | 1,288.591 | 1,659.929 |
| Coast's GDP as % of Dsm GDP (%) | 4.9 | 5.1 | 5.2 | 5.4 | 5.3 |
| Coast GDP as % of Tz (Mainland) GDP(%) | 0.9 | 1.0 | 1.0 | 1.0 | 1.0 |
| Dsm's GDP as % of Tz (Mainland) GDP(%) | 20.3 | 19.6 | 19.4 | 18.9 | 19.0 |

*Source:* URT *National Accounts for 1986-1994.*
*Note:* *Ratios calculated on the basis of data given.

Table 14.1 shows, among other things, the relatively poor condition of Coast Region with respect to its immediate neighbour, Dar es Salaam, and to Tanzania in general. Thus for the entire 1990-1994 period, Coast Region's

GDP was on average one fifth that of Dar es Salaam. Also whereas the share of Coast Region's GDP in the National (mainland Tanzania) GDPs was on average 1 per cent, that of Dar es Salaam was on average above 19.4 per cent for the 1990-94 period.

Table 14.2 shows the per capita income disparity between Coast Region and its neighbour (Dar es Salaam) as well as mainland Tanzania. Whereas on average Dar es Salaam residents earned nine times more than the earnings of people in Coast Region, the disparity of per capita earnings between Dar es Salaam and the whole country is on average in the ratio of 3:1.

**Table 14.2  Regional per capita GDP comparisons: Coast Region, Dar es Salaam and National ('000s T.Shs)**

| Region/ Years | 1990 | 1991 | 1992 | 1993 | 1994 |
|---|---|---|---|---|---|
| 1. Coast | 9.860 | 12.094 | 14.756 | 18.183 | 22.624 |
| 2. Dsm | 94.123 | 111.039 | 132.323 | 156.126 | 197.106 |
| 3. Tz Mainland ratios | 27.792 | 33.986 | 40.816 | 49.607 | 62.138 |
| 4. Dsm GDP per capita: Coast GDP per capita* | 9:1 | 9:1 | 8:1 | 9:1 | 8.7:1 |
| 5. Tz (mainland) GDP per capita: Coast GDP per capita* | 2.8:1 | 2.8:1 | 2.7:1 | 2.7:1 | 2.7:1 |
| 6. Dsm'per capita GDP: Mainland per capita GDP* | 3.3:1 | 3.3:1 | 3.2:1 | 3.1:1 | 13.1:1 |

*Source*: URT *National Accounts for 1986-1994*.
*Note*:  * Ratios calculated on the basis of data given.

Furthermore, in a recent statement, an official of the Kisarawe District Council revealed the state of poverty in the region by providing some exact figures. Mr Yahya Mbila, the District Executive Director, is reported to have said that the current average (1997) income earned by a resident of Kisarawe district was 82 shillings per day or 30,000 shillings per annum. This compares quite unfavourably with the national average, as he put it, of 80,000 shillings (*Alasiri*, No. 231, February 25, 1997).

## Explanation

For the remainder of this chapter I want to enumerate some of the possible reasons for the reality of Coast Region being so near to Dar es Salaam, the most developed area of the country, and yet having remained so backward and poor.

*Demography: Out-migration, Dependency and Skewed Sex Ratios*

A striking demographic phenomenon in the Coast Region is the average annual increase of population. Between 1967 and 1978 it was at 1.6 per cent. It went up to 2.1 per cent between 1978 and 1988 when the national increase was 2.8. This is explained by the out-migration from the region into Dar es Salaam city, especially of youths, which also affects fertility rates and dependency ratios of the remaining rural population. Because of the attraction to and proximity of the city of Dar es Salaam, Coast Region experiences one of the highest rates of urban migration in Tanzania. Thus in 1967, it was realized that 14 per cent of Rufiji district's population was residing in Dar es Salaam. As one writer has observed, the more the urban segment becomes viable and appealing, the more the rural sector turns into 'a nursery and old folks home' (Bantje, 1979, p. 36). Thus for example, instead of making more and more use of the Rufiji flood plain, the movement has been away from it. In Kisarawe, the picture is even more spectacular. In the remote division of Chole Samvula, as many as 75 per cent of the youths completing primary school education migrate to Dar es Salaam (Shishira, Sechambo and Sosovelle, 1988, p. 26).

In short, there are centrifugal and centripetal factors which lead to more out-migration from the Coast Region to the city of Dar es Salaam than from any other region in the country. In the case of Kisarawe youth migrants, it has been observed that,

> ... it is mainly the labour involved in working the land which pushes youths to migrate. They migrate at the onset of the cultivation season, engage in petty business, while staying with relatives in Dar es Salaam and then return briefly to their villages during the harvest period when food is normally available and only little in terms of labour may be demanded of them (Shishira, Shechambo and Sosovelle, 1988, p. 26).

Another demographic feature linked to the above is the dependency ratio. The dependency ratios for the whole region increased from 99.90 in 1978 to 104.87 in 1988. For each of the five districts the changes between 1978 and 1988 are reproduced below.

According to Shishira, Shechambo and Sosovelle, dependency ratios of this magnitude constitute a production constraint, because at least part of any surplus has to be diverted to support non-productive persons instead of being invested. In other words, the high dependency ratio means that the ability of the working people to save and invest and hence pull themselves out of the subsistence economy is limited.

**Table 14.3  Dependency ratios**

| District | 1978 | 1988 |
|----------|------|------|
| Bagamoyo | 102.92 | 103.64 |
| Kibaha | 90.79 | 94.83 |
| Kisarawe | 105.69 | 111.50 |
| Mafia | 96.53 | 96.07 |
| Rufiji | 98.18 | 105.82 |

*Source*: *Coast Region: Population Census: Regional Profile*, Bureau of Statistics, 1992, p. 30.

Apart from out-migration, population density is also very low, at 19.6 per square kilometre. This is itself a major developmental problem (Moore, 1973, p. 54).

Another interesting feature, which seems to be unique to the Coast Region, is a worsening sex ratio which has been remarked on by Caplan. In Chapter 15 of this volume she notes how the island has had a preponderance of males since 1924 (when record keeping started). With the highest population growth rate (2.9 per cent) and population density in the Region, Mafia showed a skewed sex ratio in the immediate past three censuses. In 1967 it was 103, in 1978 it was 104, and in 1988 it was 105. According to Caplan this imbalance in sex ratio is explained in terms of food, health and fertility issues. She argues that in Mafia island, there are important links between food, health and fertility which result in differential 'entitlements' for males and females, factors which explain the unusual sex ratio. Caplan depicts the plight of women in Mafia in the following manner. Women produce and process most of the food; they work considerably longer hours than men, but their entitlement to food is less. Women also have higher rates of morbidity than men, attributable to a combination of high work loads, poorer quality food, and frequent pregnancies as well as greater susceptibility to anaemia.

## Climate

Climatic factors have an important bearing on the predicament of Coast Region. Kisarawe district receives more rainfall than the others, but it is unreliable and has adverse implications for agriculture in the district. At times the short rains fail to commence as expected and this may lead to the extension of the dry season for as many as three months with serious consequences. A major aspect of rainfall is evaporation. During the dry season (June-October), loss of moisture through evaporation is excessive, amounting to twice the amount of rainfall that falls in Kisarawe district (Shishira, Shechambo and Sosovelle, 1988, p. 20).

Agriculture in Rufiji district depends not only on rainfall but the timing and duration of flooding which may not necessarily be the result of local rainfall. The two complementary factors (rainfall and flooding) have given rise to a complex relationship which one writer calls a 'double dependency agricultural system' in which there are excessive variations in agricultural production (Havnevik, 1993). Productive years alternate with shortages, and even famines are experienced in Rufiji district, depending on the extent of the floods or drought conditions (Bantje, 1979, 1980; Havnevik, 1993).

As Havnevik (1993, p. 82) has pointed out, agriculture in many African countries is affected by the lack of fully developed productive forces. On this account such countries are at the mercy of natural variations such as the ones mentioned above. And since there is no buffer against natural calamities, peasant production systems are necessarily sensitive to and affected by such fluctuations.

## Agricultural Systems and Cropping Patterns

Coast Region is endowed with a total of 1,607,600 hectares of arable land, but only 299,130 hectares are currently under cultivation. This is a mere 18 per cent of the potential, and the situation has raised concern among regional authorities as well (*Daily News*, January 17, 1997). The farm economy of the region is characterized by considerable tree cropping and smallholder mixed cultivation of food and cash crops. The latter form of agriculture is made possible by the traditionally simple hand hoe culture and manual work with all the inherent limitations. In short, there is a lack of proper implements and inputs. For example, there is no ox or tractor cultivation, and moreover better seeds, fertilizers, and insecticides are rarely used. The hand hoe is old-fashioned and inadequate and therefore restricts expansion of acreage. It also hinders productivity of labour because of limits set by manual labour and hazards of weather which diminish returns (Vuorela, 1987, p. 138). Another aspect is the scattered nature of crop trees as opposed to properly managed orchards or groves. Maghimbi (1977, p. 20) found that peasants' plots were dispersed as far apart as four miles in Masaki village of Kisarawe district. Yoshida (1972) estimated that 20 per cent of labour time was spent on walking to and from fields.

The productivity of Coast Region agriculture can be illustrated by data in Table 14.4, which dramatizes the disparity between prevailing low yields and potential returns with better management.

Recently an administrator in one of the districts revealed that tree crops could be the salvation of Coast Region peasants if only they used modern husbandry. For example, he is quoted as saying that 27 cashews could be planted in a hectare and that each tree could produce as much as 50 kilogrammes of nuts, giving a farmer 405,000 shillings a year per hectare (Y. Mbila, *Alasiri*, No. 231, February 25, 1997).

**Vermin and Pests**

It has been estimated that on average, 30 per cent of the pre-harvest crops are destroyed by vermin and pests in the Coast Region (Lukumbo, 1990). In some localities as high as 75 per cent losses are suffered which could mean

**Table 14.4 Average yields compared to potential yields (kgs) per hectare in typical coastal agriculture (Kisarawe and Rufiji districts)**

| | Average produce vs potential (with improved methods) in Kilograms | |
|---|---|---|
| Cassava | 12,000 | 30,000 |
| Maize | 700 | 2,800 |
| Cashew Nuts | 300 | 900 |
| Coconuts | 1,800 | 3,700 (nuts) |
| Fruits (Oranges) | 8,000 | 18,000 |
| Rice | 810 | 2,250 |
| Cotton | 230 | 700 |

*Source*: *Dar es Salaam/Msanga Road Feasibility Study. Draft Final Report*, Muhema, 1976, p. 21.

certain famine in areas so ravaged. The damage is caused mainly by baboons, monkeys, wild pigs, birds (*quelea quelea aethiopica*), hippos, and also elephants. The persistence of the vermin threat is exacerbated by vegetation cover and proximity to the Selous Game Park/Reserve. There is also a detectable lack of determined will and effort by residents to combat the menace, probably due to their leisurely demeanour (Maghimbi, 1977; Mchonde, 1977; Shishira, Shechambo and Sosovelle, 1988). In dealing with the problem, some residents of Coast Region utilize archaic, crude and laborious methods of guarding crops.

**Infrastructure**

The mainland districts of the region are well connected to Dar es Salaam by road though not to each other, whereas some of the interior areas are very poorly served by any form of communication. Mafia is served unsatisfactorily from Dar es Salaam by small planes, and ships plying to southern Tanzania (Mtwara and Lindi). In general, transport is a major bottleneck to both supply of inputs for production and the marketing of products from Coast Region villages. The Tanzania Railways Corporation

(TRC) and Tanzania Zambia Railway Authority (TAZARA) both traverse some parts of Kisarawe and Kibaha districts but few people living along these railway lines make any significant use of the routes for agricultural purposes. Road transport is more convenient but leaves a lot to be desired. There are a total of 3,842 kilometres of roads in the region as follows:

**Table 14.5 Road systems**

| District | T/road | R/road | D/road | F/road | Total |
|----------|--------|--------|--------|--------|-------|
| Bagamoyo | 92 | 285 | 132 | 421 | 930 |
| Kibaha | 141 | 69 | 99 | 213 | 522 |
| Kisarawe | - | 181 | 319 | 709 | 1209 |
| Mafia | - | 86 | 102 | - | 188 |
| Rufiji | 220 | 100 | 259 | 414 | 993 |
| Total | 453 | 721 | 911 | 1757 | 3842 |

*Key*: T = Trunk; R = Regional; D = District; and F = Feeder
*Source*: Regional Office, Kibaha (Pwani).

The most noteworthy feature of the road systems is that all of them radiate from Dar es Salaam and there are no inter-district roads except between Kibaha and Bagamoyo (and even this one is not passable during the rainy season). All connections to the regional office in Kibaha and between the districts has to be done by way of Dar es Salaam. Thus road accessibility, crucial as it may be, is largely lacking. And even maintenance of the existing meagre roads leaves a lot to be desired. Thus, according to the Regional (Works) Engineer, whereas in the 1994/5 financial year, the 721 kms of Regional Roads needed 618.8 million shillings for rehabilitation, only 125 million shillings were provided by the central government (*Daily News*, April 10, 1995).

**Culture and Traditions**

There are certain cultural factors which in many ways affect agriculture in the region. For instance, ritual activities take a particularly prominent role in the cycle of a resident in the Coast Region. There are numerous cultural celebrations, such as boys' circumcision ceremonies, puberty rites for girls, weddings and seasonal *ngomas* (dances) which people on the coast are bound to attend and participate in one way or another, also rites of passage, and requirements of the Islamic culture such as fasting. These events consume a lot of time and resources which perhaps the people in Coast region could cut down so as to engage more in profitable economic ventures. Indeed the then president of the country, Ali Mwinyi was so disturbed by the habit, that he is reported to have castigated the practice which to him was detrimental to economic progress (*Uhuru*, January 10, 1992).

Another inhibiting dilemma is witchcraft fears and practices. Many writers (M-L. Swantz, 1986; L. Swantz, 1990; Ishumi, 1974) have commented on the widespread existence of witchcraft beliefs and actions and their ostensible efficacy. There is an urgent need to research on this problem to understand its dimensions, implications and ramifications. At present the general belief is that witchcraft (*uchawi*) is so rampant in the region that it poses one of the greatest stumbling blocks towards progress.


## Official Attitudes

Underdevelopment in the Coast Region can be explained as one of the after-effects of colonial distortion of the structure of the overall Tanzanian economy. Colonial policy favoured some areas and neglected others, especially those which appeared unattractive to white settlement. Coast Region may have been neglected by the colonial masters because of its harsh weather and environment. During colonial rule, official attitudes towards the region and its inhabitants were replete with disdain. References to the 'lazy' and complacent native are common. Many reports refer to how natives in the area disliked manual labour, and to their conservatism. As a result, punitive measures were employed through by-laws and convictions. Indeed there was a time when one District Commissioner, John Young, who administered Rufiji for 20 years, is reported to have flogged people in the district because of their alleged laziness (*Daily News*, August 8, 1990).

Incidentally, even 'native' post-colonial administrators still harbour certain attitudes when it comes to explaining underdevelopment in the Coast Region. Thus, in describing the behaviour of the residents of Rufiji district, a District Commissioner of the 1990s likened them to a cunning people, '... with an inborn reluctance to hard work and very much self-conceited' (*Daily News*, August 8, 1990). Thus harsh by-laws were re-introduced in 1974 after the villagization exercise and peasants have been obliged to adhere to minimum acreages. Court action has on various occasions been taken for failure to weed cashew nut *shambas* (see, for example, orders by the Regional Commissioner to that effect in *Daily News*, September 14, 1992).

An agricultural officer in Zinga (Bagamoyo district) told me how young men were forced to migrate to Dar es Salaam when district authorities enacted compulsory minimum acreage requirements for peasants. In the city they end up off-loading cargo from trucks in market places and carry loads from the market for customers (*lumbesa*). The agricultural officer talked of how difficult it was for him to convince the people (youths) of the need to undertake agriculture seriously:

> There is plenty of fertile land and the local people could get everything they wanted but very few do ... They come to buy cassava, sweet potatoes, bananas, name it, from me and go to sell at the village *genge* (stall) or take the produce to the city ... I have tried to take the villagers to my farms so that they can emulate me ... They would admire and heap praise on me and promise to go home to do the same. That would be the end of the story ... they come again for the commodities ... the people who do serious farming along the coastal areas come from upcountry regions. The usual remark one hears from the indigenous coastal people about a hard working man or woman is *anafanya kazi kama Mnyamwezi*

210

(he or she works like a Nyamwezi - from Tabora region), implying that the local people are not used to such hard work.

The fact is that like peasants all over the world, the Tanzania coastal peasant is also determined first to meet the minimum need of satisfaction for himself and his family and then to satisfy additional desires with a minimum of drudgery (Von Freyhold, 1979). However, he differs from many other peasants in Tanzania by being more oriented towards cash: fishing, small business/commerce, seasonal crops, perennial crops and livestock keeping. All these are opportunities available to him and he will try to distribute his labour between them according to the seasons and the specific characteristics of his environment in such a way as to maximize security and returns on his labour. Indeed peasants in Coast Region, like others of their kind, make choices. Their decisions are based on immediate needs. They also consider labour inputs in relation to returns in terms of yields and market prices.

## Conclusion

A number of conclusions can be made from the above discussion on poverty afflicting the Coast Region of Tanzania. First, it is obvious and rather strange that an area so close to a vibrant centre of growth has failed to benefit from such proximity. The reasons for this failure are many. There are physical and environmental factors such as low soil fertility, but others are due to neglect as has been shown with regard to infrastructure. It is up to the authorities concerned to deal with any constraints which hinder the realization of the vast potential that exists in the Coast Region. As Hansen (1970, p. 131) rightly pointed out, it is essential to endow poorer regions by actively inducing economic activity, for the benefit of the residents and the national economy at large.

## Note

1. Since July, 1996, a sixth district, Mkuranga has been carved out of Kisarawe district. It comprises of Mkamba, Mkuranga, Kisiju and Shungubweni divisions.

## References

Bantje, H. (1979), *The Rufiji Agricultural System: Impact of Rainfall, Floods and Settlement*, BRALUP, Dar es Salaam.
Bantje, H. (1980), *Floods and Famines: A Study of Food Shortages in Rufiji District*, BRALUP, Dar es Salaam.
Bernstein, H. (1979), 'Overview of Coastal Regions', in D. Brysceson and N. Sachak, *Proceedings of the Workshop on Women's Studies and Development*, pp. 1-8.
Berry, B. (1972), 'Hierarchical Diffusion: The Basis of Developmental Filtering and Spread in a System of Growth Centres' in N. Hansen (ed), *Growth Centres in Regional Economic Development*, Free Press, New York, NY, pp. 108-138.

Bisanga, H. (1986), 'Untapped Economic Potential of Coast Region', *Daily News*, July 2, 1986.

Bureau of Statistics (1992), *Coast Region: Population Census, Regional Profile, Dar es Salaam.*

Conyers, D. (1970), *Agro-Economic Zones of Tanzania*, BRALUP, *Dar es Salaam.*

Datto, B. and Gray, A. (1977), 'Underdevelopment and Regional Planning in the Third World: A Critical Review', *East African Geographical Review*, Vol. 15, June, 1977, pp. 11-32.

Egero, B. and Henin, R. (1973), *Analysis of the 1967 Population Census*, Vol. III, Bureau of Statistics and BRALUP, Dar es Salaam.

Gould, P. (1964), 'A Note on Research into the Diffusion of Development', *Journal of Modern African Studies*, Vol. 2, pp. 123-125.

Hansen, N. (1970), *Rural Poverty and the Urban Crisis*, Indiana University, Bloomington, in Dar es Salaam/Msanga Road Feasibility Study Draft Final Report (1976), Muhema.

Hansen, N. (1970), 'Development Pole Theory in a Regional Context', in McKee, Dean and Leah (eds), *Regional Economics: Theory and Practice*, The Free Press, New York, NY, pp. 121-35.

Hansen, N. (1972), *Growth Centres in Regional Economic Development*, The Free Press, New York, NY.

Havnevik, K. (1993), *Tanzania: The Limits to Development from Above*, Nordiska Afrikainstitutet, Uppsala.

Ishumi, A. (1974), 'Community Education and Development', PhD thesis, University of Dar es Salaam.

Kamuzora, C.L. (1973), 'Demographic Patterns and Trends in the Coastal Areas of E. Africa and the Western Indian Ocean', in O. Linden (ed), *Proceedings of the Workshop and Policy Conference on Integrated Coastal Zone Management in E. Africa including the Island States*, Arusha.

Lienhardt, P. (1968), *Swifa ya Nguvumali: The Medicine Man*, Clarendon Press, Oxford.

Lukumbo, L. (1991), 'The Pest Problem in Kisarawe District', *Daily News*, 12 December.

McKee, D., Dean, R. and Leah, W. (1970), (eds), *Regional Economics: Theory and Practice*, The Free Press, New York, NY.

Maghimbi, S. (1977), 'Political Economy of the Peasants of Kisarawe, Coast Region', BA Dissertation, University of Dar es Salaam.

Mchonde, M. (1977), 'Peasant Differentiation and its Enhancement, Gumba, Coast Region, BA dissertation, University of Dar es Salaam.

Moore, J.E. (1973), 'Population Distribution and Density', in Egero and Henin, pp. 38-55.

Musendo, Z. (1990), 'The Rufiji River Civilization', *Daily News*, March 8, 1990.

Perroux, F. (1955), 'A Note on the Concept of "Growth Poles"', in McKee, Dean, and Leah (1970), (eds), *Regional Economics: Theory and Practice*, pp. 93-103.

Shishira, E., Rajeswaran, K. and Eriksen, J. (1984), *Kibaha District: Status for Development*, IRA, Dar es Salaam.

Shishira, E., Shechambo, F. and Sosovelle, H. (1988), *Problems and Opportunities for Agricultural Development in Kisarawe District Tanzania*, IRA, Dar es Salaam.

Swantz, L. (1970), 'The Zaramo of Dar es Salaam: A Study of Continuity and Change', *Tanzania Notes and Records*, 71, pp. 157-164.

Swantz, L. (1990), *The Medicine Man among the Zaramo of Dar es Salaam*, Dar es Salaam University Press, .Dar es Salaam.

Swantz, M-L. (1986a), *Ritual and Symbol in Transitional Zaramo Society*, SIAS, Uppsala.

Swantz, M-L. (1986b), *The Role of Women in Tanzanian Fishing Societies: A Study of the Socio-Economic Context and the Situation of Women in Three Coastal Villages in Tanzania*, NORAD, Dar es Salaam.

United Republic of Tanzania (1994), *URT National Accounts for 1986-1994*, Dar es Salaam.

Von Freyhold, M. (1979), *Ujamaa Villages in Tanzania: An Analysis of a Social Experiment*, Monthly Review, New York, NY.

Vuorela,, U. (1987), *The Women's Question and Mode of Human Reproduction: An Analysis of a Tanzanian Village*, Helsinki.

Yoshida, M. (1972), 'Agricultural Survey of the Lower Rufiji Plain', Preliminary report presented to a seminar at BRALUP, Dar es Salaam.

# 15 Where have all the Young Girls Gone? Gender and Sex Ratios on Mafia Island, Tanzania

PAT CAPLAN

## Introduction: Population Trends

When I carried out field-work for the third time on Mafia in 1985, and began investigating food, health and fertility, I was surprised to discover that the sex ratio on the island was skewed in favour of males (see table 15.1). This is an unusual situation in most parts of the world, where women generally outnumber men, although there are certain countries, most particularly in South Asia, where the sex ratio favours males; there is a large literature on the reasons for this, which are cultural, economic, and religious. In Sub-Saharan Africa, on the other hand, it is generally the case that women outnumber men, and indeed, this is true of Tanzania as a whole. My aim in the research conducted during the summer of 1994 was to ascertain the reasons why on Mafia Island, the sex ratio is so unbalanced.[1]

Table 15.1   Sex ratio, Coastal Region of Tanzania by district, plus Zanzibar

| | |
|---|---|
| Bagamoyo | 93.45 |
| Kibaha | 95.95 |
| Kisarawe | 90.91 |
| Mafia | 105.00 |
| Rufiji | 94.41 |
| Zanzibar | 94.57 |

*Source:* Population Census figures.

I had already discovered from previous research that in this area, this is not a new phenomenon, but one that dates from the very earliest years of British administration in Tanganyika. Although both the 1919 estimates for the total population and the 1922 count of the slave population showed a sex ratio in favour of females, by 1924, when what the District Book describes as 'a careful census' was made, it was plain that the sex ratio actually favoured males as table 15.2 **shows.**

**Table 15.2  Mafia population in 1924**

|  | Men | Women | Boys | Girls | Total |
|---|---|---|---|---|---|
| Non-natives | 266 | 210 | 139 | 141 | 756 |
| Natives | 3146 | 2593 | 1101 | 870 | 7710 |
| Total | 3412 | 2803 | 1240 | 1011 | 8466 |

*Source:* Mafia District Book.

The above sets of figures show more males than females for adult 'natives' and 'non-natives' and for 'native' children, with the sole exception being 'non-native' children.

The preponderance of males in the population has continued to be the case in the censuses taken subsequently, as Table 15.3 shows:

**Table 15.3  Mafia population by sex: comparison of 1967, 1978 and 1988 censuses**

|  | 1967 | 1978 | 1988 |
|---|---|---|---|
| Males | 8481 | 11821 | 16940 |
| Females | 8267 | 11283 | 16116 |
| Total | 16748 | 23104 | 33056 |
| Sex Ratio | 103 | 104 | 105 |

*Source:* Population Census Figures.

Indeed, a comparison of the last three censuses shows a rapidly rising population, which has doubled over two decades. Mafia has the highest population growth rate of all districts in the Coastal Region (URT, 1991, p. 32, Table 3). It also has the highest population density of the five districts of the Coast Region, at between 50-70 persons per square kilometre, compared with 30-50 for Kibaha and 10-30 for the remainder. Furthermore, Mafia has a worsening trend in terms of sex ratio. This situation makes Mafia unique among the coastal districts (URT, 1991, p.17).

In this chapter, I consider this issue with regard to food, health and fertility and also look at local ideas concerning the relative worth of women and men, including the marked preference for male children and its consequences.

**Explanation 1.  Women Get Less Food**

Mafia Island has long been a food deficit area although the situation differs between the northern and southern halves of the island, with the former, which has much more bush land available for shifting cultivation, producing a higher rate of subsistence crops than the latter, which is mainly planted up with coconut and cashew nut trees. Even so, a northern village like Kanga, the subject of the present study, which has a very large acreage of land available for cultivation, is not producing enough food to meet its own needs. Although it is difficult to be certain without spending a considerably longer time in the village than I have been able to do in recent visits, it is my impression that most households in Kanga village are now producing enough to feed themselves for only perhaps half of the year, and have to buy food for the remainder of the time, whereas when I first carried out fieldwork in the 1960s, most appeared to produce enough for nine months of the year.

While some food is produced by households for their own subsistence, most households depend upon bought food for much of the year. The price of food has risen much more sharply than that of other items at the same time as prices which the villagers obtain for their main cash crop, coconuts, have dropped.

If married, a woman is supposed to receive bought food and clothes from her husband, but the reality is that many men are either unable or unwilling to provide this. Men control household budgets to a large extent, and make the decisions about where the often limited cash resources will go. Women complain frequently that their husbands fail to provide housekeeping money, even when they manage to frequent tea-shops, or are known to give presents to mistresses.

Women have fewer opportunities to earn cash than do men - they own far fewer coconut trees, do not fish or trade, and virtually no women have the chance to get trained for paid jobs in teaching, the civil service or health. A few women make cooked food, such as buns (*mandazi*) and chapatis and sell these through local tea-shops, but the profits are very small. A woman's main source of cash income is the making of raffia mats, and she expects to produce between 6 and 10 per annum, which are usually sold to local traders for around Tsh. 1,000 each.

Although women are responsible for growing most of the food, and for preparing it and serving it, the norm is to give more and better quality food to males, especially husbands and fathers, a topic on which I have published elsewhere (Caplan, 1989). Women fear their husbands' displeasure if they do not serve them nice food, a fear which is not unfounded given that men have the right to divorce their wives easily. It is also argued that men need more and better food than women, partly because the work men do is seen as more important, and partly because women are thought better able to endure hunger.

Even though the fertility rate is high, and many women spend much of their reproductive years either pregnant or lactating, the special needs of women in pregnancy and lactation are not recognized, and this, coupled with women's high work-loads and high morbidity, results in women not infrequently *losing* weight during pregnancy.

A further point is that men have more opportunities for eating and drinking outside the household than women since they are the ones who patronize the tea-shops (*mahoteli*) where they can obtain tea, chapatis, buns, and cooked fish. Not only are women debarred by custom from entering such 'public' places, they would not have the necessary cash or indeed, time.

## Explanation 2. Women's Work Loads are Excessive

Women do most of the agricultural labour, and they also perform virtually all of the domestic labour (fetching wood and water, pounding grain, cooking, cleaning and childcare). Women have extremely heavy work-loads, especially during the six months of the main agricultural season. Yet in spite of this, their work is mostly unrecognized, by themselves and by the men. When asked, men would always claim that they worked harder than women, and that their work was more important. Some women concurred in this: 'The men go before (in cultivation); we women just follow behind', but others were quick to point out that 'We women work like donkeys while the men just sit about'.

Furthermore, there has been a diversion of male labour to cash crops. The total acreage, at least of bush land cultivated, is determined by how much a man clears in the first place, and many men today have other preoccupations, particularly the planting of coconut trees to yield cash crops. Partly because of the relative rise of coconut prices in the 1970s and 1980s, male labour has been diverted away from subsistence to cash crops. Thus in the production of food crops, much of the agricultural work, apart from the clearing of the bush and the building of protective fences, falls upon women.

## Explanation 3. Women Suffer from Greater Morbidity than Do Men

Most figures kept by the rural medical centre and the Maternity and Child Health (MCH) clinic do not give breakdowns either by sex or age. The Rural Medical Assistant told me that women and children are particularly subject to anaemia: 'There are very few women who are not anaemic'. This was also confirmed in an interview at the District Hospital in Kilindoni, where I was told that the major difference between males and females in terms of morbidity relates to the latter's high incidence of anaemia.

Anaemia is medically related both to malaria, to which men and women are susceptible, and to hookworm, to which women and children are more susceptible, since they rarely wear shoes or sandals, whereas men generally do. The primary reason for this is lack of cash with which to buy them. It is also, although this was not mentioned by any of the medics to whom I spoke, related to diet. Women need high intakes of iron-rich foods such as eggs and green vegetables because of menstruation and pregnancy, but rarely obtain sufficient quantities to improve their health.

217

## Explanation 4. Women Have High Fertility

In Tanzania, the average number of children per woman is still high - seven. Contraception has only recently become available at village level, with women able to get the pill or Depo-Provera by injection, and men to receive condoms. Many women are anxious to avail themselves of these facilities, but often meet with resistance on the part of their husbands. Many women said that they would like to bear fewer children, or space them more widely, but that their husbands would not agree. Women felt that they bore the main burdens of child-rearing as well as bearing, and that men did not always fulfil their responsibilities as fathers particularly in terms of contributing cash.

Utilizing the somewhat meagre records kept at the clinic, if we assume that perhaps 125 women are utilizing contraception, this represents only approximately one quarter of the women in the reproductive age range. In fact, there is other evidence from different clinic figures that the number of women practising contraception is even lower. And the numbers of men requesting condoms is a tiny proportion of the population.

Ante-natal care consists of examinations and weighing, and the giving of iron, folic acid and chloroquine tablets during pregnancy. There is a very high take-up rate of ante-natal care at the village level, although not all women are able to travel to the district hospital for the blood test which is recommended during pregnancy, largely because of the expense of the journey (Tsh. 1,000 return).

Women can have their babies in the MCH clinic attended by the midwife, but only a minority choose to do this. Most have their babies at home, or rather at the home of their mothers, for it is customary to return there in the seventh month of pregnancy and remain there for at least three months, in order to ensure that a woman gets sufficient help with other children, and some degree of rest. While this system does aid women who are pregnant or who have just given birth, it also throws quite a burden on to their own mothers. Although the MCH clinic is supposed to keep records of all births in the village, it is highly likely that a number of home births are unrecorded.

## Summary of Women's Well-Being

Women obtain less food than men, they work harder, suffer from a higher degree of morbidity, especially anaemia, and also bear many children. For all of these reasons, their 'life-chances' are perhaps fewer than those of men. But this does not constitute the total explanation for the skewed sex ratios - the problem starts much earlier with small children, to a consideration of whom I now turn.

# Children and Sex Preferences

## Children's Health

Children under five are supposed to be brought regularly to the clinic by their mothers for their growth and well-being to be monitored, primarily through weighing. The child's weight is entered on a growth-chart. Children are also vaccinated at the MCH clinic. Children's progress is monitored by weighing and the entering of data on to growth charts kept by the mothers. Most children are brought to the clinic at some time during their first year, both for weighing and for immunization. Not infrequently, however, the MCH clinic has problems with its vaccination programme, since there are sometimes periods when it cannot store vaccines because the fridge is not working, most commonly because of lack of kerosene.

In 1985 I had obtained figures on the weight of almost 100 children, which showed that almost half of them were under-weight (60-80 per cent of desirable body-weight - grey in the growth charts), and that some actually fell into the danger zone of being below 60 per cent (the red zone on growth charts). However, when the figures were broken down by sex, it was found that approximately one third of all male babies and young children were underweight, but *over half* of females.

In the reports compiled after this visit, I suggested that in this area, a process of sex discrimination starts at an early age, and was reflected both in feeding practices and in medical treatment. It also seems likely that women who give birth to female children may be pressured to get pregnant again quickly to produce a male child, and if they do so, would wean the first child as soon as they are aware that they have conceived. Thus the first child, a female, might not even be breastfed for the full two-year period normally considered desirable.

My plans for field-work in 1994 included obtaining comparative figures with 1985 regarding child health (particularly as measured by weight) and female fertility histories. Although the clinic records do not, unfortunately, distinguish children by sex, they do distinguish by age, using two broad categories of less than 1 year, and 1-5 years. The incidence of underweight is much greater in the second category (25 per cent as compared with 10.8 per cent), suggesting that underweight comes after the first few months, rather than at birth. This is confirmed by notes written by the midwife showing that none of the 66 children born in 1993 either at the clinic or under the supervision of a Trained Birth Attendant were less than 2.5 kg. Thus the problem appears to be less one of small-for-dates babies, than what happens after birth, and especially after the introduction of solid food at around the age of six months, a problem which has already been discussed.

With the help of the midwife, I obtained data on the weights of 77 children brought to the MCH clinic by their mothers during the month of July 1994. Of these children, 45 were boys, of whom 37.4 per cent were underweight, and 32 girls, of whom 35.6 per cent were underweight.

**Table 15.4 Children's weight**

|  | 1985 | | 1994 | |
|---|---|---|---|---|
|  | boys | girls | boys | girls |
| Numbers | 33 (100%) | 30 (100%) | 45 (100%) | 32 (100%) |
| Normal (80%+) | 22 (67%) | 14 (47%) | 26 (58%) | 19 (59%) |
| 60-80% | 10 (30%) | 15 (50%) | 11 (24%) | 8 (25%) |
| -60% | 1 (3%) | 1 (3%) | 6 (13%) | 5 (15%) |

*Source:* Surveys conducted by anthropologist, Kanga, MCH Clinic.

As Table 15.4 shows, then, there is very little difference on the basis of sex in the proportion of underweight children, and in this respect, the 1994 figures contrast sharply with those from 1985. However, their apparent indication of greater sexual equality is undermined by the absolute differences in the numbers of children, with many fewer girls than boys being brought to the clinic.

These findings were consistent with figures kept in 1994 at the general clinic: far fewer girls than boys were brought there, which was the same situation as had obtained in 1985.

*Food*

Although there is little evidence of overall protein deficiency on the island, it seems likely that small children do not receive adequate supplies, and are particularly at risk when they begin to be given solid foods at around 6-9 months and to an even greater degree when they are weaned at around the age of two years. The MCH clinic advises mothers to give their children porridge (*uji*) made with milk and eggs, and to give children green vegetables, but when asked, few women report that they do so. Many women said that milk was unobtainable in the village, and that they could not afford to buy eggs.

Nonetheless, some milk is obtained from the zebu herds, but it almost all goes to the several tea-shops (*hoteli*) in the village, which place regular orders with the herdsmen. Use of tea-shops is confined to adult males with the necessary cash, and thus it is they who consume most of what little milk is produced.

Children are breast-fed up to the age of two years, unless the mother becomes pregnant earlier, in which case she immediately weans the child. They begin to receive solids at six months, usually in the form of *uji*, a gruel made from cereals. Milk is rarely added to such gruel, nor do children often get eggs. Aside from a recognition that very small children need soft foods and cannot cope with fish bones, little account is taken of their particular needs. Many women say that they know from being told at the MCH clinic that their children would benefit from eggs and milk, but that they do not have the cash with which to purchase them, even if they are available. Their husbands, if they are present, are often unwilling to spend money on such items, which is not surprising, given that information about children's dietary needs is never given to men.  Thus small children often suffer from protein and other deficiencies.

This problem appears to be exacerbated in the case of girl children, since females - even babies - are said to be better able to withstand hunger than boys 'for that is how God made them'.  There is some evidence to indicate that husbands and fathers are less likely to take seriously weanlings' needs for protein if they are girls than if they are boys because of the very marked sex preference for male children on the part of men.  Furthermore, boys above the toddler stage are more likely to eat with their fathers, and thus share in the better food given to males.

In short, then, female children appeared to have lower 'entitlements' (Sen, 1990;  Papanek, 1990) to food and health care, resulting in a skewed sex ratio.

*Fertility*

In the light of the above, it was not surprising to find that a sample of women attending the clinic reported that they had more live male than female children.  In 1985, 53 women in a sample whose fertility histories I obtained reported having 103 live male children, but only 79 female children.  In 1994, I was able to conduct another small survey of 41 women visiting the clinic and obtain their fertility histories.  The two samples show the following:

**Table 15.5  Fertility histories of women, 1994 and 1985**

|  | 1994 | 1985 |
|---|---|---|
| Number of women | 41 | 53 |
| Live male children | 66 | 103 |
| Live female children | 48 | 79 |
| Deceased male children | 13 | 37 |
| Deceased female children | 9 | 38 |
| Total male children born | 79 | 140 |
| Total female children | 57 | 117 |
| Total live children | 114 | 182 |
| Total deceased children | 22 | 75 |
| Total births | 136 | 257 |
| Average number of births per woman | 3.3 | 4.8 |

*Source:*  Surveys conducted by anthropologist, Kanga MCH Clinic.

Either the sex ratio at birth on Mafia is quite abnormal, which seems unlikely, or women are much more likely to 'forget' the birth of female children who die, and more girls than boys die.

## Explanation for Sex Preferences

Sex preferences for male children remain clearly marked on the part of men, and women too want male children to please their husbands. This sexual preference ties in with the health and well being of children, with a clear trend that more boys than girls survive childhood. One reason for this may well be connected with the distribution of food at the household level, as discussed in section 1, and especially during the crucial weaning stage when bought food, such as eggs and milk, can make an important difference to ability to thrive. Another is the fact that male children are more likely to be taken both to the Rural Medical Centre and to the MCH clinic than their sisters.

What kind of explanations do people give for preferring sons to daughters?

### a) *Sons look after you in your old age*

People say constantly that '*Watoto ni mali* - children are wealth'; 'they are the ones who help you out and look after you when you are old'. Men, particularly, were likely to say that this was the job of sons who would have greater access to cash incomes than daughters. Yet it is statistically relatively unlikely that adult sons will live near to their fathers. In many instances known to me at the village level, elderly people were being supported by their daughters in terms of goods and services, even money. Here then we can see a contradiction between the ideal role of adult sons - to support parents in old age - and the reality of many parents actually being cared for by their daughters, a fact which is rarely publicly acknowledged.

### b) *You need a child of your own sex to assist you with tasks*

Given the sexual division of labour, both men and women want children of their own sex so that they can be assisted in their tasks. Women know that they can only command the labour of small boys - soon enough they will evince reluctance to help their mothers, whereas daughters are viewed as a constant source of support. Yet in fact, frequently, daughters themselves require the help of their mothers - when they are pregnant or giving birth, or in the case of their divorce when mother's mothers are the most likely people to take the children of the broken marriage.

### c) *You need a child of your own sex for companionship*

But there are other cultural factors which predispose men to having sons. Men and women are seen as being very different, and men spend much of their time with other men, women with women, which is explicable both in terms of the sexual division of labour, and also in terms of companionship - men talk to other men, women to other women. The word used - *mwenzako* - has the connotation both of someone who is *with* you (a companion) and *like* you. Furthermore, children of the same sex 'belong' to that parent more than children of the opposite sex. As one woman said, 'The boys belong to their father, but the girls are really mine'. Both men and women want *mtoto mwenzangu* - a child which is 'like me' and therefore 'really mine'.

## d) *Sons have more prestige than daughters*

Men see having boys as a symbol of prestige and virility, and they hope that sons will be successful and get well-paid jobs away from a village, an ambition which is in fact achieved only by a small minority. Even so, the chances of this happening are much greater with sons than with daughters.

Furthermore Islam accords special privileges to men. Such a view is not confined to men, it was one held by many women, as the following quote from an elderly woman, a leader of the *tarika* (Sufi mystical order), makes plain:

> Only men can be Sheikhs. According to our religion, only a man can stand in front and lead the prayers. If a group of women pray, they all pray together, shoulder to shoulder. But if a group of men pray, they can have one of their number stand in front. And the Imam is always a man.

## Conclusion

In considering skewed sex ratios in other parts of the world, explanatory weight has been given to factors such as women's role in production, forms of marriage payments (whereby as with dowry women take property on marriage, rather than bringing it in), or the need for sons to perpetuate lineages and family names and perform funeral rites for parents. None of these explanations holds good for Mafia Island. Women are significant food producers. Marriage does not involve the payment of dowry. Sons are not needed to perpetuate lineages because in this area, descent groups are cognatic, being traced through both parents, rather than patrilineal. Sons are not required to perform funeral rites adequately. Sons may or may not care for parents in old age, but daughters do so at least as often.

So what kind of explanation are we left with? First of all, there is no one single explanation, but rather a whole constellation of small factors which together add up to a situation in which women's life chances are less favourable than those of men. The fact that women work harder, have less leisure, suffer greater morbidity, bear many children and often receive not only less food than men but less than they need does answer the 'how' question of the skewed sex ratios in this area.

The 'why' question, and particularly that of why Mafia Island is more problematic. What is there unique about this coastal area which produces these kinds of figures? We cannot adduce, as scholars have done for a similar situation in south Asia (cf. Miller, 1981), that the explanation lies in women's contribution to productive labour or lack of it. Rather, it appears that the intrinsic worth of women and men is different, and it is thus not surprising that their entitlements should also be different.

**Note**

1. Fieldwork in 1985 and 1994 was supported by the Nuffield Foundation.

**References**

Caplan, P. (1989), 'Perceptions of Gender Stratification', *Africa*, 59, pp. 196-208.

Caplan, P. (1995a), 'Children are our Wealth and we want them: A Difficult Pregnancy on Mafia Island, Tanzania', in Bryceson, D. (ed), *Women Wielding the Hoe: Lessons from Rural Africa for Feminist Theory and Development Practice*, Berg, Oxford, pp. 131-49.

Caplan, P. (1995b), '"In my Office, we don't have Closing Hours": Gendered Household Relations in a Swahili Village in Northern Mafia Island', in Creighton, C., and Omari, C.K. (eds), *Gender, Family and Household in Tanzania*, Avebury, Aldershot, pp. 118-38.

Government of Tanzania (1967, 1978), *Population Census*.

*Mafia District Book*.

Miller, B. (1981), *The Endangered Sex: The Neglect of Female Children in Rural North India*, Cornell University Press, Ithaca NY.

Papanek, H. (1990), 'To Each less than she needs, from Each more than she can do: allocations, entitlements and value', in Tinker, pp. 162-81.

Sen, A. (1990), 'Gender and Cooperative Conflicts', in Tinker, pp. 123-49.

Tinker, I. (ed) (1990), *Persistent Inequalities*, Oxford University Press, New York NY.

United Republic of Tanzania (URT) (1991), *Population Census, 1988: (a) Basic Demographic and Socio-economic Characteristics (b) Regional Profile: Coast,,* Bureau of Statistics, Dar es Salaam.

# 16 Rural Tanzanians and the National Elections of 1995

JOHN SIVALON

## Introduction

In 1995, Tanzania had its first multiparty elections since the early 1960s. This led to a proliferation of political parties, mainly centred in Dar es Salaam, with various platforms and policies for developing the country. While urbanization is increasing, Tanzania remains primarily a rural society with the large majority of the population living in small rural settlements. The rural population consists almost exclusively of smallholder families producing both cash and food crops, with limited opportunities for earning off-farm incomes. Because of this position in Tanzania's social structure they have unique interests which at best are often not heard and at worst are consciously ignored. The focus of the project whose findings are presented in this paper was to understand better the political interests of these women and men peasants and facilitate the incorporation of their interests into the political debate leading up to the national elections.

In the period before the national elections, there were two earlier indicators of political attitudes of Tanzanians. One was the Nyalali Commission which found that over three-quarters of Tanzanians were against the introduction of multiparty governance. Another study found that the dominant sentiment was not contentment with CCM rule, but fear of the possible alternatives, especially of violent conflict (Booth, Lugangira, Masanja, Mvungi, Mwaipopo, Mwami and Redmayne, 1993, p. 29). The findings presented in this paper show that people's attitudes towards multiparty governance became more positive over time, but peasants had real questions about the opposition parties' awareness and concern for their interests. Also, throughout the campaign period, Tanzanian peasants were consistent in their political views - reform was needed but it should take place within CCM itself.

This paper is a summary of three rounds of research that took place in December of 1993, March of 1994 and June of 1995. In each round, research assistants were sent to eight regions. These were Lindi, Mbeya, Iringa, Tanga, Arusha, Mara, Mwanza, and Zanzibar South. The research assistants were selected so as to have equal numbers of men and women, and Christians and Muslims. They were instructed to take a representative sample of adult villagers based on their age, sex, religion, education and economic status. Besides this survey style data collection, the principal researcher conducted focus group discussions in each region during the three rounds of research. In the following sections, I will summarize the findings of each round and indicate conclusions in each case.

225

## Round one

The sample of the first round was nearly 800 respondents with the following characteristics.

### Table 16.1 Age and sex of respondents

| Age/ sex | 18-25 | 26-33 | 34-41 | 42-49 | 50-57 | 58 over | Total |
|---|---|---|---|---|---|---|---|
| Female | 45 | 79 | 53 | 29 | 12 | 34 | 252 |
| Male | 80 | 132 | 102 | 79 | 48 | 73 | 514 |
| Total | 125 | 211 | 155 | 108 | 60 | 107 | 766 |

Male respondents were significantly over-represented in the sample (66 per cent vs. 33 per cent female). Over three-fifths of respondents (61 per cent) were Christians, 35 per cent were Muslims and 4 per cent claimed to be following a traditional religion. This last group is significantly lower than what was expected. The other two groups are disputable and since questions on religion have been removed from census forms in Tanzania, there is no firm national data upon which to rely.

The sample also differentiated according to economic status and education.

### Table 16.2 Respondents' education and socio-economic status

| Status/ Education | Poor | Middle | High | Total |
|---|---|---|---|---|
| No formal | 66 | 27 | 3 | 96 |
| Some primary | 41 | 40 | 12 | 93 |
| Primary | 96 | 239 | 27 | 362 |
| Some secondary | 16 | 48 | 17 | 81 |
| Secondary | 9 | 49 | 28 | 86 |
| Post Secondary | | 13 | 8 | 21 |
| Total | 228 | 416 | 95 | 739 |

The economic status of the respondents was assessed subjectively by the interviewers themselves in the context of the village environment; and a series of questions were asked on whether or not the CCM government was perceived as having fulfilled its obligations towards various social groups in Tanzania.

In this first round, the vast majority of rural Tazanians in the sample felt that the CCM government had failed them in terms of their agricultural activities. From other questions, it was clear that this failure was mainly in the availability and price of agricultural inputs and crop pricing policies. This dissatisfaction was further exhibited by the hostile responses concerning the CCM government's relationship to the rich, foreign business interests and

**Table 16.3 Has the government fulfilled its obligations to ...?**

| Social group | Yes | No |
|---|---|---|
| Women | 42% | 58% |
| Youth | 32% | 68% |
| Farmers | 12% | 88% |
| Workers | 41% | 59% |
| Students | 22% | 78% |
| Business People | 66% | 34% |
| Rich | 86% | 14% |
| Foreign Business | 84% | 16% |

business people in general. From people's responses and focus group discussions, rural Tanzanians in the sample appeared to feel that CCM had transformed itself into a party no longer of workers and peasants, but a party serving the interests of the rich and the business community.

Questions were asked concerning the change to multiparty politics, people's attitudes towards this transition, evaluation of the administration of this transition and people's knowledge of the emerging parties and their leaders.

**Table 16.4 Perceived changes since introduction of multiparty governance**

| Change/Region | No change | Change for worse | Change for better |
|---|---|---|---|
| Tanga | 75% | 1% | 24% |
| Mbeya | 54% | 6% | 40% |
| Iringa | 53% | 15% | 32% |
| Lindi | 35% | 14% | 51% |
| Mwanza | 14% | 10% | 76% |
| Arusha | 80% | 5% | 15% |
| Mara | 93% | 2% | 5% |
| Zanzibar South | 29% | 32% | 39% |
| All regions | 54% | 11% | 35% |

In this first round, two-thirds of the sample had not seen any changes since the introduction of multipartyism or they had seen changes for the worse. The age-group with the most responses claiming changes were for the better were those from 34 to 49 years old. Women had negative responses of 76 per cent compared to 58 per cent for men. The majority of those with some secondary education or above felt the changes had been for the better while only 26 per cent of those with primary or less thought there had been positive changes. Finally, 60 per cent of rich peasants were positive towards this transition compared to 25 per cent for poor peasants.

Women, the poor and those with little formal education were most negative towards the transition process. This is significant when one recalls that over 75 per cent of the sample had primary education or less. Somehow, for a political party to be successful, it has to develop strategies for responding to the interests of these groups. The above conclusions were reinforced by the answers of our sample to questions related to the future prospects of the transition and its contribution to solving the problems of Tanzania.

**Table 16.5  Attitudes towards contribution of multipartyism to development by sex, economic status and education**

**Whether a help**

| Sex | Yes | No |
|---|---|---|
| Male | 48% | 52% |
| Female | 37% | 63% |

| Education | Yes | No |
|---|---|---|
| No formal | 20% | 80% |
| Secondary | 71% | 29% |

| Economic Status | Yes | No |
|---|---|---|
| Poor | 38% | 62% |
| Rich | 61% | 39% |

Women were more pessimistic than men about the contribution that multiparty governance might make to the future development of Tanzania. This corroborates the earlier study (Booth et al.,p. 29) which found highly educated men to be those most likely to favour the change while women invariably declared themselves in favour of the status quo. The strongest contrast in attitudes towards the transition process was between those with no formal education and those with secondary education or more. There was a slightly smaller variance between rich and poor peasants, with the poor being mainly negative.

In spite of the generally negative feeling concerning the transition process, CCM leaders were given high positive ratings for their performance in the multiparty transition. This was confirmed by people disagreeing with the statement that CCM leaders were delaying the transition. Those who voiced negative attitudes towards opposition leaders mainly claimed that they were causing dissension and conflict for no purpose. Thus, most rural Tanzanians in the sample of this round were not very optimistic about the actual effect that multiparty governance would have on their lives.

Another major section of the questionnaire was designed to elicit information upon what people thought the government should be doing. In the overall sample, the four major problems facing Tanzania in order of priority were poor health care, water, poor or corrupt leadership and shortage or prices of agricultural inputs. There was not a great variation in response patterns based on gender, age, religion, education or economic status. In another question, people were asked to select the single most important role of government out of a list of seven.

**Table 16.6 Responses to the question: 'From the list below on which task should the Government concentrate its energy?'**

| Most important work of government | % of responses |
| --- | --- |
| Protecting citizens' rights and security | 29% |
| Ensure just crop prices | 25% |
| Education | 15% |
| Economic planning | 11% |
| Health care | 9% |
| Discourage class formation | 8% |
| National security | 3% |

From this table, it is apparent that the two most important perceived roles of the government were to protect the rights of citizens, including their personal security, and ensuring that just prices were paid for crops. One conclusion that could be drawn is that while people saw health care as a major problem facing Tanzania, they did not see the government as necessarily the best or only possible provider of that service. However, in terms of protecting their rights, personal security and economic interest, they then looked to the government as the only viable vehicle.

**Voter Preference for Major Presidential Candidates**

At the time of the first round of research, there were no officially nominated candidates so the researcher chose names that were being mentioned as possible CCM candidates. The six names used for CCM were Amour, Mwinyi, Malecela, Mrema, Ulimwengu and Lowassa. CCM candidates who were used where chosen on the basis of their relative strength of name recognition. Mwinyi and Amour as the two present leaders were included. Mrema and Malecela were picked as two possible strong candidates. Lowassa and Ulimwengu were included as two possible weak candidates. The opposition candidates used were Mtei, Mapalala, Fundikira, Marando, Hamad and Mtikila. While all the opposition candidates had a large percentage of name recognition, the survey demonstrated clearly that most CCM candidates could easily win against any of the opposition candidates. Augustine Mrema, who was still in CCM at this time, and John Malecela were the strongest of the six hypothetical CCM candidates. Against the strongest opposition candidates they were receiving around 85 per cent of the vote.

Certain regional patterns were identified. The regions of Tanga and Arusha were always close to the national average of around 60 per cent to 70 per cent support for CCM candidates. Iringa always had a high number of respondents declaring that they would vote for neither candidate. Mara gave support to opposition candidates only when they were running against Mwinyi and Amour. Therefore, their votes for the opposition appear to be votes *against* particular CCM leaders and for reform within CCM rather than any grassroots support for the opposition. Mbeya gave the least support to the opposition candidates. Lindi and Mwanza gave support to Mtei, Mapalala and Mtikila. The most evenly split sample was Zanzibar South, but even there, CCM candidates usually received the most support.

In summary, the strongest opposition showing against the weakest CCM candidates was slightly more than 20 per cent of the vote in this round. On the other hand, the strongest CCM showings were around 70 per cent and sometimes more. The strongest CCM candidate of those named in this round of the study for rural Tanzanians appeared to be Augustine Mrema with John Malecela a very close second.

*Conclusions of Round one*

From this first round, there are a number of important conclusions that can be made. First, most rural Tanzanians were dissatisfied with the quality of their lives. At least some of this dissatisfaction is related to the failure, according to their perceptions, of the CCM government to fulfil its responsibilities to them. Besides this, they felt that certain elite groups had been favourably treated by CCM - the rich and commercial interests. On the other hand, most rural Tanzanians in this sample felt that CCM leaders had been cooperating with the transition to multiparty governance much more than opposition leaders. In focus group discussions, there was a substantial degree of negative reactions against the opposition leaders. Thus, while most of the sample were not satisfied with CCM, they felt much better towards its most popular candidates than they did towards those of the opposition.

Mrema was the most popular CCM 'candidate'. The remarks that respondents made in selecting him indicated that he was perceived as honest, fighting against corruption and protecting the rights of the poor ordinary people. In people's opinions, as expressed in this first round, this was seen as a main responsibility of government. This is further supported by the remarks of those people who said that multipartyism was bringing changes for the better. They frequently claimed that it was making CCM much more accountable and correcting abuses. All of these points to my earlier statement: peasants were consistent in their view that reform was necessary, but that it should take place within CCM.

**Round two**

The sample of Round Two had over 770 respondents and had the following characteristics.

**Table 16.7 Age and sex of respondents**

| Age/Sex | 18-25 | 26-33 | 34-41 | 42-49 | 50-57 | 58 over | Total |
|---|---|---|---|---|---|---|---|
| Female | 44 | 93 | 77 | 36 | 12 | 9 | 271 |
| Male | 63 | 138 | 122 | 75 | 49 | 27 | 474 |
| Total | 107 | 231 | 199 | 111 | 61 | 36 | 745 |

As Table 16.7 indicates, the age characteristics of the sample were fairly close to the age distribution of the total voting age population of Tanzania with 72 per cent of the sample falling between the ages of twenty-six and forty-nine. Once again, in this sample, there was a disparity in terms of gender. Sixty-four percent of the sample were male and 36 per cent were female. This difference was much smaller in the younger age brackets with the oldest bracket having a 400 per cent difference. In this sample among those who had some secondary education women outnumbered men. This discreprancy resulted from one village in the sample which had a girls' secondary school.

**Table 16.8 Religion and regions of respondents**

| Religion/ Region | Christian | Muslim | Traditional | Total |
|---|---|---|---|---|
| Tanga | 59 | 40 | | 99 |
| Mbeya | 95 | 2 | 3 | 100 |
| Iringa | 91 | 3 | 1 | 95 |
| Lindi | 53 | 47 | | 100 |
| Mwanza | 72 | 27 | 2 | 101 |
| Arusha | 57 | 45 | 6 | 108 |
| Mara | 46 | | 9 | 55 |
| Zanzibar | 2 | 98 | | 100 |
| Total | 475 | 262 | 21 | 758 |

From the table it can be seen that Iringa, Mbeya and Mara had almost no Muslims in their samples. On the other hand, Zanzibar was almost totally Muslim with other high percentages of Muslims in Arusha, Lindi and Tanga. Mara had much fewer respondents in this round of research than in the first and compared to the other regions. This was caused by unavoidable difficulties encountered by the research assistant which resulted in the loss of nearly half her questionaires.

Seventy-five percent of the sample had primary education or less. Also, 40 per cent of the sample were classified as poor peasants and 52 per cent as middle peasants. This measure of wealth again was subjective; the research assistants were instructed to make their own judgement on the economic status of the respondent based on their appraisal relative to the standards of that particular village.

In people's responses to the questionnaire in round two, it is very difficult to get a clear and consistent reading of their attitudes toward the CCM government. On the one hand, if we look at Table 16.10 we see that most people felt the government had failed to fulfil its responsibility towards women, farmers and students.

**Table 16.9 Education and wealth of respondents**

| Status/ Education | Poor | Middle | Rich | Total |
|---|---|---|---|---|
| No formal | 48 | 33 | 4 | 85 |
| Some primary | 32 | 32 | 5 | 69 |
| Primary | 159 | 208 | 23 | 390 |
| Some secondary | 23 | 29 | 2 | 54 |
| Second. | 20 | 74 | 19 | 113 |
| Post secondary | 4 | 3 | 6 | 13 |
| Total | 286 | 379 | 59 | 724 |

**Table 16.10 Has the Government fulfilled its responsibility to ...?**

| Group | Yes | No |
|---|---|---|
| Farmers | 17% | 82% |
| Youth | 31% | 66% |
| Women | 36% | 63% |
| Rich | 79% | 14% |
| Foreign Business | 73% | 17% |
| Business | 60% | 34% |

71 per cent of the women interviewed expressed their dissatisfaction with their own treatment by the present government. The regions of Mbeya, Lindi and Tanga felt the strongest that youth had been failed by the CCM government. At the same time, Lindi, Iringa, Mara, Tanga and Mbeya (all over 90 per cent) were strongest in their feelings that CCM had failed to fulfil its responsibility towards farmers. Eighty-eight percent of poor peasants and 80 per cent of middle peasants affirmed these negative sentiments. Thus, as in the first round, based on responses to this question, CCM is perceived as a party that is primarily serving the interests of the rich and foreigners.

Some questions were aimed at isolating what role rural Tanzanians felt the government should play. Again, people were asked to identify four major problems they faced and then out of those four select the one that they saw as most important. The resulting list of problems reached 24 per cent; however, the four most often identified were poor health care (22 per cent), the economy (11 per cent), famine (8 per cent) and poor education (7.5 per cent).

Three out of the eight regions had health as their number one problem and a further three identified it as their second most important problem. Also, from the responses, water and poor health care were identified by women more than men as their major problems while corruption, inflation, and agricultural inputs were identified by significantly higher percentages of men than women.

**Table 16.11 Major problems by region**

| Region | Problem | Percent |
|---|---|---|
| Tanga | Transportation | 31 |
| Mbeya | Agricultural inputs | 37 |
| Iringa | Health | 24 |
| Lindi | Education | 30 |
| Mwanza | Health | 24 |
| Arusha | Famine | 35 |
| Mara | Cattle thieving | 26 |
| Zanzibar | Health | 38 |

Again, the respondents were asked to identify the most important role they felt government should play. The list included: the provision of education, national security, internal justice and personal security, provision of health services, economic planning, hindering class formation and ensuring just crop prices.

**Table 16.12 Most important role of government by region**

| Region | Role | Percent |
|---|---|---|
| Tanga | Just crop prices | 29 |
| Mbeya | Just crop prices | 59 |
| Iringa | Personal security and justice | 35 |
| Lindi | Education | 45 |
| Mwanza | Education | 30 |
| Arusha | Personal security and justice | 30 |
| Mara | Just crop prices | 40 |
| Zanzibar | Health | 26 |

Again, this question yielded results somewhat different from the open-ended question. The number one role for government was said to be to ensure just crop prices to the farmers (26 per cent), education (23 per cent), internal justice and security (17 per cent) and the provision of health (15 per cent). Furthermore, a greater percentage of women than men identified the provision of health care (21 per cent) as the primary role of government. A very similar discrepancy occurred in the first round of research when health was identified as the major problem facing people, but was not seen as related to the primary role of government. In fact, through group discussions, it was seen that protecting the rights and security of citizens and insuring just crop prices were considered connected. This would indicate that in both the first and second rounds of research, government's primary role as perceived by rural Tanzanians was protecting its citizens by ensuring their security, protecting their economic and political rights and providing for their just treatment. A secondary, though major role, was seen to be the provision of social services such as education and health. Protecting national security was seen as an insignificant role (5 per cent) for government to play except in the Zanzibar sample (19 per cent). This is important considering the amount of the national budget that is spent on the military.

One indication of peoples' attitudes towards the new parties was found in their feelings towards the transition to multiparty governance in general. In the survey, questions were asked about the present progress of the transition and future prospects.

**Table 16.13  Perceived changes since introduction of multiparty governance**

| Region | No change | Change for worse | Change for better | Total |
|---|---|---|---|---|
| Tanga | 70 | 18 | 11 | 99 |
| Mbeya | 67 | 3 | 29 | 99 |
| Iringa | 51 | 7 | 39 | 97 |
| Lindi | 7 | 6 | 87 | 100 |
| Mwanza | 41 | 32 | 28 | 101 |
| Arusha | 62 | 20 | 27 | 109 |
| Mara | 31 | 8 | 16 | 55 |
| Zanzibar | 35 | 42 | 23 | 100 |
| Total | 48% | 18% | 34% | 760 |

Again it was evident that there were tremendous differences among the regions. The most positive towards the present transition process in this round were Lindi and Iringa. The most negative were Zanzibar and Mwanza, while Tanga, Mbeya, Arusha and Mara have primarily seen no change. Other variables also appeared correlated to peoples' attitudes towards the transition process. The majority of those with secondary and post secondary education felt that the changes were for the better. Women (27 per cent) were less positive than men (38 per cent). Finally, rich peasants (42 per cent) were much more positive than middle or poor peasants. These responses are supported by peoples' attitudes towards the future prospects of the transition process.

The regions most favourable to the future prospects of the transition were Lindi and Zanzibar. Mwanza and Tanga were most negative with the other regions remaining fairly neutral in their appraisal. This indicates a shift in the Mwanza regional attitudes from the first round of the research. In the first round, the sample was from a population living much closer to an urban centre, while the sample in this second round was from Ukerewe Island which may not have had easy access to private media which are seen as very important in shaping peoples' attitudes. Of the other variables, the only one that significantly affects peoples' attitudes towards the future prospects of the transition process is education. 50 per cent of those with secondary

**Table 16.14    Attitudes towards contribution of multipartyism to development by region**

| Region | Yes | No | Don't know |
|--------|-----|-----|-----------|
| Tanga | 17 | 44 | 35 |
| Mbeya | 37 | 28 | 33 |
| Iringa | 32 | 31 | 35 |
| Lindi | 84 | 14 | 2 |
| Mwanza | 23 | 55 | 21 |
| Arusha | 27 | 41 | 41 |
| Mara | 20 | 21 | 14 |
| Zanzibar | 47 | 37 | 15 |
| Total | 38% | 36% | 26% |

education felt that the transition to multiparty governance would help solve Tanzania's problems. 70 per cent of those with post secondary education agreed with them, while only 20 per cent of those with no education agreed.

In the transition process, CCM leaders were seen by 53 per cent of the people as cooperating in the transition process and only 28 per cent felt that they were hindering it. On the other hand, only 40 per cent felt opposition leaders were cooperating, while 35 per cent felt they were hindering it. Again, in group discussions the criticism that was voiced concerning the opposition leaders was that they came and criticized CCM rather than listening to peoples' problems and offering their own policies and strategies.

*Voters' Preferences of Candidates*

In this round, the same six opposition leaders and six CCM candidates were used to judge the relative strength of the opposition parties over against CCM and each other. Respondents were asked to voice their preference between each opposition leader in head to head competition with each CCM candidate. In this round, while no opposition candidate ran well against the CCM strong candidates, some were competitive with the CCM weak candidates. Thus, there was some movement and this led to the conclusion that it should not be assumed that CCM could run anyone and win. Moreover, some of the opposition candidates had gained in strength from the first round of research against the CCM weak candidates.

Of the opposition candidates, Mtei was the only one who actually out-polled any of the CCM candidates. Against Ulimwengu, who had the lowest name recognition of all the candidates (both oppositon and CCM) he garnered 36 per cent of the votes as opposed to 35 per cent for Ulimwengu. The more educated were also more favourable to Mtei than they were to Malecela, Mwinyi and Amour. Also, against Mwinyi and Amour, Christian support shifted to Mtei. Finally, women voters favoured CCM candidates over Mtei much more than men.

It was evident that Mrema had a great deal more support than Malecela among the CCM candidates. In this round, Mrema beat all the opposition candidates with a greater percentage than either Mwinyi, Amour or Malecela.

However, this was not to say that he had no weaknesses. In terms of religion, more Muslims supported Mtei as the most fit to be president in the sample than they did Mrema. While Mrema ran very strong in the regions of Mbeya, Iringa, Arusha and Mara, no one in the Zanzibar sample picked him as the person most fit to be president. He had strength among those with secondary education but lost that support among those elected to higher levels. He was strong among the youngest of the sample. As a CCM candidate, Mrema could gain between 70 and 80 per cent of the vote in a national election held at the time of this second round.

*Conclusions of Round two*

The sample of round three was over 761 respondents with the following characteristics.

**Table 16.15 Age and sex of respondents**

| Age/Sex | 18-25 | 26-33 | 34-41 | 41-49 | 50-57 | 58 over | Total |
|---------|-------|-------|-------|-------|-------|---------|-------|
| Female | 65 | 84 | 59 | 36 | 26 | 16 | 286 (38%) |
| Malle | 79 | 127 | 106 | 67 | 32 | 64 | 475 (62%) |
| Total | 144 (19%) | 211 (28%) | 165 (22%) | 103 (13%) | 58 (7%) | 80 (11%) | 761 |

Table 16.15 indicates, that the age characteristics of this sample were fairly similar to that found in the total voting age population of Tanzania, with 82 per cent of the sample falling below the age of fifty. Once again, in this sample, there was a disparity in terms of gender. 62 per cent of the sample were male and 38% were female.

From table 16.16 it can be seen that a change took place from the samples of the previous two rounds. While overall more Christians are present in the sample, the regions of Tanga, Mara and Arusha had an increased number of Muslims included in their samples. Once again, it is difficult to judge whether or not this is an actual discrepancy or is truly representative of the region included.

**Table 16.16  Religion and regions of respondents**

| Religion/ region | Christian | Muslim | Traditional | Total |
|---|---|---|---|---|
| Tanga | 33 | 58 | | 91 |
| Mbeya | 70 | 3 | 1 | 74 |
| Iringa | 81 | 10 | 1 | 92 |
| Lindi | 37 | 51 | | 88 |
| Mwanza | 31 | 3 | 35 | 69 |
| Arusha | 29 | 35 | | 64 |
| Mara | 52 | 20 | 16 | 88 |
| Zanzibar | 6 | 79 | | 85 |
| Singida | 61 | 21 | | 82 |
| Total | 400(55%) | 280(38%) | 53(7%) | 733 |

**Table 16.17  Education and wealth of respondents**

| Status/ Education | Poor | Middle | Rich | Total |
|---|---|---|---|---|
| No formal | 33 | 16 | 2 | 51 |
| Some primary | 22 | 22 | 3 | 47 |
| Primary | 156 | 187 | 21 | 364 |
| Some secondary | 14 | 44 | 6 | 64 |
| Second. | 20 | 81 | 11 | 112 |
| Post secondary | 2 | 7 | 7 | 16 |
| Total | 247(38%) | 357(55%) | 50(7%) | 654 |

In this round, there were again questions aimed at isolating what role rural Tanzanians felt the government should play. First, people were asked to identify four major problems they faced and then out of those four to select the one that they saw as most important. The resulting list of problems reached 24 in length and the four most often identified were poor health care (22 per cent), corruption (12 per cent), the economy (11 per cent) and poor education (10 per cent).

**Table 16.18  Major problems by region**

| Region | Problem | Per cent |
|---|---|---|
| Tanga | Economy | 20% |
| Mbeya | Health care | 38% |
| Iringa | Health care | 21% |
| Lindi | Transportation | 30% |
| Mwanza | Health care | 16% |
| Arusha | Health care | 29% |
| Mara | Economy | 25% |
| Zanzibar | Health care | 25% |
| Singida | Health care | 32% |

Six out of the nine regions had health care as their number one problem in this round. This was a slight change from the earlier rounds when health care was the number one problem in three regions. This study indicates that as a problem it is much more widespread and even more so in that two out of the three remaining regions had it as their second most pressing problem.

### Table 16.19  Most important role of government

| Role | Percent |
|------|---------|
| Education | 13% |
| National security | 7% |
| Citizens personal security and justice | 27% |
| Health care | 12% |
| Economic planning | 13% |
| Hinder class formation | 9% |
| Wage and crop prices | 15% |
| Water provision | 2.3% |
| Roads | 2% |

Again, in this round, most respondents named the number one role of government to be 'to ensure personal security and justice'. This confirmed the findings of the two previous rounds that indicated that government's primary role is perceived to be to protect its citizens, ensuring their security, protecting their economic and political rights and providing for their just treatment under the law. Again, a secondary, though major role, was seen to be the provision of social services such as education and health.

One of the major shifts in the findings of this road of research compared to the two earlier rounds was in people's attitudes towards the transition to multiparty governance in general. In this study, as in the previous two, questions were asked about the present progress of the transition and future prospects.

### Table 16.20  Perceived changes since introduction of multiparty governance (%)

| Region | No change | Change for worse | Change for better | Total |
|--------|-----------|------------------|-------------------|-------|
| Tanga | 38 | 6 | 35 | 79 |
| Mbeya | 39 | 16 | 29 | 84 |
| Iringa | 29 | 21 | 41 | 91 |
| Lindi | 35 | 6 | 47 | 88 |
| Mwanza | 36 | 6 | 39 | 81 |
| Arusha | 37 | 5 | 23 | 65 |
| Mara | 23 | 5 | 60 | 88 |
| Zanzibar | 25 | 15 | 46 | 86 |
| Singida | 31 | 10 | 43 | 84 |
| Total | 39% | 12% | 49% | 746 |

In the previous studies, Lindi and Iringa were more positive towards the transition process while the most negative were Zanzibar and Mwanza. In this round, a dramatic shift took place in the attitudes of the people of Mara, Tanga, Arusha, Zanzibar and Mwanza. While significant numbers continued to maintain that they had seen no change, those claiming to have seen change for the worse dminished. At the same time, those claiming to have seen change for the better now outnumber the other two categories for the first time.

**Table 16.21   Attitudes towards contribution of multipartyism to development by region (%)**

| Region | Yes | No | Don't know |
|---|---|---|---|
| Tanga | 34 | 20 | 32 |
| Mbeya | 38 | 22 | 23 |
| Iringa | 52 | 15 | 24 |
| Lindi | 51 | 9 | 23 |
| Mwanza | 45 | 18 | 15 |
| Arusha | 28 | 24 | 13 |
| Mara | 60 | 13 | 14 |
| Zanzibar | 52 | 14 | 20 |
| Singida | 51 | 8 | 25 |
| Total | 55% | 19% | 26% |

As stated, these figures are significantly different from the previous rounds. More importantly, the shift has been from those who did not see this transition helping to those who see it helping while the 'don't know' category has remained the same. In the previous study, only 38 per cent of the respondents felt that the transition would help while 36 per cent felt that it would not help. The above figures show a 17 per cent shift to the more positive attitude. It appeared then that people were becoming less fearful of the transition. The regions most favourable to the future prospects of the transition were Lindi, Zanzibar, Mara and Singida. Tanga, Arusha and Mbeya remained more sceptical.

In this round, a series of Likert style questions were included concerning some of the major economic changes that were associated with the liberalization policy of CCM. These questions concerned whether or not the respondents agreed with government policy on the following issues. State planning in the economy, sale of parastatals. land ownership; and foreign investment. From peoples' responses it was evident that the majority had negative attitudes towards these changes.

As the table below presents, 85 per cent of the respondents agreed that the government should play a major role in planning the economy for the common good. This attitude was further supported by their negative responses concerning the other statements. Seventy-seven per cent disagreed with the policy of the wholesale selling off of parastatals, the privatization of land ownership (62 per cent) and the removal of any barriers that may be hindering foreign investment (55 per cent). On the final two statements, Zanzibar was different from the other regions in that it favoured the privatization of land ownership and was much less negative to the statement on foreign investment.

**Table 16.22  Attitudes towards economic changes**

| Responses/policy | Agree | Disagree | Don't know/unclear |
|---|---|---|---|
| Economic planning | 85% | 7% | 8% |
| Parastatal sale | 14% | 77% | 9% |
| Land policy | 30% | 62% | 8% |
| Foreign investment | 34% | 55% | 11% |

*Voters' Preference for Candidates*

In the survey, the names of five opposition leaders and one CCM candidate were used to judge the relative strength of the opposition parties over against CCM. The five opposition candidates were Cheyo, Mrema, Fundikira, Kambona and Che Mponda. The survey began to be conducted one day after CCM announced Mkapa as its candidate and therefore only he was included in the final survey draft. In terms of name recognition, Mrema led all candidates with 99 per cent of the respondents having at least heard his name. Mkapa followed with 91 per cent, Kambona with 83 per cent, Fundikira with 79 per cent, Cheyo with 59 per cent, and Che Mponda with 49 per cent.

Sixty-six per cent of the respondents claimed some party affiliation, as shown in table 16.23

**Table 16.23  Respondents' party affiliation**

| Party | Percent |
|---|---|
| CCM | 66 |
| NCCR | 21 |
| CUF | 6 |
| UDP | 4 |
| Chadema | 2 |
| UMD | 1 |

In the head to head competition, the respondents were asked to choose between Mkapa and each opposition candidate alone as if there were only two candidates vying for the presidency. Obviously, Mrema was the strongest among the opposition candidates (45 per cent), but his support decreased with his departure from CCM. In the previous two polls, Mrema was attaining close to 80 per cent support against the opposition candidates. Nevertheless, he remained a strong challenger and his support was further indicated by many people refusing to answer the question concerning the other head to head competitions. Many simply said 'Mrema is the only one, that's it'. The head to head competition also indicated that there was a hard core of about 15 per cent who were simply against CCM.

Respondents were also asked which party they would be voting for in the forthcoming parliamentary elections. Again the split in the whole sample was 60 per cent for CCM and 40 per cent for opposition parties. Also, the same regional differentiation appeared in responses to this question that appeared in the vote for the presidency. Tanga, Mbeya, Lindi and Arusha were solid CCM regions in this sample. Iringa and Singida in this sample were strong opposition regions and Mara, Mwanza and Zanzibar were fairly evenly split. Mara was 57 per cent CCM, 43 per cent opposition; Mwanza 47 per cent CCM, 53 per cent opposition and Zanzibar was 55 per cent CCM and 45 per cent opposition in this sample.

*Conclusion of Round three*

While the earlier rounds indicated an easy victory for CCM in 1995, as we approached the actual elections it appeared that the race was much closer. Mrema's joining the opposition had immeasurable effects. While it was not possible to predict an opposition victory at the presidential level, it was apparent that at the parliamentary level a significant number of seats from certain regions could go to the opposition. In terms of the presidency, Mkapa appeared to have a slight edge (55 per cent to 45 per cent); however, it was very close to the point which would necessitate a second run-off election between himself and Mrema.

**Final Conclusion**

Throughout this chapter it was emphasized that an apparent contradiction existed in peasants' attitudes towards CCM. Most peasants felt free to criticize CCM in terms of this party's efforts in facilitating their productive activities. Their criticisms were often harsh, expressed with emotion and highlighted with anecdotes. This negativity towards CCM was further expressed by peasants in their claims that it had become a party primarily serving the interests of the commercial class. Yet, through other questions and the section on candidate preferences, rural Tanzanians indicated a consistent support for CCM.

One element of the explanation for this contradiction was given earlier in the paper. Peasants saw a need for reform but felt the reform should take place within CCM itself. As one respondent said,

> CCM is like our father. When your father does wrong, you can't just throw him out. Maybe someone can sit and talk with him, and hopefully he will listen but you can't throw him out.

This remark highlights two factors concerning rural Tanzanians' perceptions of CCM. Firstly, CCM is associated with the parties that brought independence to Tanzania. Just as Nyerere is proclaimed the father of the nation so TANU/CCM is perceived as the party of the nation. This idea of fatherhood associated with CCM reflects a very real system of patronage that CCM has been able to capitalize on throughout the long period in which it has had a monopoly as Tanzania's single party. Jobs were given, privileges were secured and positions were attained by being members of CCM. Falling out of grace with CCM meant the loss of jobs, privileges and security.

A second element in explaining the above contradiction is the fact that CCM had a national structure. This organizational structure was strengthened over the years often either through an implicit or explicit use of government funds. Throughout CCM's monopoly period, the government was seen as subservient to the party. Many party officials doubled as government officials leading to a very grey area of party/government funds. In every village, in every corner of Tanzania, CCM was present. Besides its obvious advantage for mobilization, over the years peasants had come simply to identify governance with CCM.

The third element in the explanation of the above contradiction is the fact that in both the first and second rounds of research the opposition itself was not perceived by rural Tanzanians as being any more concerned about them than CCM. The opposition was seen as just that, an opposition. Peasants complained that all the opposition leaders did was come and make noise about the weaknesses of CCM. Rural Tanzanians also emphasized that no one came to listen to them but rather they came to tell them. In some instances, some of the opposition leaders were seen simply as people who had fallen out of favour with CCM and who were only looking for a way back into politics. Finally, it was very unclear to rural Tanzanians what the policies of the opposition parties were.

Thus, there was really no contradiction in rural Tanzanians' attitudes towards CCM. Obviously, the quality of life for most rural Tanzanians is very harsh. Because of this they are looking for a change. But, fairly realistically for the above reasons, they saw change as most probable through a reform of CCM.

Their attitudes towards the need for reform were clear in all three rounds. In both rounds one and two of the research they clearly indicated their preferences for Augustine Mrema while he was a member of CCM. He was perceived as a reformer, fighting against corruption and protecting the rights of the poor, ordinary people. However, again in both the first two rounds, rural Tanzanians expressed their respect for retired President Nyerere and it was clear that he was still influential. Thus, when Mrema left CCM and Mkapa emerged as the CCM candidate (perceived at least as Nyerere's candidate) the race became more interesting with a perceived reformer supported by Nyerere running against a reformer who fell out of grace with CCM. Again, the peasants remained consistent looking for reform but reform within CCM. By a margin of about 60 per cent to 40 per cent, Mkapa was elected mainly by rural Tanzanians because of the debacle of the election process in Dar es Salaam.

# References

Abrahams, R. G. (ed) (1985), *Villagers, Villages and the State in Modern Tanzania*, Cambridge African Studies Centre, Cambridge.

Afshar, H., and Dennis, C. (eds) (1992), *Women and Adjustment Policies in the Third World*, Macmillan, London.

Booth, D., Lugangira, F., Masanja, P., Mvungi, A., Mwaipopo, R., Mwami, J., and Redmayne, A. (1993), *Social, Cultural and Economic Change in Contemporary Tanzania: A People-oriented Focus*, SIDA, Stockholm.

Collier, P., Radwan, S., Wangwe, S. and Wagner, A. (1990), *Labour and Poverty in Rural Tanzania*, Clarendon Press, Oxford.

Cooksey, B., Malekela, G., and Lugalla, J. (1992), *Parents' Attitudes towards Education in Rural Tanzania*, TADREG, Dar es Salaam.

Forster, P.G., and Maghimbi, S. (eds) (19??), *The Tanzanian Peasantry: Economy in Crisis*, Avebury, Aldershot.

Herbst, J. (1990), 'The Structural Adjustment of Politics in Africa', *World Development*, 18, pp. 949-58.

United Republic of Tanzania (1991), *Nyalali Commission Report: Kitabu cha Kwanza, Taarifa na Mapendezeko*, Government Printer, Dar es Salaam.

243

# Index of Personal Names

References from Notes indicated by 'n' after page reference.

# Index of Place Names

# Subject Index

Names of Tanzanian ethnic groups are indicated with an asterisk.

254

## DATE DUE

| | | | |
|---|---|---|---|
| | | | |
| | | | |
| | | | |
| | | | |
| | | | |
| | | | |
| | | | |
| | | | |
| | | | |
| | | | |
| | | | |
| | | | |
| | | | |
| | | | |